ESSAYS ON
LITERATURE HISTORY & SOCIETY

ESSAYS ON LITERATURE HISTORY & SOCIETY

Selected Works of Professor Syed Naqi Husain Jafri

Compiled by

Saiyid Zaheer Husain Jafri
Syed Hasan Muzzamil Jafri

PRIMUS BOOKS

PRIMUS BOOKS
An imprint of Ratna Sagar P. Ltd.
Virat Bhavan
Mukherjee Nagar Commercial Complex
Delhi 110 009

Offices at CHENNAI   KOLKATA   LUCKNOW
AGRA AHMEDABAD BANGALORE COIMBATORE DEHRADUN GUWAHATI
HYDERABAD JAIPUR KANPUR KOCHI MADURAI MUMBAI PATNA RANCHI

First published 2010
Reprinted 2013

ISBN 978-81-908918-5-1 (hardback)
ISBN 978-93-80607-82-5 (paperback)

Published by Primus Books

Laser typeset by Byword Editorial Consultants
Delhi 110 009

Printed at Sanat Printers, Kundli, Haryana

Contents

Preface

The volume includes a selection of the essays, writings and conference presentations of Professor Syed Naqi Husain Jafri (17 April 1947—9 December 2007) which spanned a period of about three decades. Such a collection always runs the risk of appearing miscellaneous with the quality deemed to be uneven, its content viewed as overlapping and repetitious. But it is a tribute to Professor Jafri's choice of themes and clarity of thought that the reader gets a large amount of information in a lucidly analysed form. One can easily recognize a consistency of approach with new data and this makes the various essays less repetitive although written on similar themes. The broad themes which he chose revolved around the Hispano–Arabic connections, the image of the Orient in English literature, *Hindavi* tradition of poetry and *ghazal* as a form of non-conformist poetry. He was deeply concerned with the study and evolution of non-European literacy theory and the criticism thereof. Apart from literature, the themes which he gave equal importance to were Sufic themes and images in Persian and Awadhi poetry, the Urdu–Hindi controversy, *madrasa* education and its contemporary criticism.

Professor Jafri was born and brought up at Salon, a *qasba* and *tehsil* headquarter in the district of Rae Bareilley, UP, in a family which was deeply embedded in the Chishti–Nizami Sufi tradition and had established a *khanqah* which was later on known as *Khanqah-i Karimiya* way back during the reign of Mughal emperor Akbar. The institution so established was endowed quite liberally by the Mughal rulers and *nawab–wazirs* of the kingdom of Awadh. In addition to these grants, the local chieftains and even some princes of central India have also made donations and offered *nazrs* to make the family affluent enough to pursue the Sufic tradition and scholarly pursuits without any monetary difficulty. The family produced a number of scholars who were recognized for their learning and erudition among their contemporaries. Since the family had in no way 'supported' the British during the events of 1857, the inmates were 'penalized' with resumptions and stringent conditions on the renewed grants—something which initiated a long-drawn phase of litigation among the various branches of the family. The bitterness so created, by the British policies, was always felt by the later generations of the family, a fact which made them irreconcilable to the British and their colonial domination. The Independence of the country in 1947 also brought about the Partition and the abolition of zamindari and Land Reform Act of UP in 1952—a turning point in the saga of the family's history. Now it was a struggle for survival among the various branches across the border.

The father of Professor Jafri, Saiyid Shah Muhammad Husain Jafri (d. 1979) was the first member of the family to have acquired an English education along with the traditional education and had obtained the degree of laws from the University of Lucknow in 1942. In a way he became an example for his cousins to obtain an English education along with the traditional education.

His mother, Bibi Ayesha (d. 1998) was the daughter of Maulana Shah Aleem Ata (d. 1953). She was a person of tremendous qualities; was a *Hafiz-i Koran,* had studied Persian beyond the level of *Gulistan* and *Bustan* and was quite well versed in the nuances of *hadith* literature and also had some knowledge of *tafseer.* Her impact on the upbringing of the children was phenomenal. It was she who gave equal importance to the *madrasa* as well as a university education and hence was instrumental in the upbringing of her sons and daughters to acquire higher education.

It was under the guidance of his father that Naqi Husain Jafri passed his high school examination from UP Board in 1962. Incidentally, he was the only student to have passed in the first division in the entire *tehsil* from the only school, Sarvodaya Vidyapeeth. During high school his oratory and debating skills were recognized not only in the school but also at the district level competitions.

Since his father Saiyid Shah Muhammad Husain Jafri, was *Mahjub-ul Irth* (disinherited from the ancestral property), his maternal uncle, Shah Muhammad Naim Ata (d. 1966), the then *sajjadanashin* of the *khanqah,* had taken his father under his patronage and bequeathed upon him not only the *zamindari* property of several villages but also designated him as his successor and the future *sajjadanashin* of the *khanqah*. Shah Muhammad Naim Ata played a pivotal role in the making of the family of Professor Jafri and had the deepest impact upon his personality. After the death of Shah Naim Ata in 1966 the claim of Shah Muhammad Husain Jafri to the office of *sajjadanashin* was hotly contested by the family members of Shah Naim Ata. This phase of litigation ended in 1984 when the title of *sajjadanashin* was finally decided by the Hon'ble High Court in favour of Shah Muhammad Husain Jafri and his nominee, the present *sajjadanashin* of the *khanqah* Saiyid Shah Ahmad Husain Jafri. It was a time of turbulence in the Jafri family, where his opinions were of prime importance during a crisis. His alacrity and presence of mind had prevented several awkward positions in the *khanqah*.

The eclectic traits in his person have resulted from a very strong Sufi tradition which he imbibed from Shah Muhammad Naim Ata. His taste for Oriental Studies, Arabic and Persian grew quite early in life. Since the *khanqah* during his early age was a centre of traditional Islamic learning and the living Sufi tradition, where the *qawwals* attached with the *khanqah* sang the poetic compositions of Shah Naim Ata in Persian, Awadhi and Urdu replete with Sufic ideas, on all the occasions, Professor Jafri was free to develop his taste for the indigenous literature and Oriental Studies.

A major breakthrough in Professor Jafri's career came when after clearing his intermediate examination from Jubilee College, Lucknow in 1964 he joined Aligarh Muslim University. The subjects he studied at the under-graduate level were: English literature, Arabic and Islamic studies. He completed his M.A. in English literature in 1968; thereafter he left the university to take up various teaching assignments at Lucknow Christian College and Anwar-ul Ulum College, Hyderabad, AP; where he served for a period of 12 years. His stay at Hyderabad saw the maturity of his ideas, especially in the company of late Mr. Fasih ud din Ahmad where his stay became memorable.

While at Hyderabad he was always in touch with his professors at Aligarh Muslim University, especially Asloob Ahmad Ansari and Masud ul Hasan. He got himself enrolled for the Ph.D. degree in English literature under the supervision of Masud ul Hasan and completed his thesis on 'Aspects of Drayton's Poetry'. His visits to Aligarh in connection with his research were quite frequent and during his absence, his wife late Tahira Khanum provided the much-needed support to the children who were then just toddlers. She was more than a companion in his intellectual pursuits but unfortunately passed away in September 1995, a loss which he could never forget. A revised version of the thesis was published in 1988. He retained his interest in Oriental Studies and contributed a large number of articles on the poetic traditions of Urdu, Persian and Arabic. He was fascinated by the possible impact of the Arabic literary tradition *Futuwwah* and *Almawashshah* on the tradition of the courtly love and other songs and sonnets of the period of European Renaissance. He has contributed a number of articles on these themes.

His last major edited work *Critical Theory: Perspectives from Asia* has reproduced the English translation of *Ijaz-ul Quran* of Al-Baqilani, and the English translation of al-Jurjani's *Kitab Asrar-ul Balagha* to argue that Arabic literature had a literary theory and a theory of literary criticism which was well developed by the tenth century AD. His key argument was that the major literary traditions of Asia represented by Arabic, Persian, Sanskrit and Tamil had a well-developed literary tradition.

The contours of his argument and his concern for the indigenous literary and cultural tradition are well exemplified when he says:

> Colonization brought about not only political subjugation and economic exploitation but also intellectual and cultural erasure. The colonizers imposed their cultural and philosophical values on the colonized, instilling in them a sense of inferiority about everything native and indigenous. The heritage of native literature and art was denigrated and dismissed by the colonizing masters. As a consequence the colonized nations have gone through a period of cultural amnesia.

Besides contributing to English literary studies, he was equally comfortable and wrote on *Hindavi* poetry and Sufic images in the *Premakhyan* literature, on *madrasa* education and on the Urdu–Hindi controversy. He engaged with classics like the *masnavi* of Maulana Jalaluddin Rumi, *Diwan-e Hafiz*, while among the Urdu poets he had a fascination for Mir Taqi Mir, Sauda and Mirza Ghalib. He was comfortable making a comparison with these classics and the poetry of Chaucer, John Donne and Michael Drayton. He had written a lot in Urdu as well. A collection of his literary essays in Urdu poetry, biographical essays, essays on the various aspects of Sufism, and his essays on aspects of Islamic civilization are being compiled separately.

His academic and teaching career spanned about four decades (1968–2007) during which period he served three different institutions with distinction. The last institution, the Jamia Millia Islamia New Delhi (1982–2007) saw the fruition of his intellectual ideas and he translated them into articles and research papers. He was in the process of writing on a number of important themes on which he had collected a corpus of data over a period of many years.

We have collected his important articles with the help of his daughter's *Qurraut ul 'ain Tayyaba*, Khadija Mariam and his son Sayid Hasan Muzzamil Jafri, who are taking care of his books, notes and other important reprints and journals. Let's hope they are able to put the other unfinished writing of Professor Jafri in a shape. We are thankful to Professor Masud ul Hasan, who besides helping us in the thematic arrangement of the articles, has contributed an introduction to the volume. We have no words to express our gratitude to him.

New Delhi

SAIYID ZAHEER HUSAIN JAFRI
SYED HASAN MUZZAMIL JAFRI

Introduction

These miscellany of essays and reviews by the late Syed Naqi Husain Jafri are presented together to honour the memory of a warm-hearted friend and scholar of proven merit, and to provide the fruits of his ripe scholarship to readers. Further, since his literary excursions cover unconventional fields, including some Urdu masterpieces, learning about them is in keeping with the current trend of multicultural studies. Scion of a renowned spiritual dynasty of Salon (Rae Bareli), distinguished for its fusion of mystical pursuits with modern liberalism, Jafri had the unique advantage of sharing the Persian and Arabic legacy. To this he added a rich knowledge of Urdu and English literatures acquired at Jubilee College, Lucknow, and later at Aligarh Muslim University, where he earned a master's and doctoral degrees in English literature. His research work related to the pastorals of the prolific seventeenth-century poet, Michael Drayton (d. 1631). The thesis was published in 1985—*Aspects of Michael Drayton*—and was acclaimed as a noteworthy addition to Elizabethan studies.

Jafri proved an asset to the Jamia Millia Islamia University, New Delhi, where he worked as Professor of English. He had also chaired the Department of English for three years and had introduced innovative changes in the curriculum in keeping with the changing needs of the times. He won ready recognition in the academic circles of Delhi and adjoining states. Benefiting deeply from his English studies, he published a notable Urdu collection of critical essays titled *Kuch Maghrib Se Kuchh Mashrique*

Se (*Fragments from the East and the West*). Interestingly, the opening essay in this book is on Provençal poetry, the first essay ever written on that unusual subject. His critical essays are clearly indebted to the Formalist school of criticism. He wrote on diverse and widely disparate subjects in English, invariably characterized by fresh insights.

Jafri was the perfect gentleman, suave and cultured. He was a competent and affectionate teacher, a caring colleague, a conscientious parent, and a trustworthy friend. His untimely death was widely mourned, quite a few literary undertakings having been aborted. His loss is a grievous one, to academia in general and to Jamia Millia in particular. Which he served loyally and with distination in various capacities. The wound of his tragic demise during his full bloom is not likely to heal for long:

> Cut is the branch that might have grown full straight,
> And burn'd is Appollo's Laurel boughs
> That sometimes grew in this learned man.
>
> —Marlowe

The present collection includes the well-researched essay 'The Poetics and Politics of Troubadours: The Hispano–Arabic Connection'. For long the connection between Provençal and Medieval European literature had been lost in obscurity until Ezra Pound, A.R. Nykl, Frederich Goldin, Maurice Valency and Elizabeth Slater brought it to the fore. Taking his cue particularly from Pound and Nykl, Jafri expands on the theme and appreciates the influence of Ibn Hazm's *Tawqul Hamama* (AD 1020)—The Dove's Neck Ring—a collection of love poems in the Arabic genres of *mawashshah* and *zajal*. Jafri displays a discriminating awareness of Hispanic poetry and its influence on Spanish and Italian verse. The essay reflects its author's fresh insights.

A companion piece, 'Some Perspectives on the Medieval Tradition of Poetry', stretches the principal contentions of the former essay farther. It sees Provençal poetry as the shaping influence on later European poetry, even spilling over into Renaissance literature. Unlike the conventional treatment of European poetry, as an abrupt phenomenon Jafri convincingly roots for the continuity of tradition. As a subsidiary point he takes up the inadequate appreciation of the Crusades' impact on the European ethos, lately sought to be compensated by scholars like Daniel, Armstrong, and Maxime Rodinson. Jafri partly attributes the rise of allegory in the Middle Ages in Europe to Oriental beasteries and tales. But the basic traditions of Latin allegories of Ovid and Scipio Africanus have been inadvertently slurred over. He has done well to cite some specimens of the Provençal *zajal* that Indian scholars find difficult to come by elsewhere. The two essays taken together offer a rich perspective on European love poetry, so necessary for a proper appreciation of English poetry as well. It is no more advisable to segregate literatures completely on territorial or ideological grounds, as they are subliminally interrelated as the product of the human imagination, and even more so in the age of globalization.

Two papers on Michael Drayton were culled from the thesis. '*The Moone-Calfe:* An Interpretation' offers a satire on the court culture of James I. The unnatural birth of twin-monsters—half-male, half-female—is conjectured to be an attack on the fashion of feigned masculinity of women imported from France, whose princess, Mary, was now the Queen of England. Man's savagery is represented through the male moon-calf. The interwoven tales of the four midwives attending on the unnatural birth suggest the general corruption and decay of the world, a common theme in Elizabethan literature. The poems may be taken as Drayton's dystopia, where savagery flourishes and the genuine man is treated as a mere ass. Jafri points out some echoes of the Bible and of contemporary drama—for example; the wise man in the first midwife's tale is compared to Noah. Concurrently, the wise man recalls Prospero as well. The poem, however, concludes with a positive view of mankind.

The other essay attempts an allegorical explication of Drayton's highly imaginative poem 'The Muses Elizium'. In fact, it is a pastoral utopia with a perfect season cycle. It consists of nimpals or nymphs' songs. The grace of the human figure, national identity of the land, praises of youthful love, debates among the swains, celebration of a nymph's marriage, and ecological concerns figure in the poem prominently. The satyr in the ninth song laments the deforestation of the countryside—'The land thus rob'd of all her rich attire'. Incidentally, the last theme bears a direct relevance to our concerns for preserving nature. It gives a patriotic and peculiarly modern touch to the poem.

In the 'Image of the Orient in Shakespeare', Jafri perceives a comparatively liberal trend rather different from the general contemporary vogue. To the Elizabethans the Orient was represented by the Saracens, Arabs, Moors and Turks. The legacy of hostility for religious and political reasons was still alive, yet Shakespeare referred to Arabia in favourable terms, famous for its warriors, perfumes and the unique bird, the phoenix. The Turk, however, did not fare so well, and in conformity with an active national bias against the Ottomans, is associated with brutality, perfidy and connubial extravaganza. References to India are fewer, and invariably refer to her wealth, pearls, gems, and, at least once, to 'the beauteous scarf veiling an Indian beauty'. Jafri makes capital use of Shakespeare's presentation of the two Moors, Othello and the lesser-known Aaron, the scheming Moor in *Titus Andronicus*. Othello's martial excellence is widely recognized in Venice, and he is chosen to lead the Venetian galleys against the Turkish fleet. Moreover, thematically the play may be said to represent the encounter between Passion and Reason, symbolized by Othello and Iago respectively. But in spite of the contemporary tilt to Reason, Shakespeare makes no secret of his sympathy for the Moor. Aaron, the Black Moor of *Titus Andronicus*, is a blood-thirsty master schemer and murderer. Yet in the final scenes he is partly redeemed and humanized as he shows tenderness for his natural infant son and saves him from his ruthless brother. This partial redemption of the infidel is significant, and it suggests Shakespeare's comparative liberalism. Jafri attributes it to the dramatist's concession to secularism: 'He does not seem to bother about the religious beliefs of the Turks or the Saracens and is generally concerned with their political conduct and ambition, a phenomenon that is not to be found in the works of his illustrious contemporary Spenser'.

Some years ago, William Walsh, the English critic interested in Indian writing in English, queried why even after about two centuries of English studies in India, Indians had failed to evolve their own school of English studies and continued to swear *ad nauseam* by Aristotle and Western theoreticians. The situation even today is not radically different, though sporadic attempts and individual essays in critical evaluation of English works by indigenous standards are no more entirely wanting. Srinivas Iyengar, C.D. Narsimiah and V.Y. Gokak were among the early sponsors. The tradition is kept alive by scholars like M.S. Kushwaha, Harish Trivedi, S. Visvanath and R.S. Pathak. Jafri's essay on Hamlet's soliloquies in the light of the *Natyashastra* follows the same line. He begins with an examination of the function and ingredients of Western soliloquies, and discovers their more elaborate parallels in Indian poetics. In pursuit of his interest in the Eastern theory of poetics, he has also edited an anthology on the subject.

Two essays relate to American literature, 'American Poetry in the Contemporary Era' is a competent survey of the first half of the twentieth-century literature. The author rightly concludes that the age no more had one American literature but American *literatures*, and therefore multiple trends and tastes meet the reader's eye, each representing a group or school of poetry. Five principal groups deserve especial mention—the Beat poets, the Confessionalists, the post-Confessionalists, Black poets and the Native American poets. The second half of the century included War Poetry, especially after World War II, the Vietnam War and the Korean conflict. Of course, the Afghanistan embroglio, the Gulf War and the Iraqi devastation were to follow later. Pound retained a conspicuous presence because of his ever growing output, while Eliot was still accepted as a reigning laureate only by way of courtesy. The Beat poets rejected social conformity and asserted individual freedom. They also turned out to be the great debunkers of Eliot and Pound. The Confessionalists too insisted on the assertion and recognition of personal identity in keeping with the political liberty of the individual. The assassination of Malcolm X in 1965 unleashed intense reaction against the White Man's supremacy over the Blacks. The progressive movements of the Black Civil Rights and feminist campaigns lent a further boost to Black Arts and even paved the way for a theory of Black aesthetics to be formulated. Apart from significant anti-war poetry, the poetry of migrants, and mystic poetry of various denominations—Buddhist, Zen and Hindu—finds no mention. Probably, Jafri meant the essay to be a brief introduction to the general poetic scene of America. A heavier dose would turn really make the endeavour counterproductive. However, he has lucidly handled a complex amalgam, and the names and illustrations cited by him are well chosen. The essay could as well be called a junior atlas of the modern American landscape.

Jafri touches confidently on the vision and technique of Edward Albee, a leading American dramatist of the Absurd. According to Albee, the individual in society is allowed only a few options of action, which turns nature and life into an absurd, unpredictable and irrational paradigm. His apparently trivial, but really unarguable remark in *Who's Afraid of Virginia Woolf* is one such observation, and Jafri treats it as the dramatist's dominant view of life. The observation reads as follows: 'when people can't abide things as they are then . . . either they turn to a contemplation of the past . . . or they set about to alter the future, and when you want to change something . . . you Bang, Bang, Bang'. In other words, lack of tolerance of the present leads initially to its deconstruction in order to build the future, and that is one's vision. More illustrations follow from the *Zoo Story* and the *American Dream*.

Reference has been made earlier to the exclusive rule of Western critical theory in English studies in India. In view of a radically changed intellectual scenario in independent India, Jafri argues in favour of evolving a post-colonial literary theory. He deals succinctly with the colonial ethos, the arrogance and assumed primacy of Western poetics under the impact of superiority complex and a total ignorance of the sublime Indian legacy. But with the passing of the colonial keyday and the dawn of egalitarian and republic demands affecting creatine imagination is new conon is needed. He is confident of the indigenous traditions meeting the challenge. He illustrates and substantiates the point, referring to the versatile genre of the *ghazal* and quoting from masters like Ghalib, Hafiz and Faiz to prove that the genre was capable of rendering the classical as well as the modern susceptibilities with equal ease and excellence. This is true of the Persian and Urdu *masnavi*.

In another essay Jafri makes an interesting and innovative point about the non-conformist and anti-establishment character of the *ghazal*. The poet may scoff with impunity at the rigid formalism and orthodoxy of the devout or boldly laud his own bacchanialism, strictly forbidden and denounced in Islam. The *mohtasib* (moral censor), the *imam*, the *mulla* and the *zahid* are the usual butts of ridicule, as are the halls of hell and paradise. The poet enjoyed licence, and his utterances were tolerated as unsullied by contumacy or heresy. But Jafri goes a step further and makes an intelligent point little noticed by the annalists of the genre. He suggests that this debunking/satire flowed from the Sufis' typical other-worldliness and their assiduous distancing of themselves from the royal courts and patrons. Because of the Sufic associations with the *ghazal,* and because of the poets' assumed identity as lovers, they adopted the mockery of the sanctimonious and the law dispenser as a generic convention. It may be recalled that the poet invariably took the persona of the *majnoon* or *saudai* (lunatic), relieving him of the demands of decorum and discretion like the Elizabethan fool. Jafri also dilates upon the two recurring metaphors/allusion of the martyr-saint, Mansoor Hallaj, and the tragic events of Karbala in Urdu and Persian poetry.

The strain of non-conformism recurs in another scholarly essay as well—'Sufic Themes and Images in Persian and Hindavi Poetry'. The author traces with perception and diligence the elements of non-conformity in the classical Persian poets and in masters of Hindavi poetry. To him the latter embraces the poetry of all the important native languages of northern India. The renowned, poet-mystic of the fourteenth-century Amir Khusrau, excelled in humanism, was liberal in outlook, and underplayed denominational differences. Allegory was its distinctive mode, and some of the best Medieval Indian poems belonged to this genre. A few of them are *Chandayan*, *Mrigavati*, *Padmavat* and *Hans Jawahir*. By implication, Jafri seems to recognize the deep bond between Sufism and the Bhakti movement, even though the latter is not mentioned by name. The sweep of his treatment is vast, and he explains lucidly the Sufic doctrine of *wahdat-al-wajood* (immanence) from its earliest stage. From among the later Urdu poets he takes up Ghalib for special treatment from this angle. In fact, the Sufis contributed considerably to the evolution and development of Urdu/Hindi poetry. The essay indirectly suggests a comparable approach to the study of English literature.

Syed Ahmad Khan, the founder of MAO College, arouses contrary emotions of adulation and condemnation in different people depending upon their personal background and predilections. Liberal opinion holds that he was a secularist, an advocate of communal harmony, and one of the nation builders of India. On the contrary, his critics call him a vocal communalist and the original author of the Partition of India. He is severely berated for his alleged twin sins of a pro-Urdu stance and a strong anti-Congress bias. In an essay included here, Jafri analyses his role in the Urdu–Hindi controversy and tries to dispel the misgivings about him. Amrit Rai's prejudicial pronouncements against Syed is (in *A House Divided*) cited as typical of this denigration, and Jafri correlates it with the hostile imaging of the Muslims in the post-1857 era and suggests that the controversy was actually created by the alien rulers as a matter of political expediency, and Syed Ahmad only reacted to it. In support of his thesis Jafri cites the opinions of Vasudha Dalmia (*The Nationalization of Hindu Traditions*, 1997), David Lelyveld, Francis Robinson and Shamsur Rehman Faruqi (about the birth and nomenclature of Urdu).

It may be added here that possibly Hindu revivalism by the British connivance and the status-quoist over-blown complacency of traditionalists (including the Muslims) generated by the centuries of illusive calm of the Hindu public, and this shock embittered the campaign, causing unpleasant reactions.

As an enlightened university teacher constructively engaged in his social ambience—Radhakrishnan and Kothari have called academics 'the conscience of the society' and 'custodians of civilization'—Jafri was sincerely sensible of the socio-cultural issues pertaining to the segment of Indian society that he belonged to. His essay 'Modernist View of Madrasa Education in Late Mughal India' provides an instance of this interest. The essay is particularly relevant today because of the prevailing monstrous misconceptions about *madrasas* as nurseries of terrorism and communal hatred. Their history, the gradual switch over from state patronage to private maintenance, over the years and the fractional inclusion of secular subjects in their heavily theological curricula, have been brought out ably. Originally, these *madrasas* provided the state with civil and judicial officers. With the change of the administrative system, these options were no more available. So Jafri recommends curricular reforms and a modicum of modernization to revitalize the *madrasas*. He has criticized in the main body of the essay the Oriental scholars' total indifference to modern scientific advances, but modifies his view in a postscript on learning that the East was not totally blind to the Western scientific works, as he had come across an Arabic translation of Newton's *Principia* into Arabic in the eighteenth century. The postscript stands to the credit of his intellectual integrity.

A few book reviews of works on Muslim problems are also included in the present anthology of essays as they reveal the living concern of a scholar with issues connected with his community and provide us a glimpse into his mind and authentic personality. M.K.A. Siddiqi's book *Educating a Backward Community* (1984) is especially taken note of as it examines some relevant issues boldly and with imagination. Supporting statistical data adds to the reliability of the statement of problems and their possible solutions. Jafri agrees with Siddiqi in blaming external factors for the backwardness of Muslims rather than the community's own lukewarm attitude to change. The success story of an ameliorative experiment SETWIN (Society for Employment for Twin Cities in 1978–81) is an encouraging example worth emulating. But the pragmatic Jafri finds Siddiqi's suggestions too ambitious and recommends caution. The reviewer, however, shows a genuine desire and understanding of the underlying problems. Another book on Muslim minorities by M. Ali Kethani (1986) has a global range and proposes 'to help build bridges between minorities and majorities', and to convert hatred and rancour into respect and sympathy. Jafri also agrees that cooperation and mutual understanding are the needs of the hour rather than conflict.

Ghazzali's *Ihya-ul uloom*, part I deals with the *ibadat*, and is translated by Mukhtar Holland as the *Inner Dimensions of Islam*. Jafri likes the lucid style and fidelity to the original text, but he is unhappy with the terms used. For example, he suggests, 'spiritual dimensions' could have been a more suitable substitute for 'inner dimensions'.

So also 'alms giving' for *zakat* is an inappropriate term, 'regular charity' used by Abdullah Yusuf Ali in his translation of the Koran is a superior and more expressive term. Zakaria Beshir's *Hijra-Story and Signifance* deals with the Muslim's temporary relocation in Abbyssinia and Medina. But the movement was not a mere flight or fugitiveness; it had a divine and spiritual purpose as well. Beshir favours Muslims from hostile pluralistic societies move to predominantly Muslim lands. Jafri points out the impracticability of such migration in modern times. Besides, he considers it an unjustificable, even harmful, infraction of the code of pluralism.

Two novels are also under review. *Umrao Jan Ada*, a classic Urdu novel by Muhammad Hadi Ruswa, written in 1899. Recently it was translated into English by David Mathews. It is a fictionalized story of a Lucknow courtesan, who not only provided musical entertainment, but also lessons in public manners. It brilliantly portrays the Awadh culture of the later half of nineteenth century. As usual the reviewer gives a brief recap of the structure and plot of the novel, and compliments Mathews for a faithful portraiture of the ethos and spirit of the age. A couple of linguistic infelicities are however pointed out. Also, as a work of translation Jafri rates it lower than the English version by Khushwant Singh and M.A. Hussaini. The other novel is Qurratulain Hyder's *Mere Bhi Sanamkhane* translated into English by herself as *My Temples, Too*. It depicts the upper class society of Lucknow of the pre-Partition days with nascent Congress–League politics. Jafri gives a consise summary of the plot, comments on the implicit disdain of the bigger *jagirdars* for the upcoming middle class. He appreciates the novel's scenario and the composite culture. One is reminded of a near contemporary comparable English novel by Attia Hosain *Sunlight on a Broken Column*. The ethos, political scenario and character traits of the two novels have much common.

Zikr-i Mir is the Persian autobiography of the eighteenth-century Mughal poet. C.M. Naim of the University of Chicago has rendered it into English. Jafri acknowledges the thoroughness and scholarship that has gone into its making, even reproducing the archaic modes and stylistic mannerisms of the original text. Chaudhry Naim's diction, additional information given in appendices with a few minor historical corrections bear witness to his impeccable scholarships. Jafri has taken note of these virtues.

Mohammad Alavi is a modern Urdu poet of repute, author of several collections of poems. Jafri has reviewed his fifth collection—*Chautha Asman* (*The Fourth Sky*), the recipient of the 1992 Sahitya Akademi Award. Alavi's contribution to modern poetry is summed up competently, and he is represented as an authentic explorer and recorder of contemporary alienation and ennui. Some short specimens have been ably rendered into English by Jafri who traces hints of Rumi in Alavi. Mainly a poet of *nazm*, Alavi's *ghazals* are notable for their treatment of commonplace themes. At the end mention may also be made of the obituary of Ali Sardar Jafri (d. 2000) one of most important modern poets. Jafri briefly mentions his quality of idealism, and passion for Indo–Pak amity. Some eloquent verses have been translated by the reviewer, who detects an Audenesque romanticism in him.

Naqi Jafri's selective contributions to English writing may, to some, appear to be slender in volume as compared to the modern wizards of publications whose favourite menu may be long on insipid items, but thin on real savourics and nutritious confections. His interpretations and contributions to seminars and symposia were certainly a cut apart, and he will be missed for long in Delhi's literary circles. It is quite likely that some of these essays, particularly those on the Troubadours and, or Shakespeare may prove to be trendsetters, and deepen interest in them.

Aligarh   MASOOD UL HASAN

Part I

CHAPTER I

The Poetics and Politics of the Troubadours: The Hispano–Arabic Connection

The Elizabethan sonnet sequences, despite the monotony of imagery and treatment in them, fascinate the student of Arabic/Persian/Urdu literature for their celebration of love, refinement of manners and richness of poetry. The reader can easily discern the echoes of the Oriental tradition in many of the sonnet sequences published in the last quarter of the sixteenth century namely, *Astrophel and Stella* by Sidney, *Amoretti* by Spenser, *Sonnets* of Shakespeare, particularly those addressed to the dark lady, and a host of other known and lesser-known sonnet sequences. Chaucer's *Troilus and Criseyde*, one of the finest love poems in English, also treats human love in a sublime manner. The trend of sonneteering in English was set by Wyatt and Surrey and the tradition can be traced to Petrarch's *Canzone* in Italian in the sixteenth century. Was Petrarch the originator of the form or also the trendsetter of this tradition of glorification of human love? Did he share these concerns with other Italian poets like Cavalcanti and Dante? Is the cult of the dame a Christian concept? Is it a legacy of the Greco–Latin tradition or the influence of Hispano–Arabic verse? Is it Ovidian in content and treatment or traceable to other possible sources/treatises on love? The essay addresses some of the issues.

It is necessary to admit that while the Orientalists have been generous in acknowledging the impact of Hispano–Arabic literature on the early literary traditions of Europe which grew in the thirteenth and fourteenth centuries, literary critics, particularly those with an Anglo–Saxon bias, have generally expressed strong reservations about the influence of the Hispano–Arabic literary tradition on English and other European languages. The Troubadours, also known as the Provençal poets, set the trend of secular love poetry in southern France in the eleventh century. These wandering minstrels remained at the centre stage of the south European literary scene for about two centuries and, by the close of the thirteenth century disappeared from the stage as mysteriously as the arrival of their predecessors in the eleventh century. They left behind a deep impact upon the world view and aesthetics of the people and the emerging vernaculars of Europe. While there is no disagreement, among historians and critics, with regard to the influence of the Troubadour tradition on the growth and development of the courtly tradition in English and other European languages, the genesis and aesthetics of the tradition continues to engage the attention of critics. Anthony Bonner posits 'That the Troubadours wrote great poetry and are, therefore, worthy of our literary consideration was an idea that was only suggested to the English-speaking public by two critics, Chaytor and Ezra Pound, who wrote in the years immediately preceding and following World War I' (*Songs of the Troubadours*, 1972). Scholars who preceded Ezra Pound generally talked about the possible origins of the Troubadour tradition, but with Pound, it remained a lifelong passion. His essays in *The Spirit of Romance*, his translations of Arnaut Daniel in *The Translations of Ezra Pound*, other renderings in *Personae* and innumerable references to the Troubadours in *Cantos* bear a frequent refrain, emphasizing the significance and centrality of the Troubadour tradition in the understanding of European civilization.

In this connection, mention may be made of Pound's essay, 'Psychology and Troubadours' in *The Spirit of Romance*, that seeks to interpret the songs of the wandering minstrels in an entirely different way by offering fresh insight.

Nothwithstanding the accusations made against Ezra Pound about his strong political bias in favour of Italy as a repository of Roman civilization with fascistic overtones during World War II, his interest in Continent and Mediterranean life and culture dates back to 1906 when he went to France as a fellow in Romance languages to translate the works of Lope de Vega. Pound began an intense inquiry into the Medieval languages and poetry of the Troubadours, a pursuit that he never put aside thereafter and that became a major source of inspiration and reference for his work. It was in the course of mastering their language that Pound learned the poetic possibilities and impossibilities of his own. In the melodies of their songs Pound discovered for himself what lyric music is. These songs became Pound's criteria for good poetry. As there exists close proximity between the Andalusian literary tradition and the Troubadour songs, any student of the ninth or tenth century Hispano–Arabic verse is tempted to consider and benefit from the highly perceptive critical insights of Pound regarding the life and letters of Mediterranean civilization.

Before proceeding to discuss the songs of the Troubadours, a brief word must be given on the various theories about the genesis of the phenomenon. Some scholars opine that it rose out of the popular poetry of the time, while others maintain that it had its roots in the Latin culture of the church, while there is yet another section who think that it came from the Moors in Spain. In the absence of any evidence of the pre-Troubadour tradition of literature in Europe, the discussion has been restricted to the possibilities of the Latin and Arabic influence. While C.S. Lewis (*Allegory of Love*, Oxford, 1939), A.J. Denomy (*Medieval Studies*, 1944), A.R. Nykl (*Hispano–Arabic Poetry and its Relation with the Old Provençal Troubadours*, Baltimore, 1946), among others, speculated upon the possible connection of courtly love poetry with the Hispano–Arabic tradition, Theodore Silverstein and Robertson Jr. expressed reservations about its Oriental connection, and considered it to be a totally indigenous phenomenon rooted in the Iberian/Celtic tradition and Christianity. In this connection, mention may also be made of studies by Samuel Milkos Stern (*Hispano–Arabic Poetry*, ed. L.P. Harvey, Oxford, 1974), which analyse the Andalusian strophic forms of *Muwashshah* and *Zajal* and examine its relationship with the lyrics of Provençal poets. But rather curiously, none of these critics have paid any attention to the writings of Ezra Pound which seem to have posited insights and interpretations of the Provençal literature which is, doubtless, refreshing and provocative.

Approximately 2,000 Troubadour texts survive (with varied stanzaic rhyme scheme). The song was sung, the tradition has it, before an audience comprising among others, the nobility and common Troubadours, including potential rivals and enemies. The poet stood before the gaze of his friends and others. The friends would demand a song and the only way to save the song would have been to give it to every part of the audience, to friends who cherish the song and rivals who want to destroy it. The lyrics follow a more or less similar pattern. A prayer to the lady to believe that the poet, her lover, is sincere when he speaks all the other formulas. The tantalizing result is that when he makes this prayer, the true lover can only succeed in sounding exactly like the false ones, for whom it is just another platitude that one is supposed to say. The ladies are all blonde beauties, universally esteemed, unreliable and distant; the lovers are all sincere and inadequate as in the tradition that continues right up to the Elizabethan sonnet sequences. The note of personal pride is identified with the pride of class. The singer goes from one role to another, his song is a pattern of impersonations, of which 'the courtly lover' is but one. To protect this play from being spoiled, the best bulwark against the invasion of ordinary life are the enemies and their redeeming disbelief. The poet takes full advantage of the incomprehension of the enemies by frequently alluding to codes and writing in a hermetic style (*trobar clus*). According to Fredrick Goldin, the question of sincerity is aesthetically irrelevant (*Lyrics of Troubadours and Trouveres*, 1973).

The annual fair of Ukaz in pre-Islamic Arabia where masterpieces of poetic composition were recited and honoured may be mentioned here as a model of literary festival celebrated in Arabic literature. 'Rich in animated-passion, expressed in forceful and compact language, the *qasidah* (ode) is poor in original ideas, in thought-provoking imagery, and is consequently lacking in universal appeal.' The poet and not the poetry according to Philip K. Hitti, 'is more often the thing to be admired . . . a poet made a name for himself here or nowhere. The fair (*suq*) of Ukaz stood in pre-Islamic days for a kind of Academie Francaise of Arabia' (*History of the Arabs*, 1970).

The Troubadour tradition of reading out their songs before a select audience, as mentioned above, bears a strange and interesting likeness to the recitation of poetry in the fairs of Ukaz.

The Provençal literature may be described as chivalric while distinguishing it from the classical tradition. It may also be interesting to note that the period of the growth and development of the idea of chivalry in southern Europe is the same as that of the Provençal tradition. Equally important is the fact that the Troubadours begin with the period of the first crusade (1096) and are not heard of after the unsuccessful Albegesian crusade (1208–29). Quite a few of the Troubadours fought in the crusades, and those who did not take part in the campaigns seem to have strong bonds with the principal figures of the crusades, particularly with the house of Aquitaine. Guillaume IX of Aquitaine, the first known Troubadour, led a disastrous crusade into the Holy Land in 1101. He is also known to have aided the king of Aragon in a victorious battle against the Moors in 1120. Jaufre Rudel, the Prince of Blaia, a mid-twelfth-century Troubadour, celebrated by many a poet, including Petrarch, for his fine *amores*, is believed to have joined a crusade in 1147. Another Troubadour, Giraut de Bornelh (1165–1211) accompanied Amamar V of Limoges to Jerusalem. Raimbaut de Vaqueiros, a Troubadour who greatly influenced Italian literature, perished in 1207 during the fourth crusade. Peive Vidal (1180–1205) spent some time in Jerusalem and sang of arms and love. Bernart de Ventadorn (1150–80) who is considered one of the best Troubadours and has been celebrated by Ezra Pound, is known to have been a lover of Queen Eleanor of Aquitaine. Likewise, Amaut Daniel, Bertran de Born and Folquet de Marseille (d. 1231) were known to and patronised by the members of royalty; particularly the house of Aquitaine. Queen Eleanor Aquitaine, the granddaughter of William IX, the first Troubadour, remains the most fascinating personality of this age. She was first married to Louis VII, the King of France, and later, after separation, to Henry II of England. Two of her sons, John and Richard, became the kings of England successively. Thus, Eleanor enjoyed a unique position among the queens of Europe. As the queen of France, she had joined the second crusade and had visited Byzantium, where in the court of Manuel Comnenus, she was exposed to a cosmopolitan culture that was not to be seen in the Paris of Louis VII. In England, she patronised the Troubadours and jongleurs, as well as French trouvere, one of whom was Bernart de Ventradorn. 'It is pleasant to think of Eleanor', Peter Makin says, 'as being herself the model for the "April like queen" who fools her annoying husband in one of the first Provencal pieces that Pound rend.' Eleanor has also been likened to Helen quoting Aeschylus as 'man-destroyer, ship-destroyer and city-destroyer' (Canto II). As is the case with many public figures, Eleanor's image was also not free from scandals. She was suspected by her husband Louis of having an affair with Saladin, another fascinating personality of the age of Crusades who was known, though grudgingly, as the 'paragon of Chivalry', in the then Europe. Ezra Pound alludes to this scandal in Canto VI.

> And he, Louis, was not at ease in that town,
> And was not at ease by Jordan
> As she rode out to the palm-grove
> Her scarf in Saladin's cimier.

The personality of Walladah, the daughter of Al Mustaqfi must be mentioned here. She was renowned for personal charm and literary ability and was in the words of Philip K. Hitti, 'the Sappho of Spain, where Arab women seem to have shown special taste and aptitude for poetry and literature'. According to Hitti, Al Mu'aara has devoted a whole section to these women of Al Andalus in whom eloquence was a second instinct (*History of the Arabs*). Walladah's home at Cordova was the meeting place of wits, savants and poets. Among the hosts of admirers and poets who thronged the court of Walladah, Ibn Zaydun was perhaps the most illustrious. It would indeed be tempting to compare Walladah of Cordova with Queen Eleanor of Aquitaine, the lady at the centre of Troubadour literary tradition during the Second Crusade. The European men of letters and writers of chivalric songs may have found a figure in the personality of Queen Eleanor who for them provided a pattern and image of the illustrious princess of Cordova.

I now intend to refer to some of the writings of critics which complicate as well as enlighten the appreciation of the Troubadours. While attempting to explicate the songs of the Troubadours, the poet invites our attention to the theme of the relationship of poetry to history, which is very germane to the problem we intend to discuss. 'Near Perigord' asks a series of questions. With his poem, 'The Borrowed Lady', Peter Makin says, 'was Bertran trying to convert Montaignac, the key to his strategy, by making the other women jealous of Maent, and giving her pride in them? But was Bertran in love with her? And then, extrapolating the guesses, was the song an attempt at alliance with all these castles' (*Provence and Pound*, 1978). Reading the poem on an esoteric plane is basic to the interpretation of the *trobar clus* in Pound's famous essay, 'Psychology and Troubadours'.

The Borrowed Lady

Lady, since you are not interested in me
and have sent me away
Without any reason,
I don't know where to look . . .

Since I can find no lady equal to you,
who should be as beautiful or excellent, or her
fine person so happy,
with such beautiful clothes,

so gay,
or her fine worth so true,
I shall go everywhere begging
a beautiful appearance from each lady,
to make a borrowed lady
until I get you back.

I take your fresh unfaked colour
from you, beautiful Cembeli,
and your sweet loving look,
and I act with great presumption
in leaving anything behind,
because you never lacked anything good; from milady
Helis I ask her clever witty talk,
to help my lady,
then she won't be stale or dumb . . .

I want Audriart, though she wishes me ill,
to give me some of her shapes,
because clothes go well on her,
and because she is whole,
for her love never broke
or twisted awry;
of my better-than-Good I ask
her upright fresh and valued body
from what one sees
it would be fine to hold her naked . . .

Beautiful Lord, I ask of you nothing other
than that I should be as covetous
of this (borrowed) lady as I am of you:
since a greedy
love is springing up
with which my body is so avid
that I prefer asking you
to kissing another woman;
so why does 'milord' refuse me
when she knows I have wanted her so much

—Bertran de Born

Near Perigord

'Maent, I love you, you have turned me out.
The voice at Monfort, Lady Agnes' hair,
Bel Miral's statue, the Viscountess' throat,
Set all together, are not worthy of you . . .
Is it a love poem? Did he sing of war?
Is it an intrigue to run subtly out,
Born of a jongleuer's tongue, freely to pass
Up and about and in and out the land,
Mark him a craftsman and a strategist?
Oh, there is precedent, legal tradition,
To sing one thing when your song means another,
Et albirar ab lor bordon',

In connection with this passage, he says, 'No student of the period can doubt that the involved forms, and veiled meanings in the *trobar clus*, grew out of living conditions, and that these songs played a very real part in love intrigue and in the intrigue preceding warfare.' Both the amorous and the moral strains of the Troubadour canon are often veiled in metaphors, not easily explicable.

In this connection, Pound's essay, 'Psychology and Troubadours' acquires significance. Pound develops the hypothesis that the 'Chivalric love' passionately expressed in the canzones was but a code and religion, which the Troubadours of southern France veiled in romanticized metaphor. Pound identifies the Troubadours with the Pagan/Hellenic religion which, for fear of censure by the Church, they were obliged to conceal in codes and techniques, incomprehensible to the uninitiate. The 'Lady' and the 'Face of the Lady' he says, denote the secret religion they faithfully followed. Pound's observations are often sweeping. He says, 'That the spirit was, in Provence, Hellenic is seen readily enough by anyone who will compare the Greek Anthology with the work of the Troubadours. They have, in some way, lost the names of gods and remembered the names of lovers' (*The Spirit of Romance*, 1967).

While the exclusivity of the Troubadour cannot be disputed, its relationship to history, from alternate angles, available to us, may also be considered. A.R. Nykl's pioneering work, *Hispano–Arabic Poetry and its relations with the Old Provençal Troubadours*, offers insights as stimulating as those of Ezra Pound. Nykl especially mentions Ibn Hazm's *Tawq al Hamamaw* (1020), an important treatise in Arabic on the modes and treatment of secular love, written in Cordova.

The *Tawq al Hamama*[1] has been translated into all the European languages. Describing the nature and kinds of love, Ibn Hazm, distinguishes passionate love from other kinds of love. In Chapter 1, he says:

> Among them is the love of those who love each other because the secrecy with which they clandestinely meet obliges them to cover it up; and love in order to obtain pleasure and satisfy (the object of) one's desire and passionate love, the cause of which is nothing else but what is mentioned about the reunion of souls. And all these kinds cease upon the cessation of their causes, and grow in intensity if the causes grow intense, or grow less intense if the causes are diminishing. They are strengthened by their proximity and grow weaker when distant from them, except the true passionate love which takes possession of the soul: this is a love which never passes away.

Ibn Hazm does not restrict himself to the concept, he illustrates his propositions by citing examples of actual persons he knew or from the stories of lovers he heard, or read about. The treatise also contains lyrics and short poems about the various states of love. The plight of a lover who undergoes the pangs of separation is described thus:

> I guard the stars as if I had been commissioned to guard all the fixed
> stars and planets:
> And they and the night resemble the fires of passion, which
> have been kindled in my thoughts coming from the dark night,
> And it seems as if I had started in the evening as the
> watchman of a green garden. And its green plants had girt
> themselves with white narcissus.
> If Ptolemy were living he would have been certain that I am
> The strongest of men in the observation of the orbits of stars.

Submissiveness of the lover to his beloved, an important trait of the courtly love tradition, is also treated by Ibn Hazm. He says,

> Thus you will see a man of rude and quarrelsome disposition, who is very difficult to deal with, very obstinate when it comes to being led, very resolute in his purposes, very particular about preserving his dignity and refusing to be humiliated, yet the very moment he inhales the soft breeze of love and plunges headlong into its waves, and swims in its ocean, his rudeness turns into smoothness, and his

difficulty into easiness, and his resolution into weariness, and his watchfulness into surrender.

Ibn Hazm quotes his own verses to prove his point:

> Submission in love is not odious,
> For in love the proud one humbles himself:
> Do not be surprised at the docility of my condition,
> For before me Al-Mustansir has suffered the same lot.
>
> —The Dove's Neck Ring, XIV

It is indeed interesting to compare Ovid with Ibn Hazm in regard to their treatment of human love. While Ovid's aim is to show men an artful method whereby to capture women by flattery, gifts and pretence of service, he is also liberal with detailed advice to women on how to hold men's affections by deceit, dress and cosmetics. On the other hand, Ibn Hazm stresses, according to Nykl, 'spiritual aspects of love . . . Ovid is a sensual, clever dandy, who like Don Juan boasts of his ability to make conquest of women; Ibn Hazm is the fine-feeling seeker of the spiritual union, even in corporeal relations, much preferring the former.'

There are innumerable songs/lyrics of Andalusian literature from the eighth century onwards which treat the ennobling passion of human love in varied themes and forms, culminating in the eleventh century.

Strophic *muwashshah* and *zajal*, are the two forms of lyric which may be described as patently Andalusian though not quite distanced from the classical Arabic tradition. In some of these verses the lady is addressed as 'Milord' (Saiyyedi/Maulaee), a convention also popular among the Troubadours:[2]

> If my Lord will give me her love
> I am ready to take her in gratefulness
> and keep her secret, serve her,
> do and say what pleases her,
> hold her value dear
> and further her praises.
>
> I dare not send her anything by another,
> I have such fear lest she should grow angry,
> Nor dare I urge my love in person,
> so much do I fear doing the wrong thing.
> But she must choose the best for me,
> Since she knows it is with her I shall be healed.

Ibn Khaldun's observation on the genesis of the lyric form in the *Al-Muqaddama* is indeed interesting in appreciating the growth and development of the sonnet in Italian and later in English:

> When the elegance of poetry had reached its highest degree in Al Andalus, later poets there started a new genre which they called *muwashshah*. They arranged it *simt* by *simt*, and *qusn* by *qusn* and were very prolific in composing this genre, as well as in the variety of its meters. They call a number of *qusn* thus arranged one *bait* (stanza). It is obligatory to use the same rhyme and meter in these *qusn* consecutively until the end of the *qasida* (poem). The usual highest number of verses (stanzas) is seven. Each *bait* (stanza) has the number of *qusn* according to the purpose and system (of the poet); they are used for singing love or praise, just as the *qasidas* are used. The Andalusians became exceedingly refined in this genre, and all the people, both elite and laymen, found it charming because of the ease with which it could be learned and understood. The inventor of this genre in Al Andalus was Muqaddam ibn Ma'afiral Faraki.

An anthology of Moorish poetry edited by Ibn-e-Said was compiled in 1243. The text of this anthology was edited by Garcia Gomez in 1942. The anthology includes, among others, compositions of kings, princes, ministers, nobles, jurists, grammarians and litterateurs. Foremost among the poets are, Ibn Zaidun, Ibn Arabi, Ibn al Attar, Al-Haitham, Ibn Ammar and Ibn Quzam. One of the lyrics entitled 'The Handsome Knight' by Al-Mu'tamid translated by Garcia Gomez and rendered into English by Arberry reads as follows:

> And when, accourted in your mail
> and with your helmet for a veil
> That hid your beauty from the day
> You charged into the fray,
>
> We deemed your countenance to be
> The noonday sun, now suddenly
> occluded by an amber cloud
> Its radiance to shroud.
> She stood in all her slender grace
> Veiling the sun's orb from my face:
> O may her beauty ever be
> So veiled from time's inconstancy!

It was as if she knew, I guess,
She was a moon of loveliness;
And may aught else the bright sun brought veil
Except the moon's own lustre pale?

Dante, who inspired the sonneteers of English poetry in the sixteenth century, owes a lot to the Troubadours. According to Maurice Valency, 'Without the lady of the Troubadours' song, without Bon Vezi, without Vanna, there could have been no Beatrice. The idea that man could ascend to God in this manner through the pure love of a woman had occurred in turn to . . . Cavalcanti, but neither had devised the means probably because, bound as they were to the Troubadour tradition, they were, unwilling to relinquish the lover's guerdon.' Valency further says, 'Like almost all the Troubadour ladies, Beatrice is depicted in terms of the ideal. She has little to distinguish her as an individual, we know only that she was of the colour of pearl, perfect and pitiless. The lover, as always, is much more interested in himself than in the lady.' Valency further argues, 'Whatever his (Boccaccio's) connection with Dante, the lover of the *Vita Nuova* is a poetic construction of more or less conventional cut, exactly as is Beatrice. Both are personages designed to play a certain action in a drama conceived according to the pattern of a lyric, and this is their principal reality. Much the same may be said of Petrarch's Laura, and, in general, of all the ladies who in the following years became the subject of the Renaissance lyric sequences of love' (*In Praise of Love*).

The extracts from *The Dove's Neck Ring* (*Tawq*) have been cited only to suggest the importance of the rich humanistic culture of Andalus, which according to Elizabeth Salter, was cosmopolitan (*The Medieval World*, ed. Daiches, 1973). The impact of the Arab Andalusian civilization in the areas of philosophy, astronomy, geography, physics, medicine, applied sciences, town planning and architecture on the West European civilization needs no reiteration, but its impact on letters has not received due consideration. The Troubadours provide a vital link between the Andalusian poetry and the secular love poetry of West European languages from the thirteenth century onwards. The muddle about the 'feudalization of love' and the confusion about the inexplicability of courtliness arises mainly because of an inadequate understanding of Hispano–Arabic poetry. With Byzantium on the east and Andalusia on the southern boundary, Provence benefited from both cosmopolitan societies. The Crusades provided the necessary impetus with Queen Eleanor, the femme fatale, inspiring strife and poetry and her brave son, Richard the Lion Heart, at the centre stage, which, among other things, exposed Western Europe to the Orient. There was unprecedented interaction at various levels of thought and feeling and this resulted in a kind of civilizational encounter. The purpose of this argument is only an attempt at re-evaluation. 'Pound's writings help us immensely in putting across the various historical and cultural vistas in focus in his own manner, that is, exploring the relationship of poetry to history.'

Notes

1. The English translation by A.J. Arberry is my reference for the present. The *Tawq* is divided into thirty chapters: (1) The Prologue and the discourse on the nature of love, (2) Singing of Love, (3) Falling in love in sleep, (4) Love from description, (5) Love at first sight, (6) Love coming only after long association, (7) About those who fall in love with a quality/virtue, and afterwards do not like another differing from it, (8) Allusion in speech, (9) Hints with eyes, (10) Exchanging messages (correspondence), (11) Obedience (submissiveness), (15) Opposition, (16) Fault Finder, (17) The Helping friend, (18) Watcher (*raqeeb*), (19) Slanderer, (20) Union, (21) Avoidance, (22) Faithfulness, (23) Betrayal, (24) Separation, (25) Contentment, (26) Illness, (27) Oblivion, (28) Death, (29) Ugliness of illicit practices, and (30) Excellence of continence. In the (other) kinds (of love) things like mental preoccupation, pain, constant obsession, change of innate character, mutation of firmly impressed nature, emaciation, sighing, and other indications of deep sorrow, as happens in passionate love do not occur.

2. A reading of the songs of the early Troubadours, especially of William IX of Aquitaine, will easily bear out the influence of the themes and poetic devices frequently used by the Arabic lyric poets or Andalus and codified by Ibn Hazm in *The Dove's Neck Ring*. The allusion to the enemy/rival in the Troubadour songs may also be understood in the light of its conventional usage in Arabic poetry.

CHAPTER 2

Some Perspectives on the Medieval Tradition of Poetry

Medieval literature, which is sometimes described as 'debased classicism' or 'the primitive stage of the several national literatures', unlike Medieval science is not only highly refined in taste and tradition but also rich in variety and fertile in imagination. The almost sudden outbrust of a people, relieved from the strains of classical disciplines and discovering their new moorings and cultural ethos through the medium of newly developed Roman languages, may be considered the first bloom in the imminent Renaissance of Europe. It is interesting to note that while the Renaissance paved the way for a more rational, all-inclusive and organized effort towards the development and progress of science and empirical studies, it (the Renaissance) considerably changed the sources from which the human mind had been fed for long. William Morris' observation[1] that the Renaissance affected the course of literary tradition in Europe in the wrong direction; betrays a kind of truth the veracity of which cannot be easily questioned. It may sound presumptuous, but one gets a sense that the literature of Medieval Europe is richer in variety, more vast in sweep and deeper in expression of thought and feeling when compared with the literature of post-Renaissance Europe. When I say this I realize the implication and import of this statement as it underscores the significance and value of the literature of the principal Roman languages in the succeeding four centuries. I have in mind the works of Dante, Petrarch, Boccaccio and Ariosto from Italian, the Troubadours, Chretien de Troyes, *Roman de la Rose*, from Provençal and French, Cervantes in Spanish, Langland's *Sir Gawain and the Green Knight*, Chaucer, Gower, Spenser, Surrey and Shakespeare in English when I refer to the Medieval literature of Europe. Though AD 1400, the year of Chaucer's death is considered by scholars to mark the end of the Medieval age in England, its tradition of poetry retains its foothold till the close of the sixteenth century.

A close look at the catalogue of authors referred to will show that I have the major authors of roughly four centuries of West Europe, i.e. from the thirteenth to the sixteenth century excepting Shakespeare who lived to write till 1616 and Cervantes' *Don Quixote* which was published in 1606. The categorization of these authors in one group demands an explanation and identification of the various Medieval virtues in literature. But before we attempt to identify the Medieval virtues, it would be useful to cast a glance at the religious and socio-political condition of Western Europe on the eve of the Medieval Age. It is said that the real recovery of Europe from what can justifiably be regarded as the 'Dark Ages' dates from the latter half of the tenth century when the Germans halted the Magyar nomadic hordes from Asia, who had conducted their raids across the length and breadth of the continent. The establishment of the Moorish kindgom in Spain early in the seventh century, which produced one of the earliest and greatest civilizations in the history of Western Europe influenced the course of the cultural history of Europe in great measure. The Arabs with their rich literary heritage found themselves busy assimilating and disseminating Latin knowledge which had hitherto been preserved in cathedrals. Hitti records that 'When the University of Oxford still looked upon bathing as a heathen custom, generations of Cordovan Scientists had been enjoying baths in luxurious establishments.'[2] Being next door to France, close to Italy and across the English Channel, it is impossible to imagine that Hispania denied the fruits of its intellectual and literary pursuits to them and postponed their recovery from the Dark Ages for long, particularly at a time when the movement of scholars, courtiers and seminaries was not only not restricted, but free and unhampered.

Another important factor which contributed towards the establishment of a new social order was the gradual formation of a Christian culture based on the universal acceptance of the faith and typified in the twelfth century by the rise of scholasticism, cathedral building, and the gradual transition to what we call universities. In the Middle Ages 'a certain marriage of Christianity and the world—Christianity with the whole mundane Order—produced a supra-national religious society that was itself an amazing structure and can now be envisaged as a work of art.'[3] Needless to add that the greatest source of this society was the institution of the Papacy. This was a period when religion was so imposing and powerful with it's external apparatus of symbolism, rituals, biblical personalities and famous saints, its associations with a peculiar pattern of the cosmos, even its view of the hand of God in history, that one could entertain the idea of a 'Christian Civilization', which culminating in the thirteenth century, affected the landscape of town and country, governed the calendar of the year, touched the home, the craft guilds, the universities, and even put a stamp of its own ideas about the nature of personality and about the right posture to be adopted by human beings. It provided the conditions for the development of piety and the inner life—for the deepening of religious thought and religious experience—and for the expression of all this in cathedrals in painting, and in poetry. One feels tempted to compare the life of thirteenth-century Europe in the university towns of Bologna, Salerno, Paris and Oxford to the Byzantium of W.B. Yeats which the poet discovers to be a meeting point and the centre of the religious, aesthetic and practical life.[4] Charles Homer Haskins' contention that the European Renaissance did not begin in Italy in the fourteenth century but in the later half of the eleventh century and that it reached its culmination in the middle of the thirteenth century deserves our attention.[5] He further says that compared to the great transformation that took place in Europe from the eleventh to the thirteenth century, the fifteenth–sixteenth-century Renaissance is not more than a ripple. He mentions the establishment of universities, rise of humanism and the efforts at translating the works of Aristotle, Ptolemy, Euclid and Boethius and the free movement of scholars from one place to the other as the factors which brought about a sea change in people's attitudes and interests.

The period of the Crusades from 1095 to 1258 is generally seen as the period of conflict between two great faiths and as an ignoble phase of Christian history. Be that as it may, this phase of European history could also be taken as another important factor in establishing a new cultural ethos in Medieval Europe. The Crusades provided to the people of the Western continent and England their first ever and long exposure at different levels of thought and feeling to the peoples of the East and their institutions and seats of learning. The holy city of Jerusalem could not be taken back from the Arabs, but the Europeans must have returned more accomplished and richer from their campaign and pilgrimage of Palestine and the fabulous Orient. Moreover, the crusades strengthened and reinforced the unity and supra-national Christian society of the European peninsula. In this connection mention may be made of Eleanor of Aquitaine (1122–1204), first married to Louis VII of France and later betrothed to Prince Henry of England, afterwards known as King Henry II. Queen Eleanor, two of whose sons, John and Richard, ruled England one after another, played a significant role in shaping the literary sensibilities of, both the French and the English. She was with Louis VII during the second crusade and had taken a troup of Troubadours from Paris to Jerusalem. She is credited with patronizing the Troubadour poetry which contributed to the growth and development of the cult of the dame in English literary tradition. It may be interesting to note that it was Eleanor's son Richard, later known as 'the Lion Hearted', whose meeting with Saladin during the course of the military campaign, has been celebrated by many authors including Sir Walter Scott, who is probably one of the first English authors to have treated Saladin, the victor of Jerusalem, with respect and consideration in the *Talisman.* Saladin was one of the greatest legends of his time and was treated as the 'Paragon of Chivalry' both by the Muslims and Christians alike. The cult of chivalry, which finds its examples in the tales of Chretien, Ariosto, Chaucer, Langland, Spenser and in a different sense in Cervantes, had its archetype in the historical-cum-fictional character of Saladin. *Futuwwah,* which has been described as the original and the Oriental form of chivalry, was popular in and practised by Arabs even before the advent of Islam. *Muruwwah* was the pre-Islamic equivalent of *Futuwwah* and carried all the connotations of 'chivalry' with an added emphasis on 'revenge', which was dropped as a consequence of the influence of Islam.[6]

This was the backdrop which laid the foundation of a society and set a new tradition of literature. The formation of a Christian culture in the relatively safe and secure boundaries of the continent, the social intercourse with the more civilized Arabs both in war time and peace time in Spain and the East, the gradual availability of the works of Ovid, Aristotle, Horace, Virgil, Boethius, Macrobius and Catullus through translations and the exposure of the European people to the highly refined and indigenous Hispano–Arabic verse, the Troubadours, the growth and development of Roman vernaculars contributed towards the establishment of a supra-national, continental Christian consciousness never seen or witnessed in Europe. It provided the author a stimulus and inspiration to explore the possibilities of expression in various modes and conventions. As has been pointed out, 'a religion that has soaked itself into the minds of men and almost become second nature of them, can work like a chemical in a society inspiring original thought giving wing to the imagination and inciting the believer to strange adventure, curious experiments in living'. The works of St. Augustine Macrobius, Boethius and St. Thomas Aquinas attracted the minds of the age as they provoked and inspired seminal debates about some of the perennial issues of life, death, predestination, free will, sin and redemption and which provided a basis and ground for scholastic affirmation of the Christian faith. What stimulated the formation of a Christian society to such heights, also contributed towards the evolution of a new aesthetics in Medieval Europe.

The evolutionary stage of any language sometimes offers to its authors an opportunity to explore and discover the possibilities of expression with vigour and variety without the constraints of tradition. To establish this contention, various examples can be cited from world literature. When Greek had been developed as a medium of communication early in the seventh century BC, the possibilities of expression had been almost exhausted in the dramatic and poetical modes of Euripides (485–406 BC), Sophocles (496–406 BC) and Homer (before 700 BC). The history of early Latin writings, that is, the works of Virgil (70–19 BC), Ovid (43–17 BC), Horace (85–88 BC), and Catullus (85–84 BC) point to the same pattern. In the Orient also, the kind and quality of poetry that was produced in the early period of Medieval Iran, is still considered the greatest and the best by the lay readers and scholars of Persian. These include the poetry of Firdausi (d. AD 1020), Omar Khayyam (d. 1243), Saadi (d. 1200), Attar (d. 1230), Rumi (d. 1273), and Hafiz (d. 1390). The Arabs still regard the pre-Islamic *Mu'allaqat* as the *magnum opus* of their poetry. It can, therefore, be stated that in at least four major classical languages, viz., Greek, Latin, Arabic and Persian, their best poetry had been written and modes of poetic expression greatly explored and richly exploited as soon as these languages had been developed as a means of communication in the early phase of their evolution. It is a different issue whether the language was developed as a result of the flowering of its literature or its literature was developed because the language had been found to be an effective means of expression. A third possibility could be attributed to the fact that it was mainly the genius of these authors which brought about and set in place the great tradition, the capability and evolutionary phase of the language notwithstanding.

Medieval literature may be classified into three distinct phases: '(1) the formation of a Catholic culture out of diverse Semitic, Persian, Coptic, Hellenic, Italic and Celtic cultures with a focus upon the life and miracles of Christ and his apostles, (2) the transmission of classical learning and scholastic studies into Roman tongues by the regular and secular clergy and, (3) a secularizing period in which verbal arts found their fullest expression in various forms of literature.'[8] For secular themes the authors had the choice of various national heroes: King Arthur epitomized the matter of Britain, Alexander, Trojan wars and its heroes were treated as the matter of Rome, and Charlemagne and his knights represented the national aspirations of the French. For legends and lores the authors drew upon various indigenous sources, the foremost and chief being the grail legend.

Weston's book, *From Ritual to Romance* which gives a fascinating account of the grail legend, offers to the modern reader a view of the Medieval world and the myths which influenced its literature. Vegetation themes, the celebration of spring festivals, annual triumphs of summer over winter and courtly passion are some of the popular themes treated in *Roman de la Rose*, a work of joint authorship of Guillaume de Lorris and Jean de Meung in the thirteenth century which influenced the Medieval French and English literatures in great measure. It is an allegory within a dream-vision. It also comprises ribald and anti-clerical tales presented in a mocking spirit.

Allegory as the mode and dream-vision as the convention are probably the most recognizable features of Medieval poetry. It is a paradigm which encompasses the earliest Medieval literature, from *Roman de la Rose* to the last major work of the great Medieval tradition, namely *The Faerie Queene* of Spenser. Allegory was a form that jacketed such diverse themes as courtly passion and the seven deadly sins. It was a convenient but powerful medium in the hand of the poet to celebrate, mock, ridicule and sermonize. Likewise, the convention of dream-vision which was frequently employed in poetry, demanded a certain measure of poetic vigour and inventiveness on the part of the poet. An example may be cited here of William Langland's *Vision of Piers Plowman*, whose beauty and strength partly lies in the poet's employment of dream-convention. The fluid movement of the poem, the sudden shifts of time and space and the inconsequentiality of Piers's dreaming contribute to the richness of the poem.

Bird fables and bestiaries are also common in Medieval literature. Ibn-al-Muqaffa's *Kalilah wa Dimna*, believed to be the Arabic version of a lost original of the *Panchatantra* set the tradition of bestiaries in Medieval

Europe. Its first adaptation was done by Anglo Firenzuola and Doni in Italy and was later published in a French translation. Sir Thomas North brought out the *Morall Philosophie of Doni* in 1570 in English directly from the Italian version. This too was seen by the Medieval poet, like allegory, as a convenient medium to treat a subject which may have invited the wrath of the authorities. Chaucer's *Parliament of Fowles* and *Nun's Priest's Tale*, Spenser's *Mother Hubberd's Tale* and Drayton's *The Owl* provide some of the specimens of Medieval poetry.

However, Fariduddin Attar's *Mantiq al Tayr* which is a 'grandiose' poetic elaboration of the *Risala-al-Tayr* of Ahmed Ghazzali surpasses them all in its superb handling of a simple bird fable for the theme of a highly mystical debate.

The more easily recognizable feature of Medieval poetry may be seen in its treatment of love, in the romantic and courtly tradition. Romance or the Romantic tradition was loosely applied to all kinds of writing in European vernaculars. It had the elements of fantasy but tended to the natural. Chretien turns men's gaze inwards and allegorizes courtly passion, whereas Guillaume de Lorris in *Roman de la Rose* removes the heroine entirely and her character is represented through personifications. Moods and aspects of the lady are personified. If she takes no part in the action, it is because her heart is the scene of action. Similar treatments are found in Spenser's *Faerie Queene* where the poet combines the diverse traditions of romance into a new form and pattern. Spenser's work is modelled on Ariosto's *Orlando Furioso*, a romance dealing with Orlando's feats of chivalry against the Saracens. The romance maybe taken as the Medieval version of the classical epic in many a respect. Poetry in the Medieval Age was meant to be recited rather than read in a closet. The oral tradition necessitated a 'prologue' and an 'epilogue'. Some of the major works of this age are divided into various books, books into cantos and cantos into numerous sections and stanzas. The division was warranted by the culture of the oral tradition which required the reading of a tale or 'passus' in one long sitting in a lord mayor's or baron's house.

The sudden emergence of the courtly love tradition in eleventh-century Provence remains an inexplicable phenomenon in English literary history. C.S. Lewis, while discussing the possible elements which may have gone into the shaping of this ennobling passion, observes in *Allegory of Love:* 'It is, at any rate, certain that the efforts of scholars have so far failed to find any origin for the content of Provençal love poetry. Celtic, Byzantine, and even Arabic influences have been suspected; but it has not been made clear that these, if granted, could account for the results we see.'[9]

But Elizabeth Salter the noted Medievalist, expresses her reservations on the entirely sceptical attitude of the literary historians with regard to Arabic influence. She considers the influence of Hispano–Arabic poetry upon that of southern France 'a serious probability'.[10]

It may be noted here that Orientalists like Philip K. Hitti, Nicholson and H.A.R. Gibb noticed the impact of Hispano–Arabic poetry on Provençal poets. *Zajal* and *muwashshah* the two forms of lyric poetry with markedly platonic treatment of love, emerged in Spain in the early eighth century and elicited native Christian admiration. The Arabic lyric form was developed into Castilian, popular verse, *villancio* and, it is said, was extensively used for Christian hymns and carols. Likewise, the Troubadours imitated their southern contemporaries, the *zajal*-singers, and contributed towards the growth of the cult of the dame in the Western literary tradition, which later came to be described as 'courtly love'.

In Al-Andalus Arabic developed verse forms absolutely different from those of other Arabic speaking countries, namely, *muwashshah* and *zajal*, the former when written in classical Arabic and *zajal* when written in Andalusian vulgar Arabic. From the fourteenth century comes a song in archaic Spanish which is still very popular in southern Spain and is a perfect example of *zajal*. Set in traditional Hispano–Arabic mode, the song is called 'The Three Muslim Maids of Jaen'.

> *Tres morillals enamoron en Jaen*
> *Aixa, Fatima Y Marien,*
>
> *Ibne a coger manzanas*
> *Y Fallaron las cogidas en Jaen*
> *Aixa, Fatima Y Marien*
>
> *Tres morillas tan garrides*
> *Iban a Coger Olives*
> *Y fallaron las cogides en*
> *Jaen Aixa Fatima Y Marieh*
>
> *Sevoritas quienes sois*
> *Que mi, vida destrozaiz*

Cristianas que eramos en Jaen
Aixa Fatima Y Marien

(I am in love with three Muslim maids in Jaen, Aisha, Fatima and Marien. Three Muslim maids so attractive went to pick olives, Olives were not picked, in Jaen, Aisha Fatima. . . . Young ladies who are you who are destroying my life? We are Christian girls who once were Muslims in Jaen, Aisha, Fatima and Marien.)[11]

One might suspect that the *zajal* form is of Persian origin, but scholars have so far failed to discover its Arabic/Persian model and there is agreement on the fact that it is indigenous to Spain. According to Hispano–Arabic tradition, the *zajal* was invented by Muqaddam of Cabra, a tenth-century bard who composed both in Romance (Lisanal Ajaro) and vulgar Arabic. This seems to indicate that the said form passed from Romance to Arabic. However, classical Latin verse knows nothing similar. Some critics find its roots in antiquarian Celtic verse. That would imply that the original of the *zajal* form passed from Celtic to vulgar Latin and from vulgar Latin to Roman vernaculars and thence to Arabic. The *zajal* consisted of several stanzas in which the rhymes were so arranged that the master-rhyme ending each stanza and running through the whole poem like a refrain were continually interrupted by a various succession of subordinate rhymes: aa/bbba/ccca/ddda/. The form appears to have richly contributed to the growth and development of Provençal poetry which began a new tradition of love poetry in Romance languages. Some examples are given:

I dare not send her message by another:
So do I fear to anger her:
Nor do I dare, for fear of doing wrong,
To show my love . . .
When the new grass and leaves appear,
And the flowers bud in the gardens,
And the nightingale, loud and clear,
Raises its voice and sings its song,
I've joy in bird, and in my lady more;
On every side by joy I am constrained,
But she's the joy from which all others flow.

And I would imprint her mouth with kisses
So that the marks would be seen a whole month.

—Bernart de Ventadorn

The love that consumes me is as pure as the
Visages of the elect . . .
I laid my face against the ground that it
Might be as a footstool to my lady

She said:
Rejoice, for you may set your lips upon my veil!
But my heart would not consent: for she
Entrusted to the nobility of my feelings
The care of her honour[12]

—Ibne Darrach (d. 976)

The courtly love tradition which found its culmination in the Elizabethan sonnet in England, contributed towards the Platonic theory of love in the literature of Roman languages. Troubadour song has been traced to carols sung to Venus by peasant girls of Poitou and Limousin in the May festivals. 'Out of this spring time love and the glorification of women', says Katherine M. Wilson, 'the troubadours developed their conventions of love'.[13]

For she knows that she alone can cure me

I have a love; I don't know who she is,
For, in all truth, I've never seen her
— Guilhem of Poitou, the first Troubadour

Far away are the castle and tower
Where she and her husband live . . .

Let no men think it strange that I
Love one whom I shall ne'er behold.
No other love as dear I hold
Save her on whom ne'er looked my eye.

Who's never told me truth or lie,
Nor know I if 'twill e'er be told . . .

She strikes a blow of joy that kills,
A wound of love that steals my heart . . .
No men with such sweet ills
E'er died, rejoicing, from lov's dart.

Despairing, rejoicing will I go
That I may see my distant love,
But I know not how that may be
Our Country are so far apart.
Countless are the ports and roads!
and therefore, I cannot forecast . . .
But all will happen as God wills!
Their love lasted a long time before the Viscount,
noticed it.

—Jaufre Rudel of Blaye (d. 1447)

The following translation from a courtly lover's verse reflects the trend that was to become a rage with the Elizabethan sonnet writer:

Bitter the breeze that strips the forest boughs:
Whose leafage once, with sweetness was fulfilled,
And strikes the back of every bird on branch,
Mated and single, to stammer or be mute.
Why have I striven' word and deed to please,
In all, that she who has my high estate brought love.
Of which I die unless she end my grief.[14]

Commenting upon the significance of Provençal poetry and its profound impact on the succeeding ages, Lewis says, 'French Poets, in the eleventh century, discovered or invented, or were first to express, that romantic species of passion which English poets were still writing about in the nineteenth century. They effected a change which has left no corner of our ethics, our imagination, or our daily life untouched, and they erected impassable barriers between us and the classical past or the Oriental present. Compared with this revolution the Renaissance is a mere ripple on the surface of literature.'[15] He further contends that the courtly love traditions did not have its origin in any of the indigenous sources nor in the classical Latin. As has been pointed out by Elizabeth Salter, it was mainly the influence of Hispano–Arabic verse which influenced the cult of the dame in Roman languages.

The virtues of Medieval literature can therefore be identified to its treatment of love, a certain measure of poetic vigour and an all-embracing exuberance and novelty of form and expression. Its literature abounds in fantasy but tends to be natural in the treatment of human passions and moods. A certain sense of mystery, a quest for the unknown, an exploration of the inner states of mind and heart characterize the spirit of Medievalism. Medievalism was found to be on its way out as soon as its virtues were replaced by the Renaissance temper and the attempts to rationalize and define life and human behaviour. The Renaissance temper suited empirical studies and scientific knowledge. It affected and checked the smooth but strong currents of humantistic culture of the Medieval Age that had been built round the edifice of the cathedral and the cross-fertilization of Roman–Arabic literature, though Medievalism was replaced by a new literary taste/culture during and after the Renaissance and a new kind of aesthetics appears to have become popular, a backward movement to recapture and re-create the Medieval aesthetics seems to recur frequently. Blake's reaction against the rationality and Aristotelian logic as expounded by Newton, Bacon and Locke, and his building of a system and new poetics, in a certain sense, may be seen as an effort to revive the Medieval spirit. The elements of Hellenism, Medievalism and all that negated the virtues of the Age of Reason, in the poetry of Romantics may also be interpreted as a trend towards Medievalism. Later, in the nineteenth century, the pre-Raphaelite movement and the Symbolist movement of France influenced the course of poetry both in England and America to the same logic, that is, to revive and re-create fantasy and dreaminess of Medieval literature. It can therefore be stated that with its freshness and vigour, quality and variety and the variety of themes, Medievalism has attracted the English authors, though only a few of them appear to have succeeded in introducing the Medieval spirit in the otherwise prosaic, didactic and sometimes unispiring literary annals of English poetry. The names of Spenser, William Blake, Byron, John Keats, William Morris, W.B. Yeats, and Walter de la Mare may be mentioned as the authors who consciously and successfully contributed in reviving and re-creating the spirit of Medieval literature.

Notes

1. 'He (William Morris) wished to go back to the Middle Ages, not because he was retrogressive, but because he thought civilization had taken the wrong turning, and that to regain the right path it was necessary to go back to where the ways had parted.' Richard Ferrar Pattersan, ed., *Six Centuries of English Literature*, vol. VI, Gresham, London, 1933, p. 46.
2. *History of the Arabs*, Macmillan, London, 8th edn, 1964, p. 526.

3. Philip P. Weiner, ed., 'Christianity in History', *Dictionary of the History of Ideas*, vol. I, Charles Scribners, New York, 1937, p. 384.

4. 'I think that in early Byzantium, may be never before or since in recorded history, religious, aesthetic and practical life were one.' W.B. Yeats, *A Vision*, 1917, quoted by John Unterecker in *A Readers Guide to W.B. Yeats*, Thames and Hudson, London, 1969, p. 172.

5. Warren Hollister, ed., *The Twelfth Century Renaissance* (Major Issues in History Series), New York, 1969.

6. See Ibn Al Sulami's (325/936–412/1021), *The Book of Sufi Chivalry—Futuwwah*, being the first English translation of Sulami's *Kitabal Futwwah*, by Sheikh Tosun Bayrak al-Jerrahi Al-Halveti, East West Publications, London, 1983 and Goldziher's chapter on '*Murruwwah*' in *Muslim Studies*, vol. I.

7. Philip P. Weiner, op. cit., p. 383.

8. Alex Preminger, ed., *Princeton Encyclopedia of Poetry and Poetics*, Macmillan, 1974, Entry 'Medieval Poetics', p. 429.

9. C.S. Lewis, *Allegory of Love*, Oxford, 1936, paperback edn, 1969, p. 11.

10. 'Courts and Courtly Love' in David Detaches and Anthony Thorlby, eds., *The Medieval World*, World Civilization Series, Aldous Books, London, 1973, p. 426.

11. For the Spanish lyric and its translation into English I am indebted to Michael McClain who kindly lent me his unpublished paper on 'Arabic-learning in Spain'.

12. Quoted by Elizabeth Salter in 'Courts and Courtly love' in *The Medieval World*, op. cit.

13. Katherine M. Wilson, *Shakespeare's Sugared Sonnets*, George Allen and Unwin, London, 1974, p. 12.

14. Quoted by Katherine M. Wilson, ibid. p. 13.

15. C.S. Lewis, op. cit., p. 4.

CHAPTER 3

Sufic Themes and Images in Persian and Hindavi Poetry: A Re-ordering of Universe and Re-adjustment of Impulses

The phenomenal spread of Islam in the seventh and eighth centuries brought in its wake political domination and immense wealth, which was to last for centuries. This accounted for the shaping of the Muslim sensibility and world view to such an extent that political power and prosperity came to be seen as the consequence of true faith, so much so that dissenters in Islamic society were not only disfavoured but persecuted and vilified. Abuzar Ghifari,[1] Ammar ibn Yasir,[2] Husain ibn Ali,[3] Umar ibn Abdul Aziz,[4] Ahmad ibn Hanbal[5] and Husain ibn Mansur[6] fall in the category of such eminent persons who dared to question the actions of caliphs and rulers. It was, therefore, all the more necessary for men like Hasan of Basra,[7] Junaid of Baghdad,[8] Abu Said Abul Khair,[9] Abdul Qadir Jilani,[10] Al Ghazzali[11] and others like them to distance themselves from court and state politics and invite the Muslims back to the Prophetic model of austerity and ascetic life. The Prophet took pride in *faqr (al-faqr-o fakhri)*. Followers of Islam were encouraged to shun the life of extravagance and unnecessary expenditure. The early preceptors of the Sufi orders emphasized the Prophet's example and exhorted their followers to live a life of austerity and piety. Not only did they consciously distance themselves from the state, but they also condemned a life of luxury.

The teachings and ideas of Sufism gradually found their way into the writings and discourses of various writers. As a consequence, there was an emergence of Sufic literature and its proliferation in the eleventh century in the forms of both *risalahs* and poetry. It was in such literature that Sufi orders were generally formalized and provided with a kind of doctrine that was hitherto available only in the form of recorded observations and utterances. Sufic thought and tenets found rich and fertile soil in Persian poetry, the *lingua franca* of many countries where Arabic was not spoken. From Rumi[12] onwards to modern times, Sufic poetry has been anti-establishment and non-conformist, an essential part of the teachings of Sufis. This characteristic feature has continued unabated for centuries. In the subcontinent, Hindavi poetry, including Urdu *ghazals*, which inherited the Persian tradition, endorsed the sentiment. The tradition of the *ghazal* genre of poetry, from Persian to its Urdu version, has an uninterrupted history, spanning over nine hundred years. From the very beginning, the *ghazal* exalted the theme of secular love and targeted the symbols of temporal and political authority. This has been the direct influence of Sufism on literature.

The phenomenon has been perceived as a unique synthesis of Sufic thought and poetry. According to the noted historian M. Mujeeb, 'By the thirteenth century, Sufism had become a movement, and it would not be an exaggeration to say that it brought Islam to the masses and the masses towards Islam.' Shaikh Abu Said Abul Khair was also a poet, and the quatrains he composed mark the beginning of the Sufis' special connection with literature, enabling their profound influence on ideas, social life and culture. One of the better-known verses of Shaikh Abu Said Abul Khair reads as follows:

> He who is not my friend,
> May God be his friend.
> And he who causes me distress,
> May his joy increase.

> He who places thorns in my path,
> With malice in his heart,
> May every flower that blooms
> In the garden of his life
> Be without a single thorn.

Rather significantly, it was the same period when the Sufi *silsilas*, namely the Qadiriya, Chishtiya, Suharwardiya, Naqshbandiya, Maulaviya, Shazliya and Rifaiya, spread all over the Islamic world with unprecedented vigour. Some of the best Sufi poetry is from this period. The poets who enriched this tradition were Jalaluddin Rumi (AD 1207–73), Abu Said Abul Khair, Fakhruddin Ibrahim Iraqi (d. AD 1289),[13] Muhiuddeen Ibn Arabi (AD 1165–1240),[14] Fariduddin Attar (AD 1142–1230)[15] and Amir Khusrau (AD 1253–1325).[16] Persian poets explained Islamic doctrines in a mystical manner that was often seen as heretical and non-conformist. This form of protest and non-conformity against the established tenets of faith and practices, particularly in the Persian–Urdu tradition, gave rise to the first conflict of its kind within the Islamic fold. It was spelt out and explained in treatises like *Risala-e Qushairiya, Adaab ul-Murideen* and *Kashf ul-Mahjub*, and *malfuzat* like *Fawaid ul-Fawad* and *Khair ul-Majalis*, and collections of epistles like *Maktubat-e Sadi* and *Maktubat-e Rabbani*. Their sentiments were expressed and echoed in Persian and Urdu *ghazals*. In the process, *shaikh, waiz, muhtasib, mimbar, sajjada, tasbeeh* and *zunnar* became the images that were targeted and censured while images like *rind, maikada* and *pir-e mughan* were celebrated and glorified.

Consequently, the images of non-conformism became attractive and the images of authority became objects of derision and detestation. It is in this context that we see glimpses of the political role of Sufism in Turkey, Iran, Central Asia and India. This phenomenon may be seen as a turning point in the history of the Islamic people and may even be described as an expression of Protestantism that had a far-reaching influence on the moral and social spheres of conduct. Even today, when much of the appeal of Persian poetry and the exclusivist and ascetic lives of the inhabitants of the *khanqah* has lost its earlier charm, the Persian–Urdu *ghazal* and the *khanqah* remain the permanent points of reference to provide the other option within the Islamic fold pertaining to a life of intellectual enlightenment and spiritual fulfilment.

It is indeed an enigma that *Wahdat ul-Wujudi* thought, as articulated in Muhiuddeen Ibn Arabi's *Fusus al-Hikam*, did not find favour with the majority of Muslim scholars; but when the same thought was expressed poetically in Jalaluddin Rumi's *Masnavi*, it was appreciated and commended by a host of Muslim scholars over the ages, so much so that the *Masnavi* has been described as 'the Koran in Persian':

Masnavi-e-manavi-e Moulvi
hast Quran dar zaban-e Pahlavi

But, at the same time, the rise of scholasticism appears to have affected the real intent of Sufic thought. It was, therefore, necessary to emphasize the felt experiences as against the intellectual debate made popular by the scholastic discipline. According to Philip K. Hitti, Sufism is 'not so much, a set of doctrines as it is a mode of thinking and feeling in the religious domain. Muslim mysticism represents a reaction against the intellectualism of Islam, and the formalism which developed as a consequence. Psychologically, its basis should be sought in the human aspiration to a personal, direct approach to, and a more intense experience of, the deity and the religious truth.' This personal element was best reflected in poetry. According to the eminent scholar, Alam Khundmiri,

> The distinctive character of Indian Sufism lies in its success in resolving the tension between the polar realities of the inward mystical experience or eternity, and the Sharia and history. Indian Sufism is heir to the martyrdom of al Hallaj,[17] the sober spirituality of al-Junaid, the ecstatic vision of Bayazid,[18] the orthodoxy-oriented mystical life of al-Ghazzali, the illuminationistic gnosis of Ishraqun, the theophanist monism of Ibn al-Arabi, and the spiritual flights of Vedantic monism. By the time Sufism reached India, it had practically resolved the conflict between the transcendental and the immanentist tendencies which are not two mutually opposite tendencies, but two necessary modes of religious experience.

But perhaps the most representative expression was given to the Sufi values by Shaikh Nizamuddin Awliya.[19] He wrote:

> There is a form of obedience of the law (*ta'at*) which is intransitive and a form that is, transitive. The intransitive form is that the benefit of which remains limited to the one person who performs the acts of obedience, which are prayer, fasting, haj and the repetition of litanies. The transitive form, on the other hand, consists of providing benefit or solace to another. The merits of this are beyond limit and conjecture. Acts of intransitive obedience have to be performed with sincerity in order to be acceptable (to God), but acts of transitive obedience are acceptable, of whatever kind they may be. . . . People asked Shaikh Abu Said Abul Khair how many paths, there were to God. He replied, 'There are as many paths to God as there are particles in the universe, but no path is shorter than that of bringing solace to hearts. Whatever, I have attained I have attained on this path.'

Here it would be interesting to narrate an incident about Hazrat Nizamuddin Awliya. Once he was watching the Hindus bathe in the

Yamuna. He was wearing a tilted cap on his head. He is reported to have commented, 'Every sect has a path of its own, its faith and cynosure.' Whereupon, Khusrau supplied the antiphony: 'I have straightened my cynosure towards one wearing a tilted cap.'

Sufism spread among the masses from the *khanqahs*. Among the Sufic orders, the Chishti–Nizami order in India has been one of the most significant in influencing the social life of people across the country. It had five great saints, consecutively, whose collective impact on the teachings of the *silsila* and whose charisma contributed greatly to the shaping of the sensibilities of its followers, from Delhi to Gulbarga and Ajmer to Pandua. The five saints, namely, Hazrat Khwaja Moinuddin Chishti,[20] Khwaja Qutbuddin Bakhtiar Kaki,[21] Khwaja Fariduddin Ganjeshakar,[22] Sultan Nizamuddin Awliya and Hazrat Nasiruddin Chiragh-i Dihli[23] in succession imparted such a halo to the Chishti order that its impact can be felt even today. The Chishti colour is so bright and all absorbing, that no other shades can compare in maintaining an identity. After the departure of Khwaja Syed Muhammad Gesudaraz[24] from Delhi to Gulbarga, several centres of the Chishti order were established at Pandua, Hansi, Manikpur, Laharpur, Kichhauchha, Taunsa, Amethi, Salon, Bareilly, Phulwari, Kakori, Jais and Dewa. These *khanqahs* extended the Chishti platform throughout the Gangetic plains. The Awadhi countryside is still dotted with small and big *khanqahs* of Chishti saints.

In the early period of the Chishti order, its saints, such as Hazrat Fariduddin Ganj-e Shakar (d. AD 1265), Hazrat Nizamuddin Awliya (d. AD 1325) and Hazrat Nasiruddin Chiragh-e Dihli (d. AD 1351), set very high standards for the *khanqah*. They insisted that the *khanqahs* should be distanced from the state powers. While Hazrat Fariduddin lived in a small village Ajodhan, now called Pakpatan (in modern Pakistan), Hazrat Nizamuddin Awliya and Hazrat Nasiruddin Chiragh-e Dihli lived in Delhi for several decades without any interaction with the powerful sultans of Delhi. Tradition has it that once, when Alauddin Khalji sent word through Hazrat Amir Khusrau (d. AD 1325) that he would visit the celebrated saint, Hazrat Nizamuddin Awliya asked Khusrau to convey to the sultan that there were two doors in his *khanqah*, and that if the sultan were to enter from one door, he would leave from the other.

The strict example set by Hazrat Nizamuddin Awliya in distancing himself from the court was scrupulously followed by his successors for several centuries. One of his illustrious successors, Hazrat Shah Pir Muhammad Saloni (d. 1099 Hijri),[25] the founder of the Chishti Nizami *khanqah* at Salon, was invited by the Emperor Aurangzeb to meet him whenever he visited the city of his *pirs*. He refused the invitation and wrote to the Emperor:

> A mendicant like me finds no courage to attend the royal summons. What has a rustic to do at the imperial court? If perchance, someone happens to visit the *khanqah*, he is welcome. My *Karim* (God) made me dependent upon none. He provides for me when I feel hungry; if I am asleep, He guards; if, perchance, some sin is committed by me, He pardons. His favours are sufficient for me and to strive for more will be futile.

The emperor was so impressed by the illustrious shaikh's reply that he thought of paying a visit to Salon to meet him. Family tradition has it that he had to change the programme because of some exigencies in the Deccan. However, the emperor issued a *farman* granting some lands 'for the expenditure of the servants' of Shah Pir Muhammad Saloni. It can be surmised that the shaikh would not have accepted the grant if the *farman* had been issued in his name. It is, therefore, a rare *farman*.

Several passages and verses from the Persian poetry of the classical period celebrate the position of man in the universe. While these poets glorify secular love and the unity of humankind, they scoff at whatever is pretentious and vain. The symbols of religious hypocrisy have all along been derided in the *ghazal* tradition. In Western literature we find passages in Chaucer, Langland and Blake launching a scathing attack on the church and the symbols of the ecclesiastical order, but not an entire tradition of poetry spread over several centuries given to the exposure of the sanctimonious tendencies in religion. One shudders to think what may have happened to Muslim civil society if the Sufi orders had not so vigorously upheld the cause of true faith by consciously distancing themselves from state politics, and if the poets had not satirized the pretentious and the ritualistic tendencies in Islam. It was, in a way, a movement that wanted Muslims to go back to the Medina of the time of the Prophet Muhammad and the four rightly guided caliphs. This phase of Islam; in the eleventh and the twelfth centuries, can also be described as the first reawakening of Muslims.

II

Husain ibn Mansur remains, in the history of Islam, one of the greatest Sufis to have come into direct confrontation with the exponents of *fiqh* in the early tenth century AD. He made his felt experience of *Anal Haq* public, for which he was reprimanded and censured. Mansur belonged to the fraternity of such eminent persons as Shibli[26] and Junaid. As he refused to recant his public utterance, the state and jury inflicted severe punishment on him. His execution in AD 922 at Baghdad, which had the support of a section of the court and the *ulema*, was perhaps one of the most disquieting events in Islamic history, one that has continued to haunt sensitive souls. It would, however, be presumptuous to suggest that the execution of Mansur charged and propelled generations to react adversely to the domination of *fiqh* that justified the said punishment. There could have been several other factors, which may have caused disillusionment with the edict and the support and patronage that came from the court. It is indeed intriguing that Mansur's execution did not receive the kind of notice in Arabic poetry that it did in the Persian and Hindavi languages, where it took on the dimensions of a metaphor. To quote Alam Khundmiri:

> Al Hallaj, one of the greatest martyrs of Islam in the cause of human freedom, not only represents an immortal example of the Sufi man, the gnostic being, but also expresses in a passionate manner, the Sufi ideal of man, which became the constant theme of all genuine Sufi literature. The essence of man, in which man partakes with God, is love. As Massignon has pointed out in his study of al Hallaj, the mystery of creation can only be understood if one realises that the fundamental nature of the divine essence is love, creative love, 'essential desire'.

Mansur's execution appears to have attracted the ire of sensitive souls against the symbols of religious and political authority for all times to come, a phenomenon peculiar to the Persian and Urdu *ghazal*. A scrutiny of the *diwan*s of major Persian and Urdu poets brings to notice frequent references to Mansur al Hallaj as a victim of bigotry and of a narrow interpretation of the law. The reasons for this are not difficult to comprehend.

According to Syed Vahiduddin, the eminent professor of philosophy, 'The universal impact he (al Hallaj) has left on Persian poetry still echoes through the writings of Attar and Rumi. Whatever scholars like Ibn Taimiya and others might say about him and the difference of opinion among the Sufis about his station and status notwithstanding, in whatever way his utterance "Anal Haq" may be interpreted, there was no dichotomy between the personality and the teachings of al Hallaj.'

Some of the couplets alluding to the execution of Mansur in Persian poetry are given below. Rumi writes:

Each time that an iniquitous judge lifts a pen,
There is a Mansur (Hallaj) who dies on a gibbet.

The image of Mansur has been invoked by many Persian poets. Hafiz of Shiraz[27] says:

Facing the gallows, Mansur al Hallaj repeated the mystical utterance 'Anal Haq' (I am God) which led Imam Shaafai,[28] one of the four Imams of *fiqh*, to pronounce him guilty of infidelity. Don't inquire about such recondite points from men like Imam Shaafai, for they know nothing of gnosis.

O Lord, watch out and save them from calamities. By the grace and blessings of the perfect master of exaltation, of Mansur (who, like a king amongst saints, affirmed 'Anal Haq').

Dara Shukoh (d. AD 1659), the Mughal prince, whose learning and deep knowledge of Islam and other philosophies, particularly the Vedanta, brought him into confrontation with the Muslim *ulema* attached to Aurangzeb's court, was also a poet, compiler and translator of various scholarly works. Some of his couplets listed below allude to Mansur:

Did not Husayn (ibn Mansur al-Hallaj) say I am Truth and go to the gallows.
'Tis the evil and malicious spirit of the mullahs which
Has tormented every saint and prophet.
The gnostics are always in a new ecstatic state.
They are religious leaders not followers.
Lions eat only on what they have preyed;
The fox eats the carcass abandoned in the sun.

Mirza Asadullah Khan Ghalib (AD 1796–1869) also alludes to Mansur and his execution in several of his couplets directly as well as obliquely. However, there is one couplet wherein he accuses Mansur of not having been able to contain himself (*tunuk zarfi*):

Haq goyam wa nadan ba zabanam dehed azar
Ya rab che shud aan fatwa bardar kashidan
(I speak the truth but the ignorant continue to torture me, O God!
Why should the decree drag me to the gallows?)

Dil-e har qatra hai saaz-e anal behr
Ham uske hain hamara puchhna kya
(The essence of every drop of blood sings to the tune of 'I am the
sea'; we are a part of Him, and it is useless to ask our identity.)

Ze geer o dar che gham chun ba alam-e ke manam
Hunoz qissa-e hallaj harfe zere labeest
(Why should I grieve anyone's hold on me as the tale of the
passion of al Hallaj is still on my lips.)

Qatra apna bhi haqeeqat mein hai darya lekin
Hamko taqleed-e tunuk-e zarfee-e Mansur nahin
(Our drop-like existence also proclaims to be the Sea, but we
better not follow the example of Mansur who could not
keep to himself his ecstatic experience.)

Na har ke khoonee o rahzan ba paae Mansur ast
Badeen hazeeze tabee-e ze auj dar che huz
(It is indeed difficult to be cheerful and happy at the gallows;
killers and robbers can never attain the status of Mansur.)

Ibn Insha, an Urdu poet from Pakistan alludes to Mansur in a rather
ironical manner: To champion the cause of truth is fine—it were better if
someone else fought for truth. Why follow the example of Mansur and get
crucified, it's better to keep quiet.

III

But references to Mansur are only a refrain in Sufic poetry,
signifying empathy and admiration for the slain Sufi. Sufic thought
encompassed much more and one of its greatest bases was the *Wahdat ul-
Wujudi* thought, i.e. the Doctrine of Immanence. Love and compassion
were so overpowering in the life of a Sufi that he would frequently become
oblivious of all other distinctions. Rumi, in his *diwan*, dedicated to Shams
Tabrez,[29] offers diverse examples of his unparalleled universality and love
of humankind. In one of his poems he negates all identities of religion,
race, elements, directions, genesis, and even life hereafter. Some of the
bayts (distichs) from the poem are given below:

What is to be done, O Muslims, for I do not know my own identity;
I am neither a Christian, nor Jew, neither a Zoroastrian nor Muslim.

I hail neither from the East nor the West, neither from land nor sea;
Neither from the mine of Nature nor from the revolving spheres.

Neither from dust nor from water, neither from air nor from fire
Neither from the throne of god nor the earth, neither from existence nor eternity

Neither from India nor China, neither from Bulgaria nor Scythia
Neither from the land of two Iraqs, nor from the province of Khurasan

Neither from this world nor the next, neither from heaven no hell
Neither from Adam nor Eve, neither from paradise nor the Garden of Eden

The placeless is my place, the traceless is my trace
I have neither body nor soul for I belong to the soul of the beloved.

Another extract from one of the *ghazals* of Hafiz of Shiraz is also worthy of consideration. It exalts the straying and the wayward, while castigating the conventional worshipper and pretender.

Where is the pious doer and I
The estray'd one, where.
Behold how far the distance, from
His safe home to here.

My heart fled from the cloister,
and chant of monkish hymn.
What can avail me sainthood,
fasting and punctual prayer.
What is the truth shall light me
to heaven's strait thoroughfare.

Whither O heart, thou hastest.
Arrest thee and beware.
See what a lone adventure is thine
unending quest.

Fraught with what deadly danger.
Set with what unseen snare.

Say not, O friend, to Hafiz,
'Quiet thee now and rest.
Calm and content, what are they.
patience and peace, O where.'

I know this perilous love lane
Know whither the traveller leads
Yet my fancy the sweet scent of
Thy tangled tresses feeds.

In the midnight of thy locks
I renounce the day
In the ring of the rose lips
My heart forgets to pray.

Plunge into your angry waves
Renouncing doubt and care;
The flowing of the seven broad seas
Shall never wet thy hair.

Sufism has a paradoxical dialectical relationship with its sources, and this paradoxical relation becomes very manifest in Sufi poetry, particularly that which belongs to the early period of the Sufi movement when it had not yet assumed the character of an ideology, offering a supra rational justification to the established social order by calling upon all believers to leave the world to the mighty Caesars and to become meek observers of the cosmic order. In this regard, Ibn Sina's[30] 'Ode to the Soul' is a fine illustration of the soul's quest for its original state that has been, to use William Blake's phrase, spoiled by the 'state of experience':

Why then was she cast down from her high peak
To this dreading depth. God brought her low,
But for a purpose wise, that is concealed
E'en from the keenest mind and liveliest wit,
And if the tangled mesh impede her,
The narrow cage denied her wings to soar
Freely in heaven's high range, after all

She was a lightning flash that brightly glowed
Momently o'er the tents, and then was hid
As though its gleam was ever glimpsed below.

In the *Conference of the Birds* (*Mantiq al Tayr*), written in the thirteenth century, Fariduddin Attar speaks about man:

He has a lofty spirit, his body comes from the lower element, clay.
Thus he is the meeting point of the humble clay and the pure spirit.
Since the humble and the high have become partners
Man has become a wonderful mystery.

Hazrat Amir Khusrau (AD 1253–1325), like Attar, in one of his Persian *ghazals* gives vent to a similar sentiment that characterizes the hallmark of *tasawwuf*-inspired poetry of that age. It may also be attributed to the philosophy of *Wahdat ul-Wujudi* (Doctrine of Immanence) widely accepted as the cornerstone of many a Sufi order:

I am a pagan and a worshipper of love—Islam I do not need;
every vein of mine has become taut like a wire,
the pagan's girdle I do not need.

Arise from my bedside, O simple physician. The only
cure for the patient of love is the sight of his beloved;
other than this, no medicine does he need.

The people of the world say that Khusrau worships Idols.
So he does, so he does; the people, he does not need;
the world he does not need.

Another *ghazal* by Khusrau is remarkable for its musicality and thought content:

O thou, whose beautiful face is the envy of the idols of Azar,
Thou remainest superior to my praise, praise thee as I may.

All over the world have I travelled, many a maiden's
love have I tasted, many a beautiful star have I seen
but thou art something different and unique if I may say so.

A face lovelier than thine my eye has not seen.
Art thou the Sun or the Moon or Venus or Jupiter?
What thou art, 'tis hard to say.

Ever since the sky began making images on earth
On no one else was such charm bestowed;
Art thou a fairy or an angel, a daughter of angel or nymph?
What thou art I cannot say.

I have become thee, thou hast become me,
I have become the body, thou hast become the soul
So that 'I am different from thee, thou art different from me.'
None hereafter may be able to say.

The verses quoted are fine examples of the blending of *majaz* (appearance) and *haqeeqat* (reality). While, at one level it exalts secular love, the poet completely identifying himself with the beloved—to the extent that their separate existence has been obliterated; the verses, on the other hand, signify a state of *fana* (mortality) in the soul's journey along the path of life. Almost all the Sufic orders spell out the said journey in the tripartite dimensions of the *Shaikh* (preceptor), the *Rasool* (the Prophet) and Allah. Persian and Hindavi poetry abounds in such verses where the objects of love and reverence are interchangeable.

Mirza Abdul Qadir Bedil (AD 1644–1720), one of the most prolific poets in Persian whose works are said to comprise 90,000 verses, has been one of the great influences on Persian writing in India. No less a person than Ghalib declared his indebtedness to Bedil for the ingenuity of his style and his thought processes. In one of his poems he says:

I have heard that the saint Bayazid was once conversing with love,
Saying, what gift worthy of acceptance
Can a good for nothing fellow like me
bring unto thee, O God.

To which the Lord of Glory replied, 'The two worlds
Of perfection are a footstool here;
For prayers and devotional practices, of whatever kind they be,
The unblemished kingdom of God needs them not.

No commodity other than defect is required,
Thy perfection here has no buyer at all.
But the broken stuff, the more broken it is,
The higher is its value at this threshold.

Thy defect here will be stripped of its imperfection,
For this sea of bounty is a fracture restorer from one end to the other.

The illimitable ocean which creates the elegance of pearls
Needs naught from the waves save their breaking.

Infrangibility goes not well with the structure of the waves,
For breakage is the beginning and the end a/the wave.
The vernal cloud sheds tears on that rose
Which did not acquire the state of breaking.'

Ghalib remains till this day the greatest Urdu poet of India. He freely indulged in the adventure of ideas and the interplay of orthodoxy and heresy. While adhering to the classical Persian *ghazal* tradition, he wrote *ghazals* in a refreshingly new style. His Urdu *diwan*, comprising no less than 1,600 couplets, offers insights that are thought-provoking and stimulating. He was, to say the least, an admirer of novelty but not without vigour, an admirer of conventional wisdom but not without fresh insights. He often proclaimed himself to be a Sufi, frequently embellishing the *wujudi* philosophy in his couplets. Some of his couplets (in English translation) are given below:

Once I gave up the tavern it matters not
If it's a monastery, academy or mosque
When there was naught, existed God

If all turn void, he'd still be there
Doomed am I, for I am
Whatever could be if I were not

—Translated by Qurratulain Haider

If punishment there needs must be
For sins I have committed
Give me my need of praise, O Lord,
For sinful longings unfulfilled.

What is the temple, what is the Ka'ba
Baffled passion for union constructing
Myths and illusions, asylums to shelter
Its ardour, its hopes, its dreams and despair.

God is one, that is our faith;
All rituals be abjured.
'Tis only when the symbols vanish
That belief is pure.

This universe is nothing but
Thyself in peerless glory,
We exist, since duty takes
Delight in seeing itself.

What heartlessness to make us see
Life's spectacle and not enjoy or learn;
What misery to yearn for things
When soul and body both are naught.

The nodes of life and death
Pitched high or low
Are but a screech,
Sober and mad
Are fatuous distinctions.

Foolish, this brag of knowledge,
Futile, this prayer and fasting;
Dregs of a stupefying cup
Our Here and our Hereafter.

—Translated by M. Mujeeb

IV

Another aspect of the Chishtiya-Nizamiya order that deserves attention is the change in the medium of expression from classical Persian to Hindavi as a vehicle for communication of Sufi thought. Hazrat Amir Khusrau, as far back as in the early fourteenth century, had shown his clear preference for Hindavi against Persian:

cho mun tootie-e-Hindam az rast pursi
ze mun Hindvi purs ta naghz goyam.
(To speak the truth I am a bird of song (*toote*) from India
I would love to sing only in Hindavi)

In his Hindavi, Khusrau includes all the vernaculars spoken from Punjab to Gujarat and Rajasthan to Bihar, viz., Multani, Saraiki, Punjabi, Braj, Gujri, Awadhi and Khari Boli and its variants, that is, Urdu and Hindi. This was indeed a linguistic revolution brought about by Hazrat Amir Khusrau, a process begun by Hazrat Baba Farid Ganjeshakar whose

Multani *kalam* (verses) is preserved in the *Guru Granth Saheb*. This linguistic revolution also contributed significantly in 'taking Islam to the masses and the masses to Islam'. It may also be called popular Islam, insofar as the medium and communication are concerned. The *Chakkinameh* attributed to Hazrat Khwaja Syed Muhammad Gesudraz may also be read as a step in the same direction where *chakki* (millstone) acquires the status of a metaphor, effectively conveying the daily chores as a means of understanding abstract values and higher reality.

The themes of Sufic thought are conveyed in poetry through images that are purely Indian in origin. The images of *gori* (beloved), *sej* (bed), *panghat* (riverbank), *chunri* (head cover), *rang* (dye) and *rangrez* (dyer), richly employed in Sufi folk literature have never lost their charm at *Sama* sessions (hymns and devotional music). The metaphor of *panghat* in colloquial Urdu and Hindi continues to be used as a powerful and profound expression with all its connotations:

bahut kathin hai dagar panghat ki

Here *panghat* (the riverbank), a large well or any reservoir of water stands for the objective and destination of life, spiritual or temporal. The *dagar* the approach road or the lane is neither smooth nor straight and quite often circuitous with a rough terrain. But the visual image of a well, to which womenfolk make a beeline to fetch water, is always present in popular imagination. The metaphorical meaning of the line quoted above that it's a daunting task and we better equip ourselves with the requirements and accomplishments of a true seeker has acquired the status of an idiom.

In classical Indian aesthetics, the beloved is always the male principle. Radha and the *gopis* are passionately in love with Lord Krishna. The Sufi folklore tradition adapted the same model of the lover and the beloved.

However, the major works in Sufi poetry such as Mullah Daud's[31] *Chandayan* (AD 1379), Qutban's[32] *Mrigavati*, Malik Muhammad Jaisi's[33] *Padmavat* (AD 1540), Manjhan's[34] *Madhumalti*, and Shah Qasim's[35] *Hans Jawahir* revert to the Arabic–Persian model of the male seeker and the female object. It may be mentioned here that almost all these poets are from the Chishti–Nizami order. Mullah Daud was the disciple of Shaikh Zainuddin, the nephew of Hazrat Shaikh Nasiruddin Chiragh-e Dihli. Malik Muhammad Jaisi was the disciple of Hazrat Makhdoom Jahangir Ashraf Simnani,[36] while Shah Qasim Daryabadi was a *murid* of Hazrat Shah Ashraf Saloni.[37] This impressive galaxy of writers in the Chishti–Nizami fold wrote in the Hindavi tradition spelt out by Hazrat Amir

Khusrau in his famous couplet mentioned earlier. It may be suggested that they were not only the transmitters of Sufic thought and teachings, but the harbingers of a linguistic revolution in India. The emerging ethos was unfortunately lost in the Urdu–Hindi controversy in the middle of the nineteenth century under instigation from some British officers of doubtful scholarship. Consequently, Deccani, Gujri, Awadhi, Multani, Saraiki, Braj and Sindhi were left out of the Hindavi umbrella. Last, but not the least, mention may be made of Syed Abdul Wali Uzlat (AD 1692–1775),[38] the great-grandson of Hazrat Shah Pir Muhammad Saloni, whose Urdu *diwan* is prefaced in Hindi and not in Persian as was the practice at the time. It was admittedly a pioneering idea in the tradition of Hindavi writings introduced and popularized by Chishti–Nizami saints.

In the context of the passage that follows, *gori* is the seeker of the higher object and the lover of the preceptor. *Chunri* is her habit and costume, that is, her physical appearance and life which is stained and without any attraction and charm. The preceptor (*Shaikh*) is the *rangrez* who alone can dye the *chunri*, i.e. transform the seeker's life to a higher spiritual station thereby making her or him worthy of attention and valuable. One of the popular songs sung in the Chishti–Nizami *khanqahs* is a similar invocation attributed to Hazrat Amir Khusrau in which he addresses his Shaikh, Hazrat Nizamuddin Awliya:

Tori surat ke balihari, Nizam
Sab sakhyan mein chunar mori maili
Dekh hansen nar nari
Ab ke bahari chunar mori rang de
Sadqa Baba Ganjeshakar ka
Rakh lo laj hamari

(O Nizamuddin, my life is dedicated to the sight of your face.
As compared to others my garment is stained
    because of which I am ridiculed.
This spring you may kindly dye my garment
    so that I don't lose face among friends.
I ask you to be kind to me
    in the name of Ganjeshakar, your preceptor.)

It may be interesting to mention here that Kabir[39] also uses the image of *chadar* or *chunar* as a metaphor of life. In one of his verses *jheeni jheeni beeni chadariya*—he says that the *chadariya*, that is, the life given to him by the Almighty has been returned stainless.

Jheeni jheeni beeni chadariya
Kahe kay tana kahe kay bharni
Kaun tar se beeni chadariya

Ingla Pingla tana bharni
Susman tar se beeni chadariya

Aath kanwal dal charkha dolay
Panch tatwa gun teeni chadariya

Sain ko siyat maas dus laage
Thok thok kay beeni chadariya

So chadar sur nar muni orhin
Orh kay maili keeni chadariya

Das Kabir jatan se orhin
Jas ki tas dhar deeni chadariya

The passage may be translated as follows:

(Who weaves this mantle, thin and fine.
What the warp, what the woof,
What the spindle,
And what the thread,
Weave this mantle.

The awakening nerves are the warp and woof
And the spindle;
The prime nerve of enlightenment
The thread;
Weave the mantle.

Eight stages, five elements,
And three attributes
Go into the weaving of the mantle.

The Master Weaver took ten months
To perfect the mantle with stress and strain;

Worn by gods, saints and men
The mantle was soiled.
Kabir, the servant (of God) wore it
With utmost care
And left the mantle spotless and untainted.)

As is evident in the passage cited, Kabir's imagery is drawn from the life of weavers and interwoven with allusions to the Hindu philosophical system of *hatha yoga*. The references to *ingla pingla* and *susman tar* respectively allude to the nerves of awakening and the prime source of enlightenment. *Aath kanwal* refers to the eight stages of spiritual enlightenment, from the navel to the highest point on the top of the head, stages being symbolically conceived in the shape of a lotus. *Panch tattva* refers to the five elements while the *gun teeni* are *sattva*, *rajas* and *tamas* (goodness, passion and darkness). Kabir's poem is representative of Sufic poetry in which the commonplace and the profound coexist. The images and vocabulary from everyday life acquire philosophical, religious and mystical dimensions.

In the *Khanqah-e karimiya* at Salon several Awadhi songs are sung during the annual 'urs of Hazrat Shah Mehdi Ata[40] from the 8th to 9th Jamadi ul Awwal. One of the rituals performed is the *gagar* (earthen cups) ceremony held on the 9th Jamadi ul Awwal in the forenoon. As the *sama* congregation reaches mid-way, mendicants in traditional robes enter the hall with scores of earthen cups (which are later distributed by the *sajjadanasheen* to the family members, *khalifahs*, *ulemas*, *mashaikhs* and *murids*). While *qawwals* continue, the *sama*, the congregation forms a procession, and holding the empty earthen cups in their hands, move towards an old well near the *Idgah*, less than a kilometre away. The procession moves slowly in solemn dignity, with the *qawwals* continuing to sing. It halts at different, specific points, and specific passages are sung at specific halts. Tradition has it that the *gagar* ceremony owes its origin to days of the illustrious saint Makhdum Husamul Haq Manikpuri[41] of the Chishti–Nizami order when he, during a *sama* congregation, on being informed that there was no water in the *khanqah* kitchen, rose with an earthen cup in his hand and moved towards the nearby Ganga to fetch water in a state of ecstasy. The members of the congregation followed suit and so did the *qawwals*. The entire assembly walked to the Ganga and filled their containers, or whatever vessel they could lay their hands on, with water. The event was so moving and ecstatic that the following year the *murids* of Shaikh Husamul Haq requested for a repeat of the same experience—of fetching water from the Ganga in a procession. The ritual is observed at several *khanqahs* of the Chishti–Nizami–Husami order, as in the *khanqah* of Salon, the only difference being that an old well serves as a substitute for the Ganga. The Awadhi verses sung on the occasion are very rich and profound in imagery, such as the following:

Kou aai sughar panihar, kuana umand chala
Ke tum gori sanche ki dhari, ke tumhe garha re sunar
Na mein gori sanche ki dhari, na mohe garha re sunar
Mai bap ne janam diyo hai, roop diyo kartar
Kou aai sughar panihar kuana umand chala

(Who is this accomplished water-fetcher at whose approach
   the water in the well rises to the surface?
Greatly enamoured by the beauty of the dame,
   the bystander asks, 'Are you made of gold?
Which goldsmith has created you?'
The dame replies, 'Neither am I made of gold
   nor is any goldsmith my creator.
I am born of a mother and a father
   and my looks are the gift of God Almighty'.)

A text is autonomous and not bound by any specific interpretation; so are the lines cited earlier. The passage is beautiful and can be appreciated only on a literal plane. The present *sajjadanasheen* of the *dargah* Nizamiyah, Khwaja Hasan Sani Nizami, who comes from one of the oldest families of Delhi from the times of Hazrat Nizamuddin Awliya and is immersed in the Sufi tradition, once attended the *urs* ceremonies at Salon. After listening to the verse mentioned earlier he very insightfully interpreted it as a passage in praise of the Prophet. He later wrote down the meaning of the passage as he understood it in his travelogue published in *Munadi*. He wrote: 'It seems to me as if these words have been composed especially in praise of the Prophet.'

The verses perceptively describe the Koranic revelation: 'This day have I perfected your religion and completed my favour upon you. The well had always been there; the water was also there; only the coming of the accomplished water-fetcher was awaited by the thirsty. She arrived and such was her perfection and overwhelming mercy that everyone was satisfied.'

It is indeed an interpretation that opens up new dimensions of the song composed in Awadhi hundreds of years ago. Taking a cue from Khwaja Hasan Sani Nizami, we can say that the well symbolizes the eternal grace of God that had been waiting for the Perfect Man to come and fetch water from it. The *kuan* got so enamoured of the beauty and perfection of the water-fetcher that it began to well up, keen to shower all its glory and plenty on him. The people were so struck by the charisma of the man that they unhesitatingly attributed divinity to him. The last line depicts the Prophet's response, which, in *Surah Kahf* of the Koran, is recorded in the following words:

> Say: 'I am but a man
> Like yourselves. (but)
> The inspiration has come
> To me, that your God is
> One God; whoever expects
> To meet his Lord, let him
> Work righteously, and,
> In the worship of his Lord,
> Admit no one as partner.'

—XVIII: 110, tr. Abdullah Yusuf Ali

There are several verses in the Koran emphasizing the humanity of the Prophet. In the Koran, the Prophet is exhorted to tell his followers that he is a human being like them (XXV: 7; LXI: 6). In some contexts, God says that Muhammad is no different from the messengers sent earlier (LXVI: 9) and his passing away or sudden death will not in any manner change the message of God. It is indeed remarkable that the essential teachings of the Koran were beautifully and correctly incorporated in Hindavi Sufi poetry. By rendering the Koranic message about the status of prophethood in Awadhi, Sufi Hindavi poetry played an important role in bringing home the essential tenets of Islam in the consciousness of the masses.

There is an entire tradition of literature in Awadhi dating back to the fourteenth century, which includes some of the path-breaking poetry of Mullah Daud, Malik Muhammad Jaisi, Qutban, and Manjhan, and extending to the early eighteenth century with the poetry of Shah Qasim Daryabadi. Mullah Daud's *Chandayan* (AD 1379) and Jaisi's *Padmavat* (AD 1540) are works of considerable linguistic and thematic value, insofar as the interplay of poetry and Sufic thought are concerned.

Padmavat is the first epic written in Awadhi that synthesizes legend and folklore with history. A major part of the epic is concerned with the love story of Ratansen and Padmavati, while the latter treats the story of Alauddin Khilji's fascination for the Rajput queen, who was ultimately rescued by Gora and Badal, the two brave chiefs. The story ends with both Padmavati and Nagmati committing *sati* when Ratansen dies in the battlefield. After storming the fort, Alauddin plunges into grief at finding that the object of his love has performed *jauhar* (the Rajput custom of self-immolation). *Padmavat* offers several Sufic insights during its narrative, which are new to the vernacular Indian literature. The epic begins with invocations to God, the Prophet, the four caliphs, the author's *pir*, Hazrat Jahangir Ashraf Simnani, and two illustrious shaikhs from Jaunpur, Syed Muhammad Jaunpuri[41] and Makhdum Shah Bahauddin Natthan Jaunpuri[42] and the sovereign of the day, Sher Shah Suri. It is rather significant to find a mention of Mansur al Hallaj and his ecstatic utterance, 'Anal Haq', in the epic. It is perhaps the first ever reference to the exalted, though controversial, saint in any of the Indian vernaculars:

Ka bha jog kahani kathen
Niksen na ghew baju dahi mathen

Jo lahi aapu hirain koi
Tau lahi heart pau na soi

Prem pahar kathin bidhi garah
So pai chareh sis so charah

Pant surinh kar utha ankuru
Chor chareh ki chareh mansuru

Tu raja pahirasi kantha
Tore ghatahi mah das pantha

Kam, krodh, trsna, mad gaya
Pancho chor na chharahi kaya

Nav sendhe ohi ghar majhiara
Ghar muse hi nisi kai ujiyara

Abahun jagu ayanai hot av nisu bhor
Puni kichhu hat na lagihi musi janhi jab chor

('There is no use narrating the tale of *yog*.
The yogurt does not become ghee without churning.
Till one himself is not lost he will not find the one
    he is following. God has raised the summit of love tough and
    high;
    he alone can reach it who scales the hard way.
The path is strewn with saplings' of gibbet.
Either thieves are hung on it or Mansur mounts it.
If thou art a king why should you cover your body
    with rich garments.

There are as many as ten ways to your body.
Lust, anger, desire, pride and illusion are
     the five thieves who would not leave you.
In this house there are nine entrances
     through which thieves rob your body day and night.
O ignorant one, it is still not late to wake up,
     the dawn is drawing near.
After the thieves have plundered, nothing will be left'.)

There is another reference to Mansur in another canto, *Ratnasen Suli Khand*:

Jogi ker karahu pai khoju
Maku yah hoi na raja bhoju
Jas marai kahn baja turu
Suri dekhi hansa mansuru

(This *yogi* should be thoroughly recognized,
lest he may be found to be a lusty king.
As soon as the bugle was sounded for the king to be executed,
he smiled like Mansur looking at the gibbet.)

The parrot Hiraman describes the beauty of Padmavati first to Ratansen's queen Nagmati and later to the king, which sets Ratansen on his journey to find Padmavati. The context has been interpreted in the Sufic terminology of *shaikh*, *salik* (seeker), and God, with Hiraman initiating Ratansen into the Sufic way of finding Padmavati, the Supreme Reality. Since he was the *murid* of Makhdoom Jahangir Ashraf Simnani, it is quite likely that Malik Muhammad Jaisi designed his grand epic with Sufic teachings and terminology as its archetypes. Rather significantly, Alauddin Khalji is treated in the poem as a symbol of illusion (*maya*), without any sympathy for his quest to possess Ratansen's lawful queen. History tells us only that Alauddin Khilji did lay siege to the fort of Chittor during the reign of Ratansen, lasting six months. He ultimately succeeded in capturing Chittor in AD 1302–3 after vanquishing the great chiefs Gora and Badal, but the existence of Padmavati and the related incidents described in *Padmavat* have not been proven historically. They are believed to be a creation of the poet's imagination. Jaisi has created a legendary tale of love and separation between Ratansen and Padmavati to express human devotion to the Supreme Being as expounded in the Sufi doctrine, according to which, love is supreme and governs both this world and the world beyond.

Likewise, *Chandayan* of Mullah Daud is another milestone in the tradition of Sufic poetry. *Hans Jawahir* of Shah Qasim Daryabadi is also a poem in the same tradition. Shah Qasim was a *murid* of Hazrat Shah Pir Ashraf of Salon and has very indulgently invoked his *pir*, the *pir's* father and preceptor and his two sons at the beginning of the work. An entire canto has been devoted to Salon and its saints. It is a popular text in the eastern districts of modern Uttar Pradesh, and portions of the poem comprise an oral tradition; these are still recited at gatherings by the elders of villages and towns.

The introduction and treatment of Sufic themes and imagery in the Hindavi vernaculars is an important dimension of the Chishti–Nizami order, and deserves to be studied in some detail, not having received the attention it deserves.

The reference to and treatment of Mansur in Persian and Urdu poetry and even in the Awadhi masterpiece *Padmavat* demonstrates the manner in which it has acquired the dimension of a metaphor over the last nine hundred years of poetical tradition, recurring quite frequently. Besides expressing reservations obliquely about the legitimacy of political authority and the supremacy of *fiqh* (jurisprudence), this metaphor appears to have contributed significantly towards developing a general resentment against political and temporal authority.

V

But early Sufic orders were not reactionary altogether. Theirs was indeed, in some measure, a very sincere effort to revive the Medinan model of the first Islamic commonwealth established by the Prophet himself. This model was soon lost in the quagmire of unprecedented wealth and phenomenal political expansion. The call aimed at restoring austerity (*faqr*), complete trust in God (*tawakkul*), and total submission to the will of God (*razi ba raza*) as the chief features of piety. There was great insistence on distancing from centres of power, which consequently strengthened negative perceptions about the establishment and authority and brought them into disrepute. We have seen that the Sufic themes and images have been a resistant refrain on both the Persian and Hindavi poetry. Likewise, the concept of *jihad bin nafs*, literally translatable as 'fight against self', has always been vigorously pursued in all Sufic teachings. To be able to contain and control the desire of the self is perhaps the prerequisite of self-discipline after a person has been initiated into a Sufic order. It is neither suppression nor repression of legitimate ambition and permissible desires but a self-imposed discipline aimed at controlling and containing the irresistible temptations in accordance with the dictates of the *shariah* and the way of the Prophet. The Koran categorizes the self into three kinds: the *nafs-e ammarah*, the *nafs-e lavvamah* and the *nafs-e mutmainnah* (that is, the rebellious self, the repentant self and the contented self). The rebellious self is more in the service of the Devil rather than of God. In order to control it, one has to fight it out. One can do so only when a ceaseless *jihad* is fought against it, and this, in the Sufi terminology, is called *jihad bin nafs*. The Sufis of all principal orders have greatly emphasized the ceaseless fight against such a self. This *jihad* is said to be of greater importance and merit than the *jihad* against an external enemy. It may not be out of place to refer to the well known sonnet by John Donne, 'Batter my heart, three-person'd God . . .' wherein a war is declared against the 'self, which is "captive" and betrothed unto your (God's) enemy'. Donne prays to the Divine force to 'break, blow, burn and make me new', obviously suggesting a total metamorphosis of his self, which is presently in the possession of God's enemy. *Jihad bin nafs* may be compared to a condition similar to that in which Donne finds himself, to a kind of relentless struggle against the rebellious self. No seeker of truth can succeed in his path to enlightenment and contentment without undergoing this struggle.

The teachings of the Sufis were disseminated through poetry written both in Persian and Hindavi, invariably by employing images with native appeal. This ushered in the values of tolerance, love, accommodation and adjustment among peoples of diverse ideologies and sects. The masters of Sufic thought and sensibility had realized, and foreseen, even in the early period of Islam, the rapid changes that were taking place, and were likely to take place, in the society as a result of the unprecedented political spread of Islam over the three known continents of the world. They realized the need for a re-ordering of the universe, failing which the intrinsic message of Islam, and the glorious example set by the Prophet himself and his illustrious companions, would be lost. It is in the writings and personal examples set by Hasan Basri, Ma'aruf Karkhi,[44] Sirri Saqti,[45] Ibrahim Adham,[46] Junaid Baghdadi and Abu Said Abul Khair that one gets the first intimations of the new moral dispensation and a certain re-ordering of the universe, that is, the prioritizing of moral and ethical values *vis-a-vis* the dictates of state and polity. Sufic poetry written in Persian and Hindavi played a significant role in accomplishing this feat and in introducing this re-ordered and re-structured universe to the masses. In addition, such poetry gave rise to a liberal attitude, which brought about a further re-adjustment of impulses.

Notes

1. One of the illustrious companions of the Prophet. He was expelled from Medina for questioning the misuse of the public treasury during the period of the third Caliph Othman, and later from Damascus for similar reasons during the reign of Muaviyah.

2. One of the companions of the Prophet. He was consistently vilified and maligned by the camp followers of Muaviyah.

3. One of the grandsons of the Prophet and the second son of 'Ali. He was persecuted and finally slain along with the male members of his family at Karbala in AD 761 for refusing to take an oath of allegiance to Yazid, son of Muaviyah.

4. One of the most illustrious of the Umayyad (Marwanite) caliphs, respected for his piety and sense of justice. During his brief rule he discontinued many practices aimed at smearing the reputation of 'Ali and his progeny. He was, however, poisoned by his own kinsman for deviating from the Umayyad state policy.

5. One of the four Imams of Sunni jurisprudence. He was persecuted and publicly whipped for joining issue with the Abbasid Caliph Al Mamun in the controversy regarding the nature and status of the Koran.

6. One of the greatest Sufis of all times, twice tried and finally sentenced to death for his ecstatic utterance 'Anal Haq' ('I am the God') at Baghdad in AD 922. He has remained in the Muslim consciousness as an unjustly treated man of God. While a large majority of poets and Sufis have glorified him as a blessed soul, a few others have found no sympathy for a person who openly defied the injunctions of the *Shariah*.

7. One of the disciples of 'Ali and the preceptor of several Muslim mystics. He is the link to 'Ali in the Chishti order.

8. The *Saiyid ut-Taifah* (Leader of the 'Brotherhood') and a common link among several principal Sufi orders.

9. One of the earliest Sufis. His quatrains mark the beginning of the union between Sufism and literature.

10. The preceptor of the Qadri order, and one of the greatest influences on Sufi thought and practice throughout the Muslim world.

11. One of the greatest thinkers of Islam in the eleventh-century Baghdad. He addressed the sources of revealed knowledge while analysing the problems of philosophy by writing 'A Refutation of Philosophy'. He put Islamic sciences on firmer ground by highlighting the limitations of philosophy. His works include *Ihya ul-Ulum al-Din, Tahafut a-Falasifah* and *al-Iqtisad fi al-I'tiqad*. According to Philip K. Hitti, 'Thomas Aquinas, one of the greatest theologians of Christianity, and later Pascal were indirectly affected by the ideas of al Ghazzali'.

12. One of the most celebrated Sufi poets of his time whose *Mathnavi* and *Divan Shams Tabrez* have been reigning influences on Sufic thought and Persian poetry.

13. One of the well-known poets of thirteenth-century Iran. His poetry is rich in humanistic culture.

14. The famous sufi philosopher who propounded the theory of *Wahdat ul-Wajudi*.

15. The author of *Tazkira-ul Awliya*, the well-known Sufi biographical dictionary compiled at Nishapur.

16. A poet, courtier and soldier of thirteenth-century Delhi. In Sufi circles, he is better known as a very distinguished *murid* of Hazrat Nizamuddin Awliya. He is the author of several important works in Persian, the propounder of the Hindavi style and dialect, and a great maestro of Indian music. He is credited with having invented the Indian *sitar*.

17. Husain bin Mansur (executed in AD 922) better known as al Hallaj. He became a legend in his lifetime for his controversial utterance, 'Anal Haq'.

18. One of the celebrated mystics of Islam who lived in Baghdad. He was a contemporary of Shibli and Junaid.

19. One of the most celebrated saints of the Chishti order in India. As the *khalifa* and successor of Hazrat Farid al-Din Ganj-e Shakar, he set a very high example by distancing himself from the imperial court and living a life of austerity and total dependence on God. It was his long spell as a Chishti saint in Delhi that laid a strong foundation for the said order in the subcontinent. His *malfuzat* have been accorded in *Fawaid-al Fuwad*, collected by the famous Persian poet, Amir Hasan 'Ala, Sijzi.

20. The propagator of the Chishti order in India. His tomb at Ajmer is visited by hundreds of thousands of people. His *'urs* falls in the first week of the lunar month of the Hijri calendar, *Rajab*.

21. The *khalifa* and successor of Hazrat Khwaja Moinuddin Chishti. He is buried at Mehrauli in Delhi, later developed as the Qutub Complex.

22. The *khalifa* and successor of Hazrat Khwaja Qutubuddin Bakhtiar Kaki. He established his *khanqah* at Ajodhan, a small village in Punjab, now called Pakpatan and in present- day Pakistan. He is popularly known as Baba Farid. Many of his *sakhis* are included in the *Guru Granth Sahib*.

23. The *khalifa* and successor of Hazrat Nizamuddin Awliya. Like his shaikh and predecessor, he distanced himself from the imperial court and invited the wrath of Sultan Ghiyasuddin Tughlaq, His *malfuzat* have been recorded in *Khair ul Majalis* by Hamid Qalandar.

24. The *khalifa* and successor of Hazrat Nasiruddin Chiragh-e Dihli. After presiding over the *khanqah* of his predecessor in Delhi for several decades, he moved to Gulbarga, where he established a *khanqah* and became an important source of popularity of the Chishti order in the south. His *malfuzat* have been recorded in *Jawami al-kilam*.

25. The founder of the Chishti Nizami *khanqah* at Salon, District Rae Bareli, Uttar Pradesh. He was a descendant of Hazrat Makhdum Minallah Jaunpuri, who was a descendant of Hazrat Qazi Hamiduddin Nagauri, and *khalifa* and successor of Hazrat Shaikh Abdul Karim Manikpuri, the illustrious saint of the Chishti–Nizami–Siraji order. He was a celebrated scholar of rational sciences and of traditional knowledge. It is reported that no less than three hundred *ulemas* of his time were his *murids*. The tradition of learning and piety continues in the family.

26. One of the illustrious Sufis of ninth–tenth-century Baghdad. It is reported that Mansur al Hallaj, during the period of his intense suffering on the gallows, felt agonized when he found Shibli a part of the crowd witnessing his execution.

27. One of the most celebrated poets of Iran. His *diwan*, rich in love themes and esoteric dimensions, has enjoyed an enviable status in the Persian-speaking world as a book of

omens. The poetry of Hafiz, rich in humanistic values and culture, elicited a response from the great German poet Goethe and achieved the status of a cult in nineteenth-century America.

28. One of the four illustrious imams of Islamic jurisprudence. He is believed to have justified the execution of Mansur.

29. The preceptor of Maulana Jalaluddin Rumi. It is said that Rumi, the great scholar turned into a mystic upon meeting Hazrat Shams Tabrez who was not even literate. Rumi has dedicated his *diwan* to Shams Tabrez.

30. Known as Avicenna in Europe, he was the grand shaikh, who mastered several disciplines including philosophy, medicine and surgery. His treatise *Qanoon* enjoyed the status of a seminal text for centuries in Europe.

31. One of the earliest poets of Awadhi, he belonged to Dalmau, a small town in District Rae Bareli, Uttar Pradesh.

32. He lived in the last quarter of the fifteenth and the first half of the sixteenth century. His only work *Mrigavati* (AD 1503) has elicited considerable critical response as a major text of Medieval Romantic Awadhi poetry. He was a disciple of Shaikh Burhanuddin, a saint of the Suharwardy order during the reign of Husain Shah Sharqi.

33. One of the greatest poets of Awadhi, his *Padmavat* (AD 1540) inspired Tulsidas to use the same poetic meter in composing his *Ramcharitamanas*. The epic, besides being a well-wrought narrative, offers allegorical dimensions with patently Sufic cosmology and overtones.

34. Another major Awadhi poet in the Sufic mould. His work *Madhurmalti* (AD 1545) treats eternal and profound love as a subject of the poem.

35. An eighteenth-century poet in the Sufic mould whose work *Hans Jawahir*, in the oral tradition, has been much acclaimed and is a popular narrative often recited in the eastern parts of modern Uttar Pradesh.

36. An illustrious shaikh of the Chishti–Nizami order who established his *khanqah* at Kichauchha in Faizabad District, Uttar Pradesh. His *malfuzat* have been recorded in *Lataif-e Ashrafi*.

37. An illustrious shaikh of the Chishti–Nizami order, the *khalifa*, son and successor of Hazrat Shah Pir Muhammad Saloni.

38. One of the earliest poets of Urdu who received very favourable mention in Mir Taqi Mir's account of poets. His father Syed Saadullah Saloni was known as one of the great scholars of his age who taught *hadith* for twelve years at Madina before settling down at Surat. For details, see Mujeeb's *Indian Muslims*.

39. Born in AD 1440, Kabir is, by common consent, one of the greatest poets of Hindavi who by his relentless satire, castigated both Muslims and Hindus for their hypocritical and ritualistic adherence to religion devoid of its true spirit. In many of his verses, as in the passage cited, he uses weaving imagery to bring home his sensibility and message. A Persian chronicle, *Mirat-ul Asrar* (AD 1647) compiled by Abdul Rehman Chishti, describes him as a shaikh of the Firdausi order revered by both Hindus and Muslims. It is indeed unfortunate that his Hindavi poetry did not become a part of the Urdu canon.

40. The seventh *sajjadanasheen* of the *Khanqah-e Karimiya* at Salon, Rae Bareli. A *risalah* titled *Nala-e Anfas-e Gham* or *Gham-e Qibla-e Alam* written by Hafiz Syed Taqi Husain commemorates his death in AD 1900.

41. The founder of the Chishti *khanqah* at Manikpur (presently in District Pratapgarh,

Uttar Pradesh). He was the successor of Makhdoom Nurul Haq of Pandua, in Malda, West Bengal.

42. The founder of the Mehdavi movement in India. One of the most illustrious saints of the age of Sher Shah Suri and Akbar, he became a cult figure. His followers were persecuted in many Indian towns.

43. An illustrious Chishti saint and the grandfather of Hazrat Makhdum Minallah Jaunpuri. His *malfuzat* have been recorded in *Sahaif ut-Tariqa*, edited by Mian Muhammad Said, published in 1995 from Lahore.

44. The first Sufi of the Baghdad school. He was a devout man and venerated as a saint in his lifetime. His tomb at Baghdad on the west bank of Tigris is a great destination for pilgrims. He was initiated into mystical knowledge by Imam 'Ali Riza and is the link between Qadiri and Suhrawardy orders.

45. The disciple and successor of Hazrat Ma'ruf Karkhi, also considered to have been the link between Qadiri and Suhrawardy orders.

46. One of the greatest influences on several Sufi orders, particularly the Chishti and an exemplar of quietist asceticism. He is said to be a prince who, 'while hunting heard some mysterious voice warning him that he was not created for such a purpose. Thereupon, the princely sportsman dismounted and forever abandoned the path of worldly pomp for that of asceticism and piety. . . . After his Sufi conversion, Ibrahim migrated to Syria where Sufism had its earliest organization, and lived by his own labour.' – Philip K. Hitti, *History of the Arabs*.

References

Ali, Abdullah Yusuf, translation and commentary, *The Koran*, Madina, 1992.

Ansari, Asloob Ahmad, ed., *Nazr-e Manzur*, Aligarh, 1990.

Ansari, M.T., ed., *Secularism, Islam and Modernity: Selected Essays of Alam Khundmiri*, New Delhi: Sage Publications, 2001.

Daryabadi, Qasim Shah, *Hans Jawahir*, publisher not mentioned, n.d.

Faiz, Faiz Alunad, *Poems by Faiz* (translated by V.G. Kiernan), London: George Allen and Unwin Ltd., 1971.

Ghalib, Asadullah Khan, *Whispers of the Angel*, New Delhi: Ghalib Academy, 1969.

Hasan, Hadi, *A Golden Treasury of Persian Poetry*, New Delhi: ICCR 1966.

Hitti, Philip K., *History of the Arabs*, Macmillan, 1970.

Jafri, S. Zaheer Husain, *Awadh from Mughal to Colonial Rule: A Study in the Anatomy of Transformation*, Delhi: Gyan Publishers, 1998.

Jaisi, Malik Muhammad, *Padmavat*, ed. Vasudev Sharan Agarwal, Chirgaon: Sahitya Sadan, 1998.

Jamshidipur, Y., ed., *Selected Poems of Hafiz: Persian Text and Translations*, Tehran, 1963.

Mujeeb, M., *The Indian Muslims*, Delhi: Munshiram Manoharlal, 1995.

Mujeeb, M., *Ghalib: Makers of Indian Literature Series*, Delhi: Sahitya Akademy, 1974.

Nicholson, Reynold A., *Introduction to Rumi with Commentary and Annotations to the Mathnavi-e Manavi*, Teheran University Publications, 1971.

Nizami, Khwaja Hasan Sani, trans., *Fawaidul Fawad*, Delhi: Urdu Academy, 1990.

Qureshi, Abdul Razzaq, ed., *Divan-e Uzlat*, Bombay: Adabi Publishers, 1962.

Ram Malik, ed., *Divan-e Ghalib*, Azad Kitab Ghar, n.d.

CHAPTER 4

The Persian/Urdu *Ghazal*: A Mode of Non-Conformist Utterance

Ghazal has been defined as a song, elegy of love, often, also the erotic-elegiac genre. The term is Arabic, but passed into Persian, Turkish and Urdu and acquired a special sense in these languages. In its present form it consists of a few *bayts* (verses, or distichs), generally not less than five and no more than twelve, with a single rhyme (often accompanied by a *radif*); the first *bayt*, called *matla*, both hemistichs to rhyme together; the last *bayt*, called *maqta*, contains the nom de plume (*takhallus*) of the author; the contents of the *ghazal* are descriptions of the emotions of the poet in front of love, spring, wine, God, etc., often inextricably connected.[1] As an illustration, the English translation of one of the *ghazals* by Hafiz of Shiraz (d. 1390) is given below:[2]

1. Once more the age of youth has returned to the garden and the sweet singing nightingale receives the good news of the flower.
2. Oh, gentle breeze! should you once more reach the budding plants in the meadow, give my greetings to the basil, the rose, the cypress tree.
3. The young son of the magi, the vintner, appears before me in such charming motions that I am ready to sweep with my eyebrows the dust of the tavern.

4. Oh, thou who coverest with purest amber the face of the moon do not perturb yet more this man perplexed by love.

5. I greatly fear that those who laugh at wine-bibbers may at last make a tavern of their faith in God.

6. But mayest thou remain a friend of the holy men, for in the Ship of Noah there is still a handful of Mud that knows how to defy the Deluge.

7. Go out from this Dwelling, that has the Heavens for roof, and do not ask it for Food, for that Vile one at the end shamelessly kills her guest.

8. And say to those whose last resting place will he a handful of Dust: 'Friends, what avails it to raise high palaces to the skies.'

9. Oh, moon of Canaan! the throne of Egypt has been allotted thee; it is now high time that thou shouldest say farewell to the Prison!

10. Oh Hafiz, drink wine, and be a libertine, and live joyfully, but take care not, as others do, to make a snare of the Book of God.

The said *ghazal, raunaq-e-ahad-e-shabab* talks of the conventional relationship between the nightingale and the rose and celebrates the coming of spring. In the third couplet the significance of the tavern in the life of the poet has been highlighted, making it almost a parallel to the place or worship. The fourth couplet celebrates human beauty and love. In the following couplet, wine-bibbers have been praised with a prophecy that a day may come when the tavern will be the means to reach God. The sixth couplet glorifies the 'mean and the sundry' by alluding to the handful of mud on the Ship of Noah which remained a friend of the pious and defied the Deluge. The next couplet derides the materialistic tendencies of people whose only aim in life is to crave for worldly comfort. The eighth couplet may be seen as poetic expression of conventional wisdom with regard to the futility of pomp and show. The last but one couplet alludes to the unknown hand of destiny, as it was in the case of Joseph, awaiting his royal reception in the Egyptian palace while he was still in prison. The last couplet, that is *maqta*, celebrates drinking wine and indulgence in earthly joys as a better engagement than the efforts of the holy men, doctors of divinity, who interpret the Koran in such a manner that it loses its significance and becomes incomprehensible for the lay person.

It is indeed a strange coincidence that the evolution and rise of the Persian *ghazal* takes place at the same time when the Sufi orders were established. While the Sufis in the ninth and tenth century, and in later ages, sought to establish their seats of learning and meditation away from the centres of power and distanced themselves from the temporal as well-religious authority,[3] the poets celebrated human love and earthly existence in their verses. On a superficial plane it appears contradictory but a deeper insight into this phenomenon brings out a uniform stand and similarity of approach. The Sufis and the poets, sometimes speaking for each other, played the role of conscience keepers of society.

As the sudden emergence of the courtly love tradition in the form of Troubadour continues to baffle scholars and critics alike, the establishment of Sufi orders in the tenth/eleventh century with new vigour and, the proliferation of the Persian *ghazal* with a patently anti-establishment stance targeting the symbols of religious orthodoxy and political authority, may also be seen as a strange phenomenon, defying any acceptable justification. Interestingly, there is no such trend in Arabic poetry during the same period of time. The Persian-speaking Muslims, subjugated by Arabs in the early seventh century had a sense of hurt pride and were conscious of their civilizational strides in the pre-Islamic Iran. Their first national poet, Firdausi, gives vent to this emotion when he refers to the Arabs as 'camel drivers'. The *ghazal* tradition experimented and perfected by Sana'i, Nizami, Iraqi and Sa'adi that reached its peak in the hands of Hafiz of Shiraz continues to fascinate readers of Medieval humanistic culture. The tradition found new roots in India when Amir Khusrau introduced a new style of Persian–Hindi *ghazal* later popularized as *Sabk-i Hindi*. The Indian variant of Persian reached its golden period in the seventeenth/eighteenth century at the hands of Sa'ib, Kaleem, Anand Ram Mukhlis, Abdul Qadir Bedil and later in the nineteenth century, Mirza Ghalib. The poets of *Sabk-i Hindi* were very proud of their Indian Persian and did not accept any magisterial account of Indian writing in Persian from the Iranian scholars and poets. It is worth recalling that the debate about the literary merit of Indian writing in English that began in the middle of the twentieth century was similar in nature and context about the literariness of *Sabk-i Hindi*, that is, Indian writing in Persian in the eighteenth century.

The Urdu *ghazal* was not different from the Persian *ghazal* in its thematic concerns. It also celebrated human love and earthly existence in its infinite variety. It derided whatever appeared to be pretentious, ritualistic and vain. Like the Persian classical *ghazal*, the Urdu *ghazal* also continued the convention of an anti-establishment stance with fresh vigour. Thus, we have a poetic genre, that is, the Persian–Urdu *ghazal* which has a history and a tradition of eight hundred years. It is difficult to find any parallel of the *ghazal* tradition in any language. In the eight hundred years of the history of *ghazal* there may have been several instances of puerile imitation, monotonous themes, hackneyed and stereotyped images and word play but, nonetheless, the prime concerns of *ghazal* writers have not changed. The innovativeness of the form has allowed experiments with and extensions of the limited vocabulary and meter available to the poet from time to time. The symbolism of the *ghazal* writers during the Medieval Age is transcendental and mystical. In our times, in the hands of Faiz Ahmad Faiz, it acquires patently political overtones.

As has been suggested in the beginning, the sudden emergence in the eleventh century of this form, which glorified humanity and man, and derided political and religious institutions, continues to engage the attention of teachers and students alike. One of the plausible explanations of the phenomenon may be seen in some tragic and crucial events between the seventh and tenth century. This was a period of unprecedented expansion of Islamic empires from Spain to Sind, and the establishment of one of the greatest civilizations that ushered in a new era of scientific temper and reasoning with its great seats of learning at Baghdad, Cordova, Granada, Bukhara, Cairo and Shiraz. However, the assassination of Hazrat Husain Ibn-e Ali at Karbala in AD 671 and the execution of Husain Ibn-e-Mansoor Al Hallaj in the year AD 922 at Baghdad, were, among other factors, some of the most disquieting events that continued to haunt sensitive minds. Both the events had the support of a section of the court and *ulema* (religious scholars). It is presumptuous on my part to suggest that these events charged and electrified generations of people to react unkindly to the regimes that perpetrated the said misdeeds. There could have been several other factors, which may have caused discontentment and loss of faith. It may have directed the ire of the sensitive poets towards the symbols of religious and political authority for all time to come.

A perusal of the *diwans* of major Persian and Urdu poets brings to notice several references to Husain and Mansoor. The allusion to Karbala and the treatment of the theme of martyrdom of Hazrat Imam Husain Ibn-e Hazrat Ali did not acquire the dimensions of suffering and supreme sacrifice in the early Persian *ghazal*, which marks their treatments in Urdu poetry in the twentieth century. The poetry of Iqbal, Josh, Nasir Kazmi, Khalil-ur-Rehman Azmi, and in our times, Shahryar and Irfan Siddiqi, among others, offer diverse treatments of Karbala as a metaphor. References to the unjust and most sacrilegious execution of Mansoor, as a poetic idiom and symbol may be traced in the poetry of Rumi, Hafiz, Ghalib, and several other modern Urdu poets. Rumi says: 'Each time that an iniquitous judge lifts a pen, there is a Mansoor Hallaj who dies on a gibbet.' Hafiz writes: 'On the gallows, Mansoor Al Hallaj made the beautiful recondite point. "Anal Haq" ("I am God" which led Imam Shaafai, one of the four Imams of *fiqh* to pronounce him guilty of infidelity); don't enquire about such recondite points from men like Imam Shaafai (for they know nothing of gnosis). O Lord! watch out and save them from calamities. By the grace and blessings of the perfect master of the exaltation of Mansoor (who like a king amongst saints affirmed "Anal Haq").'

One of the poets of our time, Ibn Insha says: 'To fight for truth is fine, it were better if someone else was to fight for truth why follow the example of Mansoor and get crucified, it's better to keep quiet.'

Rumi in his *diwan* dedicated to Shams Tabrez offers diverse examples of his unparalleled universality and love of human kind. In one of his poems, he negates all identities of race, religion, elements, directions and genesis. Some of the *bayts* (distichs), from the said poem read as follows:

1. What is to be done, O Muslims, for I do not know my own identity: I am neither a Christian, nor Jew, neither a Zoroastrian nor Muslim.
2. I hail neither from the East nor the West, neither from land nor from sea; neither from the mine of Nature nor from the revolving spheres.
3. Neither from dust nor from water, neither from air nor from fire; neither from the throne of God nor the earth; neither from existence nor entity.
4. Neither from India nor China; neither from Bulgaria nor Scythia; neither from the land of the two Iraqs; nor from the province of Khurasan.
5. Neither from this world nor the next; neither from heaven or hell; neither from Adam nor Eve; neither from paradise nor the Garden of Eden.
6. The placeless is my place; the traceless is my traceless; I have neither body nor soul for I belong to the soul for the Beloved.[4]

The verses cited are indeed matchless and have been composed by no less a person than Maulana Jalaluddin Rumi, the mystic poet *par excellence*. But there are scores of similar passages by other Persian poets, which celebrate the station of Man in the universe. While on one hand, these poets glorify human love and unity of humankind, on the other, they scoff at whatever was pretentious and vain. The symbols of religious hypocrisy have all along been derided. We find passages in Chaucer, Langland and Blake with scathing attacks on the church and the symbols of the ecclesiastical order but not an entire tradition of poetry spead over several centuries devoted to exposing the sanctimonious tendencies in religion. One shudders to think of what may have happened to the Muslim civil society if the Sufi orders had not so vigorously upheld the cause of true faith by consciously distancing themselves from state politics, and the poets had not satirized the pretentious and the ritualistic tendencies in Islam. It was, in fact, a movement which wanted Muslims to go back to the Medina of the time of Muhammad (peace be upon him) and the four rightly guided calilphs. This phase, that is the eleventh and twelfth century, may also be seen as the first Renaissance of Muslims.

I take this opportunity to highlight the aspects of the *ghazal* tradition that have generally been ignored by Western critics. Besides being a form of verse wherein the celebration of human love reached its pinnacle in a large number of Persian and Urdu poets, it is also a form of poetry which celebrates secular life in a way which is indeed unprecedented in literature. The *ghazal* tradition scoffs at whatever is status-quoist, superficial, vain and hierarchical. The very form of the *ghazal* is such that it cannot accommodate any thought or expression, which supports the authority, political or religious. It is anti-convention, anti-establishment, unyielding, and wary of whatever is pretentious or ritualistic. The beauty and love of the beloved in infinite variety is its soul and sustenance, nothing else is. Such an important form of poetry continued to be treated disdainfully by quite a few European scholars because it did not conform to the poetics of English poetry and was generally compared to the ode form without any rhyme or reason. Love and religion shared, 'besides a common emblem in wine', in the words of Kiernan, 'another refinement of gross fact into ideal essence'.

The following verses from the English translations of Hafiz, Mir, Ghalib and Faiz clearly bring out the essential concerns of *ghazal* tradition. The celebration of human love and the rejection of temporal and religious censure are the common denominators in *ghazal* from the twelfth century to the present day. The form has undergone changes of various hues and shades but its principal concerns remained unchanged as the basic instincts of human life. This may partly explain the variety and vigour of the tradition that has stood the test of time for the last eight centuries. Says Hafiz:

Where is the pious doer? and I the strayed one, where? Behold how far the distance, from his safe home to hear!

My heart fled from the cloister and chant of monkish hymn. What
can avail me sainthood, fasting and punctual prayer?
What is the truth that shall light me to heaven's straight thorough
fare?
Whither 'O heart thou hastest'?
Arrest thee and beware!
See what an adventure is thine unending quest!
Fraught with what deadly danger!
Set with what unseen snare!
Say not, O friend, to Hafiz
Quiet thee now and rest!
Calm and content, what are they
Patience and peace, O where?
I know this perilous love-lane
No whither the traveller leads,
Yet my fancy the sweet scent of
Thy tangled tresses feeds.
In the midnight of thy locks, O renounce the day: In the ring of thy
rose-lips
My heart forgets to pray.
Plunged in your angry waves
Renouncing doubt and care;
The flowering of the seven broad seas
Shall never wet thy hair.

—Translated by Elizabeth Bridges

Mir says:

Shaikh says his prayer? Don't be deceived by that
Prayer is a load he lowers from his head.

I grant you, Sir, the preacher is an angel
To be a man, now that's more difficult.

It is God's mercy that we sinners speak of;
Fasting and prayer are never mentioned here.

To enter love's dominion is to throw your life away
For love makes no allowances, and beauty does not spare.

Now and then she passes smiling and for me the roses bloom
All the advent of the spring is the grace of her approach.

—Translated by Ralph Russel

In Ghalib's words:

Once I gave up the tavern it matters not
If it's monastery, academy or mosque
When there was naught, existed God
If all turned void, He'd still be there
Doomed am I, for I am
Whatever could be I were not
I would recall the vast number of blighted hopes
Lord, You'd better not ask to account for my deeds,
From slumbering Fate
I could purchase
A dream or two,
But how would I pay their price
Admire me, too, O Lord!
For the desire of vices missed
If there be the punishment of my committed sins.

—Translated by Qurratulain Hyder

And Faiz says:

At times, in remembrance faintly old scenes reviving. Things once so
    near and so far from heart vision, eye vision striving.
At times, in desire's parched sands, caravans come halting, With
    tokens laden to seal all bargains of lovers driving.
For eye or heart what repose, what slaking of joy an anguish.

—Translated by Victor Keirnan

A few more examples from Persian poetry which satirize the symbols
of religious authority—*shaikh* (religious head), *waaiz* (preacher), and
mohtasib (censor), etc., are given for a better appreciation of the *ghazal*
tradition:

Come to our tavern, O Shaikh, and drink that wine which is not
found even in the stream of Paradise.
A thousand points, finer than the finest hairs are present here; not
every person who knows how to shave his head is a hermit.
The prayer from the pure hearts of drunken revellers is a key
wherewith many a locked door shall be opened.
The mystery of God which the gnostic never confided to anyone it
surprises how and whence the wine came to Know.
I am not that libertine who forsakes his mistress or forgoes his cup of
wine; the Proctor knows that such acts are hardly in my line.

I am a law-breaker seduced by the cup of the tulip and the intoxicated eye of the narcissus have many charges to face, O Lord, whom should I charge with arbitration?

Bring wine; lover fears not the *fatwa* or rather, the decree of the Royal Court as well.

The Censor knows that Hafiz is a lover—a fact known to the Asaf of the kingdom of Solomon, as well.

Come to the tavern, O Hafiz that I may acquaint thee with a thousand prayers which never remain unanswered.

Last night I went to the tavern in a drowsy condition; wet with wine was my hermit's cloak and my carpet of prayers as well.

I am not the only exile from the house of piety; my ancestor also let the eternal paradise slip from his hands

When there is no purity, the Ka'ba and the idol-temple are alike; no virtue exists in that home where chastity is wanting

O my heart, learn from the Censor the art of drinking; he is gloriously drunk but who can suspect him of drinking?

The preachers who assume such airs on the pulpit and the rostrum, appear in a rather different role in the bosom of their home.

Speak not here of honour and dishonour, for we consider ourselves disgraced by honour and honoured by dishonour

The comfort of the two worlds is a commentary of these two words; kindness to friends; consideration for foes.

O Lord, keep a watchful eye on my faith and heart!

O worldly kings! What is the sense in making an exhibition of your regal insignia before the (gnostic) bondsman? O Lord! Watch out and save them from calamities. But the grace and blessings of the perfect master of the exaltation of Mansoor (who like a king amongst saints affirmed 'Anal Haq'), in composing these verses, Hafiz became the standard-bearer in the realm of poesy (leader of the gnostic cause).

Vahiduddin posits:

We have substantial evidence on the life and teachings of Al Hallaj on the basis of Massignon's celebrated work *The Passions of Al Hallaj*. The universal impact the *Al Hallaj* has left on Persian poetry still echoes through the writings of Attar and Rumi. Whatever scholars like Ibn Tayymiya and others may say about him and the differences of opinion among the Sufis about his station and status notwithstanding, in whatever way his utterance 'Anal Haq' may be interpreted there was no dichotomy in the personality and world view and teachings of Al Hallaj.[5]

The writers of literary history in Urdu have also not been fair to the *ghazal* as a genre. They regard it as an imitative art form, artificial, insincere and false. It is said to be 'rootless with no affection for the soil of its location'; and 'a mask' and 'a burrowed face'. The *ghazal* form has been accused by some insensitive critics of bringing about stagnation in the flowering of human experiences. The European critics found it 'incoherent', 'lacking in unity of expression', 'betraying psychopathic behaviour'. Quite a few of them have tried to categorize it as lyric or ode.

The early Urdu *ghazal* no doubt shows a curious state of creative apprenticeship. But despite the obvious limitations, it is perhaps the best source material for the study of Indo–Iranian culture. There is an intense outgrowth in self-expression in the fibre of the language, which asks for speech. In its formative years Sufism was much inspired by the wisdom of *Wahdat ul-Wujudi* of Ibn Arabi (1164–1240). The philosophy remains to this day one of the inherent paradigms of the *ghazal* traditions. The concept of unity of being and its framework based on the categories of the phenomenal and the real provided the world picture, and helped in seeking the knowledge of the visible worlds and everything else it contained. The Urdu *ghazal* in the seventeenth century is rooted in Indian soil as most of the images used by the poets reflect Indianness. It was, for a change, different from the Persian *ghazal* of the Iranian and Indian poets. However, things changed, as rightly observed by Gilani Kamran, in the eighteenth and nineteenth century.

The compulsions of the temporal reality deeply affected the view of the protagonist of the Urdu *ghazal* as a consequence of the turbulent times and the hostile political situation in eighteenth and nineteenth century India.

According to Gilani Kamran:[6]

The conventional Beloved, the abstract Thou of the consciousness became different, cruel and hostile, and correspondingly, the behaviour of the protagonist became a detailed account of suffering. The attitude appears in the *ghazal* vocabulary as 'separation' (*hijr*) and instead of the protagonists' central position in the framework of *ghazal*, another character, the 'rival' (*raqib*) emerged as a parallel principle of union with the Beloved. In the process the *ghazal* became more Persianized in technique and treatment. However the protagonist of Ghalib's *ghazal* succeeded in releasing himself from the compulsions of immediate temporal reality and thus made an upward progress in the framework of Ibn-Arabi's Sufism.

The modern Urdu *ghazal* in the hands of Faiz and Ahmad Faraz and later Nasir Kazmi Shahryar and Irfan Siddiqi has evolved new imagery and symbolism without divesting the genre of its earlier concerns.

Notes

1. See *Encyclopaedia of Islam*, new edn, vol. II, 'ghazal', ed. Benard Lewis et al., Leiden: E.J. Brill, London: Luzac and Co., 1965.
2. Translated by M. Kazwini and K. Ghani, cited in the *Encyclopaedia of Islam*, vol. II.
3. Reference may be made to the early period of the Chishtiya order in India. Hazrat Farid-ud-din Ganj-e-Shakar (d. 1265), Hazrat Nizamuddin Awliya (d. 1325) and Hazrat Nasiruddin Chiragh Dilli (d. 1351) set very high standards of the Chishti Khanqah as a centre distant and away from the powers that be. While Hazrat Farid-ud-din lived in a very small town, Ajodhan, now called Pakpatan (Pakistan), Hazrat Nizamuddin Awliya and Hazrat Nasiruddin Chiragh-e Dihli lived in Delhi for several decades without any interaction with the sultans of Delhi. Tradition has it that once when Alauddin Khalji sent word through Hazrat Amir Khusrau (d. 1325) that he would visit the celebrated saint, Hazrat Nizamuddin asked Khusrau to convey to the sultan that there were two doors in his *khanqah*, if the sultan would enter from one door, he would leave from the other. For more details see M. Mujeeb's *Indian Muslims*, Delhi: Munshiram Manoharlal, 1996.
4. All references to the Persian couplets are taken from Hadi Hasan, *A Golden Treasury of Persian Poetry*, ed. M.S. Israeli, ICCR, 1966.
5. '*Ghalib ka husn-e-fikr aur haqeeqat-e aagahi*', *Nazre Manzoor*, ed. Asloob Ahmad Ansari, Aligarh, 1990.
6. Gilani Kamran, *South Asian Muslim Creative Mind*, Lahore: National Book House, 1980.

CHAPTER 5

A Modernist View of *Madrasa* Education in Late Mughal India

Madrasa—Nursery of Civil Service in India from Late Mughal Times to Independence

A scholar (*'alim*/pl.: *ulama*) or graduate from a traditional *madrasa* in the subcontinent, while proficient in revealed knowledge, principles of jurisprudence and aware of some disciplines like logic and history of Islam, is not generally conscious of the civilizational strides which have contributed to the making of the modern sensibility. The *dini madaris*, as traditional Muslim educational institutions, have nevertheless served as a nursery of the civil service in Mughal India, as they produced the jurisconsultant (*mufti*) and the judge (*qadi*/pl.: *qudat*), the two offices for which the *madrasa* graduates qualified, and which were considered high civil offices in society.[1] That seems to indicate a preference for principles of jurisprudence and Islamic law (*fiqh*) in curricula of *dini madaris* during this period.

Also, in the actual regional successor-states of the Mughal empire, most prominently in north Indian Awadh, Muslim religious scholarship was entrusted with the task of producing graduates that could be integrated into their state administration. In this regard, the school of the Farangi Mahall in Lucknow deserves mention.[2]

In the aftermath of the events of 1857, however, the British East India Company (EIC) removed the legal anomaly which recognized the Mughal Emperor Siraj ad-Din Bahadur 'Shah 'Alam II' (d. 1858) as a *de jure* ruler while the EIC constituted the *de facto* government. Even though this put an end to the sponsorship of Muslim scholars by the Mughal court, the EIC followed in its footsteps by continuing to employ *madrasa* graduates in the civil service of their Crown colony.

However, the end of state patronage over Muslim religious educational institutions and the virtual dissolution of the religious revenue system (*awqaf* sg.: *waqf*) by the colonial administration in the second half of the nineteenth century[3] led to the establishment of a number of *madaris* independent from the state, which cater to particular ideologies and frameworks (*masalik*/sg.: *maslak*) and which expect its graduates not to deviate from their allotted role.

This inner-Islamic controversy made it difficult for the British colonial administration to evaluate the usability of *madrasa* graduates for the civil service. Moreover, the affinity of some *masalik* to Muslim reformist movements in the Middle East, namely to the Wahhabiyya on the Arab peninsula and the Salafiyya in Egypt and Syria, aroused suspicion among the EIC officials. Relations with the Wahhabiyya proved to be especially fatal for Indo–Muslim scholars—for the British the military successes of the Arabian movement in the early nineteenth century linked it to the ideas of armed *jihad* and the oversimplified dichotomy of the 'abode of Islam' (*dar al-islam*) *vs.* the 'abode of war' (*dar al-harb*), and were responsible for the application of this term to similar activities in British India. The labelling of Muslim religious movements which were regarded as disloyal to the Crown as 'Wahhabi'[4] was not without its effect on Muslim intellectual elites—they began to adopt the term to designate streams within the community of *ulama* which vehemently protested against local customs and even against certain legal opinions that they considered unlawful innovations (*bid'a*).[5] The historical affinity of the movement of the Ahl-i hadith—characterized by its strong opposition against the widespread veneration of saints and their graves as well as against the adherence to a particular 'school of Islamic law' (*madhhab al-fiqh*)—with the Arabian Wahhabiyya made it easy to polemically apply the 'Wahhabi' label to them.

The dispute between the Deobandis and the Barelwis—the latter adhering to their loyalty to Mawlana Ahmad Rida Khan (d. 1921)—over the legal question of the veneration of saints and their tombs moved the Deobandis closer to the Ahl-i hadith, and thus enabled the term 'Wahhabi' to be applied to them too, despite the existence of a prolonged controversy between the Hanafite Deobandis and the Ahl-i hadith over a number of legal points.[6]

However, the British colonial administration was in some need of a Muslim religious educational institution that could serve them as a forge for cadres for the civil service. As such, they supported the establishment of a council of Muslim religious scholars that could serve as an umbrella organization by integrating current streams of Muslim scholarship in India and conciliating their internal conflicts. The Nadwat al-'ulama', inaugurated in Kanpur in 1893, was at first believed to be such an institution, which is why the British took quite a number of the graduates of its *Dar al-'ulum*, established in Lucknow in 1908, into its civil service.[7]

Things changed dramatically with the beginning of the 'Indian Independence Movement' in the early twentieth century. Leading *ulama* of whatever *maslak* actively took part in the 'Khilafat movement'; renowned Deobandi scholars drew nearer to the 'Congress movement' by setting up the 'Society of Indian Muslim Scholars', the Jam'iyyat-i 'ulama'-i Hind. This way, they enjoyed a certain level of respectability as nationalist Muslims. For the British colonial administration, however, these developments put an end to the employment of *madrasa* graduates in the civil service.

The Problem after Independence

The employability and social status of the *madrasa* graduates has been narrowed even more after the Independence. While in earlier times they had the option to aspire to the office of *mufti* or *qadi*, in the present scenario, the office of the *qadi* having been abolished in India, the only available position is that of a *mufti*, which is neither official nor secular. Today, quite a few of them join a madrasa or *Dar al-'ulum* as faculty; the majority go to serve the mosques as leaders of the prayers (*imam*) and preachers (*khatib*). Some graduates, however, are admitted to such institutions of higher learning so as to allow them to continue their education at the undergraduate level, like the universities of Lucknow and Aligarh, the Jamia Millia Islamia in Delhi, and a few others. Rather significantly, *madrasa* graduates in the streams of humanities and social sciences do fairly well. It is when the knowledge of classical Arabic literature is profitably applied to modern disciplines that the graduates from *madaris* excel over their counterparts from government administered schools and colleges. But such instances are few. Even *madaris* which belong to modern *masalik* do not seem to cater to the requirements of the Indian secular polity. Thus, for example, the Madrasat al-Islah at Sara'i Mir, A'zamgarh— often called the nursery of the twentieth century's religio-political movement, the Jama'at-i Islami, in India—has been said to be an institution excelling in Koranic knowledge,[8] but seems not to provide sufficient knowledge and practical skill demanded by the Indian state.

Mainly because of the emphasis on religious subjects in the syllabi, the majority of *madrasa* graduates do not get an opportunity to enter into university systems, and thus remain deprived off the benefits of liberal education in an emphatically secular state. It is by no means suggested that university graduates necessarily imbibe a liberal outlook and catholicity of approach, just as all the graduates of the *madrasa* system are not narrow-minded and conservative in approach. But it is expected that a university graduate who reads courses in humanities, social sciences, philosophy and modern natural sciences will have an open-minded approach and generally will not be indifferent and hostile to other systems of thought. The university system, now spread all over the world, has established its bonafides as the most viable and practical system of education, both for employability in the civil and financial domain and as a reservoir of knowledge that fosters free inquiry, tolerance and better understanding of the world around us. It is in this context that the *madrasa* graduates seem to be lagging behind and this often results in a siege mentality and near total alienation from society.

In another sense, and this is particularly true of the subcontinent, the *madrasa* graduates who eventually acquire leadership roles are better trusted by the overwhelming majority of Muslims in India than their counterparts from university systems. Muhammad 'Ali Jinnah (d. 1948), however, was an exception to the rule.[9] The majority of the Indo–Muslim leadership had gone through the *madrasa* system of education. Even today, representative bodies of Muslim leadership comprise mostly those who have graduated from *madaris* or possess some knowledge of Islamic systems of thought and are hesitant to deviate from the received opinions. However, it is my personal conviction that if those leaders happen to be backward-looking scripturalists devoid of any imagination and creative thought, they will not only misrepresent Islam but also mislead the community. Muslims in the subcontinent have generally been at the receiving end and in a disadvantaged position mainly because they have not been led by an able, imaginative and thoughtful leadership. Highly illustrative of this fact, the Jama'at-i Islami in India did not for a long time permit its members and followers to participate in the general elections, calling the democratic system unholy and therefore unacceptable. Likewise, the Indian version of secularism as enshrined in the Constitution was termed as not corresponding to the authoritative sources of Islam and therefore unacceptable.[10]

It may not be inappropriate to recall that the Indian *ulama* continued to debate the propriety of Western education and did not permit their children to study in schools and colleges for at least three generations after the coming of Western-model colleges in India.

Rather interestingly these retrograde measures were in total defiance of the teachings of the Koran and the *ahadith*—it is nowhere suggested in the Koran and the sayings of the Prophet Muhammad that Muslims have to shun attending educational institutions which disseminate new knowledge. The Koran exhorts the believers to ponder over the mysteries of the universe. There is a constant refrain in the Koran to observe and study the phenomena of nature. The Prophet of Islam also exhorted Muslims to seek knowledge and made this obligatory for every child, female and male. The almost electrifying consciousness of knowledge and the stores of knowledge that were opened as a consequence of the translation work done at the cities of Damascus, Baghdad, Toledo, Granada, Cordova, Monte Cassino (in southern Italy), Bukhara, and Isfahan could not have been possible without the inspiration of the Koran and the *ahadith*.

It is admitted that scholarly pursuits declined after the fall of Baghdad in AD 1258. But before the sack of Baghdad by the Mongols, the famous Medieval Muslim scholar Abu Hamid Muhammad al-Ghazali (d. 1111), by refuting the relevance and usefulness of philosophy in understanding revealed knowledge, had in fact questioned rationality (*'aql*) as the foundation of philosophy as an academic discipline within the realm of religious education. He pleaded for reliance more on intuition (*kashf*) as a mode of understanding creation and revealed knowledge. The arguments of al-Ghazali were ostensibly focused in favour of revealed knowledge and its primacy, but were misconstrued by later scholars for the mere rejection of philosophy. There was no problem in probing and investigating secular disciplines from the paradigms of philosophy. It seems as if no clear distinction was made or construed between the dictates of revealed knowledge and secular sciences, a fault-line which continues to distract Muslim scholars, particularly in the *madaris* and *Diyar al-'ulum*.

By the time the Arab-Iranian legacy of scholarship reached the subcontinent, it had already lost its eminence of earlier times: The support of *hadith*-centred traditionalism in the legacy of Ahmad b. Hanbal (d. 855 BC) since the reign of the Abbasid caliph Ja'far al-Mutawakkil (d. 861 BC) put an end to the dominance of the rational theologies of the *Mu'tazila*, the *Ash'ariyya*, and, to some extent, the *Maturidiyya* in the eastern realm of the empire.[11] The spirit of free inquiry and empirical investigation had, to quite some extent, been replaced by literal interpretation (*taqlid*) and strict adherence to the doctrines within the Islamic fold. One discovers a clear denominational divide from this time onwards. It had inevitably led to a consciousness of self-righteousness and rejection of the 'other'. Exegesis of the Koran and collation and compilation of the literature of *hadith* and the principles of jurisprudence, however, flourished with renewed vigour.

In the post-Independence era, the study of the so-called 'rational sciences' (*ma'qulat*) has lost the focus it earlier had for considerable periods, and the curricula of the *madaris* shrank further. Today, there appear only sporadic engagements with matters affecting daily life, but the holistic approach as emphasized in the Koran and prophetic Sunna vanished. It is against this backdrop that one may examine the legacy of the Mughal period in the context of education.

The Need for a Change in the Syllabi in Late Mughal Times

In the term '*madrasa* education' one may include advancement of knowledge and promotion of intellectual traditions as reflected in the curriculum of the *madaris*. Like their counterparts in the Ottoman Empire and Safavid Iran, the Mughals were also interested in the advancement of learning, which was expressed by the fact outlined earlier, that *madaris* often served as nurseries for the Mughal civil service. The interest of the Mughal rulers in the matter was reflected in the predominant systems of education, as well as in the priorities of the individual sovereigns, which finally set the criteria for royal patronage. While the *madrasa* curricula generally focused on principles of jurisprudence and revealed knowledge, the ruling elite showed greater interest in fine arts, architecture, literature, jurisprudence, medicine, calligraphy, forms and designs of interior decoration, costumes, gastronomic refinements, pottery, horticulture and many other arts and crafts which contributed to the perfection of good life. Forging of metal and related industries were developed partly as a requirement of the military establishment.

However, insofar as reception of new ideas and technologies was concerned, the Mughals, as the following examples show, did not display much interest. Akbar (reigned 1556–1605), after seeing the pages produced by the printing press and presented for the royal perusal by a delegation of Portuguese missionaries, is reported to have shown total lack of interest, as he found the pages printed by the machine unattractive as compared to the fine specimens of calligraphy.[12] In another instance, Emperor Jahangir (reigned 1605–27) displayed similar indifference to a mechanical clock presented to him by the leader of the French royal delegation, while he highly appreciated the French paintings. He was, however, so charmed by these French paintings that, he summoned the court painters and commissioned them to replicate the originals, which they had indeed managed, to the great admiration of the emperor. If Jahangir had evinced a similar interest in the mechanical clock we could speculate that similar, if not even better clocks would have been manufactured at imperial Agra. It may also be suggested that if Akbar had shown some interest in the printing press it may also have been popularized in India long before its introduction in the nineteenth century.

These two instances have been cited only to suggest how the rulers and powers that be guided and shaped the priorities of a nation. Unlike the earlier examples of the centres of learning in Damascus and Baghdad, and later in Toledo, Granada and Cordova, when Arabs mastered the Syriac, Greek and Coptic languages, the Muslims of later ages, particularly in Ottoman Turkey, Safavid Iran and Mughal India showed no, or at most little, interest in acquiring any competence in foreign languages (in the present case, European languages).[13] How else could one explain the ignorance of Muslims throughout Asia, Africa and Europe about the epoch-making discoveries by Copernicus, Newton, Galileo and Kepler? The discoveries and inventions of these men were available in European languages, i.e. Italian, French, German, Spanish, and English. Latin continued to be the medium of scholarship, though the new treatises were also available in the developing vernacular languages. And, as suggested earlier, Muslims not acquainted with any of the European languages did not know the pace and scope of scientific thought. Sir Syed Ahmad Khan's (d. 1898) treatise *Qawl al-matin dar ibtal-i harakat-i zamin* (*Sound Argument in Refutation of the Theory of Revolution of the Earth*), published in 1854, is a case in point. After all, Sir Syed was one of the most well-read and well-informed persons of his age and quite favourably inclined to new ideas, and would not have written the said treatise if he had sufficient in formation on later scientific developments in the West. Indeed, he wrote this treatise only because Copernicus' works had not been translated into, or referred to, in Arabic and Persian languages until that time.

We learn from some of the recent studies that Mawlawa Tafaddul Husayn (d. 1800) of Lucknow translated Newton's *Principia* (1687) into Arabic in the late eighteenth century and was, thus, obviously familiar with progress in European science. It was during the period of the late eighteenth and early nineteenth centuries that, according to Robinson, 'Lucknow became a major intellectual centre training scholars who took pleasure in engaging with European science.'[14] This makes Sir Syed's treatise in defence of Ptolemy's geocentric theory even more enigmatic, even though he recanted his position by writing another treatise the following year, when one of his friends had brought the findings of Copernicus, empirically supported by Galileo, to his notice.

It seems that the corpus of rational sciences that developed during the fifteenth and sixteenth centuries in Europe was not, or at the most only scarcely, accessible to Muslim scholars at their respective centres of learning and was therefore not incorporated in their syllabi. There are historical reasons for the changes brought about by the scholars, but none of them can be justified. While in the sixteenth-century Suleyman 'the Magnificent' in the Ottoman Empire (reigned 1520–66), Shah Isma'il in Safavid Iran (reigned 1502–24) and Akbar in Mughal India were among the greatest rulers in the world at this time, their academic institutions had ceased to be pioneers in the advancement of knowledge and ideas. The situation did not change for another two hundred years, i.e. until the close of the eighteenth century, by which time Europe had, due to the Enlightenment acquired intellectual supremacy. The East, including Mughal India, was now at the receiving end and had not much to offer in the promotion of learning and scholarship.

The Muslim Renaissance

Widespread consciousness of the advancement of knowledge in Europe came to the East via Egypt, but not earlier than its occupation by Napoleon in the first decade of the nineteenth century. It was only at this point of time that some inkling of the real dimensions of the European intellectual advancement appeared in Arabic. Muhammad 'Ali Pasha, the ruler of Egypt between 1805 and 1849, showed keen interest in the technological progress of Europe and had planned to invite geologists from France who could identify places and regions in Egypt rich in mineral wealth. But it did not occur to the Egyptian ruler, according to the Pakistani physicist and Nobel Laureate Dr 'Abd as-Salam (d. 1996), to establish departments of geology at al-Azhar in Cairo and other centres of Islamic higher learning, whose graduates could discover and exploit the mineral wealth of their own country. The Ottoman Turks had shown similar lack of interest in establishing departments of modern natural sciences in their universities and centres of advanced studies, and only wanted experts and technicians from friendly European countries to upgrade their weaponry during the period of Sultan Selim I 'Yawuz' (reigned 1512–20).

The Scene in Late Mughal India

The case of late Mughal India was no different. We do not find an organized and consistent effort to establish and upgrade studies of rational sciences in Mughal India. As has been suggested earlier, this was partly due to the unconcern and lack of initiative on the part of the rulers as patrons of higher learning. But to insist on this would be a generalization and a sweeping statement. The situation in the subcontinent appears to be different from the European 'experiments', as in the patrimonial Mughal state everything emanated from the rulers and their personal predilections. This was perhaps not the case in the European context, where an emancipating and enlightened nobility and the newly emerging mercantile class (particularly the shipping industry) played a more active role in promoting fine arts and technologies. Akbar's courtiers included men of such eminence as Abul-Fadl' 'Allami (killed 1602) and his brother Faydi (d. 1595), and Shah Fath Allah Shirazi (d. 1589) in the later period of his life. This tradition continued during the reigns of Jahangir, Shah Jahan (reigned 1627–58) and Aurangzeb. But the point being insisted upon here is that there were only sporadic efforts at establishing institutions of learning by the rulers; perhaps this was not the priority of the nobility unlike their counterparts in Europe. The colleges and universities in most

European cities owe their existence to private efforts and support from the feudal class, a phenomenon that was not very widespread in Ottoman Turkey, Safavid Iran and Mughal India.

A positive example in this regard, however, is the Madrasat Ghazi ad-Din in Delhi, established in 1692 under the patronage of Ghazi ad-Din Khan (d. 1751), one of the nobles at the court of Aurangzeb. This institution, which later became the well-known Anglo-Arabic College or Delhi College under its principal Alois Sprenger (d. 1893), served as a prime centre of learning in pre-1857 Delhi. Besides, there were numerous *madaris* attached to the Sufi hospices (*khanqahs*), but they offered instruction predominantly in the so-called 'transmitted religious sciences' (*manqulat*) that deal with revealed knowledge, i.e. Koranic exegesis (*tafsir*), 'ulum al-hadith, literature (*sira/adab*), and jurisprudence (*fiqh*). This was seen as an all essential requirement for the reinforcement of the tenets of Islamic faith. During Aurangzeb's reign and even beyond, the collation and compilation of Islamic legal documents was carried out on quite a large scale at Aurangabad in the Deccan (where the emperor had shifted his court), which ultimately resulted in the publication of the *Fatawa-yi 'Alamgiri*.

The Farangi Mahall in Lucknow, the *madrasa* at Khayrabad, and finally the Madrasa 'Aliyya at Rampur seem to be exceptions to the general rule, as they provided instruction in the rational religious sciences at the advanced level but naturally within the confines of knowledge available in Arabic and Persian. As these two classical Oriental languages remained untouched by the advancement of knowledge available in the European vernaculars, the institutions depending upon the resources of Arabic and Persian also remained untouched by post-Renaissance European thought. Besides, we must be aware that the mentioned *madaris* blossomed only after the heydays of the Mughal empire passed, and principalities such as Awadh, where all these *madaris* were situated, managed to acquire *de facto* autonomy from the court at Delhi.

Prince Dara Shikoh (executed 1659) who stands as a beacon of light in Mughal history for introducing and incorporating the wisdom of the Upanishads in Persian does not appear to have been inspired by the examples of Taxila and Nalanda, the centres of rational sciences in ancient India. However, he must be credited for his contribution in fostering an atmosphere of tolerance and respect for other religions.

Another question that continues to baffle us is the absence of interest towards Europe and its centres of civilization and learning in the East.

While European travellers have had a passion to see the East, particularly India, from at least the thirteenth century AD onwards,[16] no such sentiment was ever exhibited among the people of the East to see Europe. There are no records of any distinguished Muslim visiting Rome and pre-1453 Byzantium, let alone Leiden, Bologna, Paris, Genoa, Venice or London. Rather significantly, the great Arab traveller Ibn Battuta (d. AD 1369) did not have any European cities on his itinerary.

While the Orientalists of the eighteenth and nineteenth centuries freely wrote and commented upon Eastern civilization, art and culture, there is little reciprocity from the East, particularly India. The Orientalists created, distorted and fabricated the East and its myths, and by the middle of the nineteenth century went to the extent of appropriating the right to speak for the East, as demonstrated by Edward Said in his *Orientalism* (1978). But the Muslims remained indifferent to anything that Europe offered in terms of ideas and institutions.[17] The first outpourings of European thought in Arabic, Persian and Urdu were not seen before the middle of the nineteenth century, and a fuller realization of their power and scope was felt only after Europe had politically conquered almost the whole of Asia and Africa.

The above scenario has only been given as a backdrop to the predilections of the managers and the academic leaders of the *madaris* in Mughal India. That they lagged behind in the advancement of ideas and thought systems was a fallout of the stagnation of the educational system after the fall of Baghdad in AD 1258 and a consequence of the political domination of Europe, particularly after the defeat and dismemberment of the Ottoman Empire in 1918.

However, it must be said to the credit of the *madaris* and the *madrasa* graduates in Mughal India that in the disciplines of revealed knowledge and so-called 'transmitted religious sciences', their contribution is indeed significant in the Islamic world as a whole. The commentaries on the Koran, the promotion of *hadith* literature, critical treatises on the tenets of Islam, the compilation and systematization of *fiqh* in the form of *fatwa*—collections of the writings of authentic and well-researched biographies of the Prophet Muhammad in Persian, and historiography as a discipline were developed in keeping with the most rigorous standards of scholarship. In this regard the contributions of Abd al-Haqq 'Muhaddith' Dihlawi (d. 1642); Shah Wali Allah Dihalwi (d. 1762) and his illustrious sons, Shah Rafi' ad-Din (d. 1817), Shah 'Abd al-'Aziz (d. 1824), and Shah' Abd ai-Qadir (d. 1827); his not less renowned grandson Shah Isma'il Dihlawi (killed 1831); and also Mawlawi Mamluk 'Ali (d. 1851), Shah Muhammad Panah 'Ata' Saloni (d. 1860), the famous *ulama* of the Farangi Mahall in Lucknow, and finally Mawlawi Fadl-i Haqq Khayrabadi (d. 1861) are worth mentioning in this regard.

Francis Robinson has given tables of curricula in Ottoman Turkey, Safavid Iran and the *dars-i nizami* in Mughal India at the close of the seventeenth century.[18] While in the Ottoman curriculum there are no headings for mathematics and medicine in the rational religious sciences (*ma'qulat*), there is greater focus on the transmitted religious sciences (*manqulat*), in particular on the principles of jurisprudence (*usul al-fiqh*) and *fiqh* itself, besides the study of *hadith* literature and *tafsir al-Koran*. The Safavid curriculum, on the contrary, includes, besides the traditional sciences, mathematics, logic (*mantiq*) and philosophy (*hikma*) in good measure. The *dars-i nizami* includes, in addition to morphology (*sarf*) and syntax (*nahw*), rhetoric (*'ilm al-balagha*), principles of jurisprudence and *fiqh*, *'ulam al-hadith* and *tafsir*, and a number of topics and books in mathematics, logic, philosophy and theology on par with the Safavid curriculum. In the Ottoman curriculum works of medicine (*tibb*) are not recorded at this stage, though they were to be included later.[19]

A cursory glance at the curricula of the three great empires indicates a general tendency towards the marginalization of the applied rational sciences, particularly of the disciplines of physics (*'ilm at-tabi'a*), astronomy (*hay'a*), alchemy (as the predecessor of modern chemistry) and medicine, wherein Muslims had made significant contributions in these fields from the eighth to thirteenth centuries AD. Even the emphasis on *ma'qulat* in the original *dars-i nizami* of the late seventeenth century became increasingly obscured in later modifications of the syllabus, aiming no longer at practical purposes but becoming more and more of an intellectual exercise with only little relevance for society. Much could be said to explain the absence of the will to engage with the latest developments in the world of ideas and developing systems of knowledge in *madrasa* education. But the fact remains that this gap resulted in the overall decline in the standards and scope of education which left its graduates competent mainly in the transmitted religious sciences, over and above the principles of jurisprudence and *fiqh*, historiography (*tarikh*) and rhetorics, besides the mastery of the classical languages, Arabic and Persian. From the perspective of today's secular polity and its requirements concerning the intellectual elites, this can hardly be considered a mean achievement in itself. If a system of secular education were also to have existed side by side, the two would have complemented each other. Why this did not happen remains an enigma that deserves to be addressed.

Contrary to the modern perception regarding the *madrasa* and the *madrasa*-educated graduates, this Islamic institution has a glorious history. For a long time the graduates of the *madaris* were the torchbearers of knowledge, revealed and secular, who transformed our world view and society in a significant manner. There was never any gap or dichotomy in the realms of the divine and the secular.

It will perhaps not be an exaggeration to say that after Latin, Arabic became the *lingua franca*, with all knowledge available in it. The fall of Baghdad and the gradual marginalization of philosophy as an academic discipline also resulted in the change of emphasis in curricula design. The Renaissance and, inseparably related to it, the advancement of knowledge in Europe remained unnoticed for a long time in the Orient, till the European military might and expansion knocked at their doors. The late realization that the Orient, though militarily and politically still formidable, lagged far behind in intellectual pursuits did not bring about any qualitative shift in their emphasis. A parallel and powerful move to shun intellectual pursuits and revert to traditional sciences brought further deterioration. It is nothing but a siege mentality inwardly and the spectre of being hunted and haunted outwardly that further narrowed down the options of *madrasa* managers and its graduates. It is only with a radically positive and healthy approach that things can be bettered. This is difficult though not impossible.

Postscript

All surmises are subject to correction and refutation. What struck me as complex and inexplicable was my reading of Syed Ahmad Khan's tract supporting the geocentric theory of Ptolemy as against the then current views in 1853 and also the fact that Syed Ahmad Khan corrected his position the very next year when he came to know of Copernicus and his arguments against the geocentric theory. It led me to my surmise that Sir Syed Ahmad Khan was at least in this regard three centuries behind the European systems of knowledge. However, the availability of Tafaddul Husayn's translation of Newton's *Principia* into Arabic done in the late eighteenth century and other relevant literature point in a different direction. Moreover, some recent publications lead us to far different conclusions. It appears that the hypothesis that Muslim interest in the Christian West began in the early nineteenth century (to which Bernard Lewis also subscribes)[20] is not very tenable. As new researches show, people from the Muslim and Christian worlds already mixed and intermingled during the sixteenth and seventeenth centuries. In this connection reference may be made to the works of George Makdisi and, even more important, those of Nabil Matar.[21] The information and argument of researches about the *bilad an-nasara* (land of the Christians) cited earlier makes it much more puzzling why the Islamic East remained unaware of and indifferent to the corpus of new ideas regarding science, literature, politics and arts that came in the wake of the rise of humanism and the Renaissance in Europe. A comparative study of the syllabi in the institutions of the Safavid, Ottoman and Mughal empires does not seem to have taken cognizance of what was being read and taught in secular realms in the institutions of European empires.

This postscript is being added by way of an apology, lest a reader be misled to accept the generalizations regarding the Islamic East's contact with the West dating back to the early nineteenth century in which I also at times indulged. I end my note with the following lines from T.S. Eliot's *East Coker*:

> The knowledge imposes a pattern, and falsifies,
> For the pattern is new in every moment
> And every moment is a new and shocking
> Valuation of all we have been.[22]

Notes

1. An example could be that during the reign of the last great Mughal emperor Aurangzeb 'Alamgir (reigned 1658–1707) high ranking *ulama* were employed to compile and standardize prevailing formal legal opinions (*fatawa*/sg.: *fatwa*) into the most comprehensive collection of legal opinions in India, the *Fatawa-yi 'Alamgiri*.
2. Even though the *nawabs* of Awadh never refused to recognize the sovereignty of the Mughal ruler over their dominion, they became *de facto* more independent from the court in Delhi. cf. Alam (1997, pp. 47–73). On the Farangi Mahall and its role for the *nawabi* state administration in Awadh, cf. Robinson (2001).
3. Cf. Kozlowski (1985, pp. 21–32).

4. Indeed, according to William W. Hunter, an EIC official who was appointed in 1881 to conduct an Education Commission investigating into the state of education in India, what was called 'Wahhabiyya' in South Asia was essentially an anti-British stance, and carried political rather than religious connotations. cf. Hunter (1880, pp. 40–77).

5. Cf. Hermansen (2000, pp. 30–4). Here it needs to be taken into account that the *khanqah*-based *madaris* held a special position as the oldest and most widespread form of *madrasa* education right into the nineteenth century. Cf. the contribution of Saiyid Zaheer Husain Jafri to the present volume.

6. It is felt that the purism of so-called Wahhabi thought was not absent from the curriculum and broad outlines of the ideologues of the founders of the Dar al-ʿulum at Deoband. However, I may submit that they can definitely not be called 'Wahhabi' in the real sense of the word, because almost all the leading Deobandi scholars had Sufi affiliations with the Chishti–Sabiri order, and in some cases with the Naqshbandiyya too. Mawlana Ahmad Rida Khan, while criticizing the basic tenets of the Deoband school, pejoratively labelled them 'Wahhabis', without taking note of the fact that they never rejected the Sufic dimension of Islam, although they were critical of some Sufi practices, such as the performance of Sufi devotional songs (*sama*) and other practices in various *khanqahs* of the subcontinent, which they considered as *bidʿa*.

7. On the history of the Nadwat al-ʿulamaʾ and its role for *madrasa* education in contemporary India, cf. the contribution of Jan-Peter Hartung (chapter 5) to *Islamic Education, Diversity and National Identity: Dini Madaris in India Post-9/11*, ed. Helmut Reifeld and Jan-Peter Hartung, New Delhi: Sage Publications, 2006.

8. Mawlana Amin Ahsan Islahi (d. 1997), a graduate of the Madrasat al-Islah and former associate of Sayyid Abul-Ala Mawdudi (d. 1979), the founder of the Jamaʿat-i Islami movement in undivided India, later differed with his master in regard to some of the basic interpretations of the Koran. His own commentary on the Koran, *Tadabbur al-qurʾan* (*Reflections on the Koran*), differs on some of the basic issues as spelt out by Mawdudi in his *Tafhim al-iurʾan* (*Understanding of the Koran*). Apart from Amin Ahsan Islahi, two more graduates from the Madrasat al-Islah, Sadr ad-Din lslahi (d. 1998) and Najatallah Siddiqi Islahi have significantly contributed to the literary corpus of the Jamaʿat-i Islami.

9. Even though Jinnah obtained his barrister's degree from the Lincoln's Inn of Court in London, where he studied between 1894 and 1896, he also received his earlier education at the Madrasat al-Islam in Karachi.

10. The leadership of the Jamaʿat-i Islami of India changed their position only as late as 1967, 20 years after India became a democracy based on a secular Constitution.

11. For the sake of justice it needs to be said that the rationalist tendencies, especially those of Islamic philosophy and Muʿtazilite theology, have over the centuries and in a highly complex process been absorbed in Shiʿite systems of knowledge. Thus, the process of traditionalization which we have outlined here belongs primarily to the Sunnite denomination of Islam.

12. It has been outlined in various sources why it might have been that Muslims failed to adopt the letter-press until the nineteenth century. Cf. Robinson (2000, pp. 68–75). It might, however, be enlightening to compare the Mughal attitude towards printing with the Ottomans. Here the case of the letter-press was already positively considered

in the early eighteenth century, when the Hungarian convert to Islam, Ibrahim Muteferriqa (d. 1745), brought forth solely Islamic arguments for the introduction of printing to Sultan Ahmed III (reigned 1703–30). Cf. Reichmuth (2001, pp. 153–9).

13. It should be said that during the Mughal period a lively activity had set in to translate works from Indian languages into Persian. These texts, however, were primarily Hindu religious and philosophical texts, which do not deal with problems that arise from new developments in the fields of science and technology.

14. Robinson (2001, p. 223).

15. Cf. Zaydi (1990).

16. Cf. Rubies (2000). Here a number of reasons for the interest in travel to the East are named, which are mainly linked to different types of travellers. Thus, the early travelling to the East by lay travellers, such as the famous Marco Polo (d. 1324) of Venice, was based on the intellectual movement of the so-called 'Florentine humanism', whereas the interest of Christian missionaries was, of course, of another kind. In the sixteenth century, finally, independent travellers became more and more sceptical of the East and, therefore, provided a fertile ground for the approaching 'Orientalism' of the eighteenth and nineteenth centuries.

17. Cf. Said (1995, 92–10). For the Indian case, cf. Inden (1990).

18. Cf. Robinson (2001, pp. 240–51) Here, it needs to be emphasized that the *dars-i nizami* owed its origin to the demands of the nawabs of Awadh during the process of their political emancipation from the Mughal court in Delhi.

19. Ibid.

20. Cf. Lewis (2002).

21. Cf. Makdisi (1981, pp. 224–91; 1990, pp. 294–347); Matar (1998, 1999, 2003).

22. Eliot (1996, p. 16).

References

Abd ar-Rahman, Sabah ad-Din (1973–80), *Bazm-I Taymuriya*, 2 vols., Azamgarh: Dar al-musannifin.

Alam, Muzaffar, *The Crisis of Empire in Mughal North India: Awadh and the Punjab*, 1707–48, 3rd edn, New Delhi, OUP, 1997.

Ansari, Asloob A., *Sir Syed Ahmad Khan: A Centenary Tribute*, Delhi: Adam Publishers, 2000.

Eliot, T. S., *Four Quartets*, Cambridge: Rampant Lions Press, 1996.

Faruqi, Diya' al-Hasan, *Musalmanon ka ta'limi nizam*, New Delhi: Maktaba-yi Jami'a, 1992.

Hermansen, Marcia, 'Fakirs, Wahhabis, and Others: Reciprocal Classifications and the Transformation of Intellectual Categories' in Jamal Malik, ed., *Perspectives of Mutual Encounters in South Asian History 1760–1860*, Leiden: Brill, 2000, pp. 23–48.

Hunter, William Wilson, *The Indian Mussalmans*, 4th edn, London: Trubner, 1880.

Inden, Ronald, *Imagining India*, Oxford: Basil Blackwell, 1990.

Jafri, Sayyid Naqi Husayn, 'Musalmanon ki 'ilmi riwayat' in *Kitabnuma*, New Delhi: Maktaba-yi Jami'a, 1994.

Kozlowski, Gregory C., *Muslim Endowments and Society in British India*, Cambridge: CUP, 1985.

Lewis, Bernard, *What Went Wrong?: The Clash between Islam and Modernity in the Middle East*, Oxford: OUP, 2002.

Makdisi, George, *The Rise of Colleges: Institutions of Learning in Islam and the West*, Edinburgh: Edinburgh University Press, 1981.

————, *The Rise of Humanism in Classical Islam and the Christian West, With Special Reference to Scholasticism*, Edinburgh: Edinburgh, University Press, 1990.

Matar, Nabil, *Islam in Britain: 1558–1665*, Cambridge: CUP, 1998.

————, *Turks, Moors and Englishmen in the Age of Discovery*, New York: Columbia University Press, 1999.

————, *In the Lands of the Christians: Arabic Travel Writing in the Seventeenth Century*, New York: Routledge, 2003.

Reichmuth, Stefan, 'Islamic Reformist Discourse in the Tulip Period (1718–30): Ibrahim Muteferriqa and his Arguments for Printing', in Caksu Ali, ed., *International Congress on Learning and Education in the Ottoman World (12–15 April 1999)*, Istanbul: IRCICA, 2001, pp. 149–61.

Robinson, Francis, *Islam and Muslim History in South Asia*, New Delhi: OUP, 2000.

————, *The 'Ulama of Farangi Mahall and Islamic Culture in South Asia*, New Delhi: Permanent Black, 2001.

Rubies, Joan-Pau (sic), *Travel and Ethnology in the Renaissance: South India through European Eyes, 1250–1625*, Cambridge: CUP, 2000.

Said, Edward, *Orientalism: Western Conceptions of the Orient*, London: Penguin (rpt), 1995.

Zaydi, Zahid Husayn and Iqbal A. Khan, eds., *Khwab awr haqiqat*, New Delhi, 1990.

CHAPTER 6

The Signs and Signifiers of the Urdu–Hindi Controversy

Sir Syed Ahmad Khan (1817–98) was one of the most integrated personalities of his time. His role as a social reformer and his contribution to the development of Urdu prose are well established. He is generally known for spearheading the movement for educational advancement of Indian Muslims and as the founder of Mohammedan-Anglo Oriental College, Aligarh, which was later, accorded the status of a university. Sir Syed is also recognized as a religious thinker and his political thought and activities have been given due consideration by scholars sympathetically, though quite often with censure of various degrees. He has also been accused of fomenting the Hindi–Urdu controversy and blamed for keeping the Muslim intelligentsia of north India away from the fold of the All India Congress Committee. The orthodox *ulema* found him guilty of a partisan attitude in favour of English and Western values and for interpreting the Koran in a rational mode. Even today, Sir Syed's compelling genius continues to elicit a response from scholars and critics of all hues and shades even about a hundred years after his death.

The misperceptions about Sir Syed are varying in nature and degree. Some of these are deliberate while others are based on misreadings of his writings and speeches. There have been attempts in India and abroad to place Sir Syed at the centre of the Urdu–Hindi controversy and the rise of separatist tendencies among Muslims, while there is an inclination among Pakistani historians to trace the demand for Pakistan to some of the writings and speeches of Sir Syed. In addition to the said categories there are apologists who defend whatever he said and did. In the absence of any critical evaluation and objective assessment of what Sir Syed accomplished in India or abroad, it is indeed difficult to form an opinion with regard to some of the controversies that grew around his personality. The present essay is an attempt at analysing some of the misperceptions specially with regard to the Urdu–Hindi controversy that continues to baffle us.

In the last chapter of his book, *A House Divided*, appropriately titled 'Aetiology of the Division', Amrit Rai has castigated Sir Syed for fomenting the Urdu–Hindi controversy, maligning Raja Shiva Prasad and Bhartendu Harishchandra, and for making a prophecy about the imminent Partition of the country. Amrit Rai has quoted extensively from the writings of Growse, Fallon, Beames, Syed Insha (*Dariya-e Latafat*), Altaf Husain Hali, Raja Shiva Prasad, Bhartendu, Grierson, Suniti Kumar Chatterji and some other linguists in support of his arguments in the context of the Hindi–Urdu controversy. He says: 'It is understandable for someone to disagree with Bhartendu and other protagonists of the movement for Hindi. But the kind of fierce intolerance evinced by Sir Syed is difficult to comprehend except in terms of a special psychological make-up which seems to be noticeably different from that of the earlier, pre-Muslim conquerors.'

In defence of Raja Shiva Prasad, Amrit Rai goes on to say: 'As it happens Raja Shiva Prasad is a much misunderstood man in both Urdu and Hindi circles. His views on the question seem to have undergone radical change with time and he made no secret of this. Thus he managed to offend combatants on either side—the Urdu side with his earlier views and the Hindi side with his later views.' After quoting from *Hayat-i Javed* wherein Maulana Hali has referred to Sir Syed's meeting with Mr. Shakespeare at Banaras, Amrit Rai says,

> This dark prophecy came true, as we know, about eighty years later. Whatever else may have been at the back of it, there is little doubt that such extreme reaction on the part of Sir Syed to a simple dispute does appear perverse. One is therefore impelled to look for its possible cause in other material pertaining to the language controversy. . . . It is well known that Raja Shiva Prasad Sitara-e Hind and Bhartendu Harishchandra played a prominent role in the movement for Hindi and Devanagari, so they naturally came in for severe punishment from Sir Syed.

Later, Amrit Rai concludes: 'one thought that a person like the Raja deserved better of Sir Syed and the Urdu world'.

As can be easily borne out from the passages cited, Amrit Rai's denigration of Sir Syed is tendentious and the book appears to have been written with preconceived judgements. Sir Syed's efforts to safeguard the interests of the Muslim elite and his espousal of Urdu as an official court language comes in the wake of deliberate attempts by the then British government to cut down the size of the Muslim bureaucracy and curtail the area of influence of Urdu by creating the language controversy. Amrit Rai appears to be blind to some of the contemporary issues that forced Sir Syed to take up the issues relating to the Muslims and Urdu language. In this connection an extract from a despatch of Ellenborough, the Governor-General of India makes an interesting reading with regard to the new policy of the British towards Muslims. It was in the context of the installation of the Deodar gates of the tomb of Mahmud of Ghazna (d. AD 1030) at the Somnath Temple in 1842, that Ellenborough wrote:

> When we are sure of the hostility of one-tenth (i.e. the Mussalmans) not to secure the enthusiastic support of the nine-tenths (i.e. the Hindus) which are faithful . . . I would make the most of our successes and of the recovery of the gates of the Temple, treating it ostensibly as a great military triumph, but knowing very well that the Hindus will value it as a guarantee, of the future security of themselves and their religion against the Mussalmans. All those who best know India tell me that effect will be very great indeed and I think it will. . . . I have every reason to think that the restoration of the gates of the Temple of Somnath has conciliated and gratified the great mass of the Hindu population. I have no reason to suppose that it has offended the Mussalmans; but I cannot close my eyes to the belief that that race is fundamentally hostile to us, and therefore our true policy is to conciliate the Hindoos.

Ellenborough was severely criticized for his views in the British Parliament but he defended and justified his policy as a politic measure. The question of 'fundamental hostility' may be better addressed to the Christians if one were to consider the context of the Crusades beginning in AD 1096. Amrit Rai appears to be unaware of the context of Christo–Anglian hostility to Muslims while denigrating Sir Syed to protect the claims of Muslims and the Urdu-speaking elite from total marginalization. The British were also extremely unhappy with the role of the Muslim aristocracy in 1857. The brunt of the British wrath was faced by the Muslims and not so much by Hindus. The British always felt greater danger from Muslims rather than Hindus which is why they began a policy of Hindu appeasement as may be borne out from the passage cited earlier on the installation of the Deodar gates at Somnath Temple. The language policy of the British also underwent significant changes first by replacing Persian with Urdu and later by de-Persianizing Urdu on the pretext of addressing the larger majority of Indians, the Hindus. In this context the views of Macdonnell, ICS (1866–72), deserve to be mentioned. He encouraged and patronized the campaign for Nagari, which was aimed at cutting down Muslim influence in the bureaucracy. 'Hindu revivalism', according to Francis Robinson, 'not only pressed the Urdu-speaking elite hard but also weakened, and in many places broke the links that held its Hindu and Muslim components together'. Robinson adds, 'Hindus such as Shiva Prasad, Jai Kishen Das and the Raja of Bhinga found it difficult to resist the claims of the new and burgeoning sense of Hindu nationality' (*Separatism Among Indian Muslims*, 1993). It is indeed difficult to see the campaign for Nagari by Raja Shiva Prasad, Jai Kishen Das and Bhartendu Harishchandra as sincere and genuine attempts towards the fulfilment of the aspirations of the masses, whose majority was more at ease with the simple Hindustani written in Nagari script. In this regard the observation made by Vasudha Dalmia merits attention: 'Thus it is important to note that the distinction between what was later known as Urdu and Hindavi had little to do with the religion of the people who used it, or with script alone. If there was a divide it was the urban-rural divide, cemented by the formal creation of Urdu-e mualla' (*The Nationalization of Hindu Traditions*, Oxford, 1997). There is no reason to believe that it was not a deliberate attempt to reduce and marginalize the position of the Urdu-speaking Muslim aristocracy, ostensibly, in the name of the true *lingua franca*. Sir Syed's defense of Urdu, which writers like Amrit Rai project as his opposition to Hindi, should be seen in the larger context of the British policy of Hindu appeasement and gradual marginalization of Muslims as an extension of their centuries-old fundamental hostility to Islam and its followers.

Vasudha Dalmia in her book, *The Nationalization of Hindu Traditions*, analyses the forces that worked behind the movement for Hindi. She extensively quotes from the writings and speeches of Bhartendu Harishchandra, especially his Ballia address, to establish that the movement for Hindi was inextricably linked with Hindu revivalism. Bhartendu drew the analogy from the combination of the British renaissance and reformation to the Hindu progress and revival. She quotes a passage from Pratap Narayan Misra (1856–94), a fellow writer and publicist of Bhartendu when he wound up his journal *Brahman*:

> If you truly desire your own welfare
> Then keep chanting this *mantra* with one tongue,
>   Hindi, Hindu, Hindustan
>
> Whether it attracts or repels the world,
> Brings respect or affront
> Don't leave off chanting with one voice
>   Hindi, Hindu, Hindustan
>
> Those who don't know their own identity
> Are like the living dead
> So sing loud this grand *mantra*
>   Hindi, Hindu, Hindustan
>
> Wise are those who don't discard their own language,
> Food and clothing
> In all its proof and good fortune,
>   Hindi, Hindu, Hindustani

The concept of national language, Dalmia says, was initially introduced by the British and applied to the Indian situation. She further adds that the evolution of Hindi as the language of the Hindus continued through the nineteenth century. It was first and foremost a process of dichotomization, i.e. separation from Urdu, coupled with the claim of absolute autonomy for Hindi. It was later standardized by means of grammars, dictionaries and social primers. The third important stage, says Vasudha Dalmia, was the process of historicization, i.e. the process of establishing historical links with literary works connected with great ideological movements of the past.

The two primary ideological constructs, according to Dalmia, 'were the British imperialists and later the Hindu nationalist'. She calls it the 'Hinduization of Hindi'. From Bhartendu Harishchandra's Ballia address to the Memorial presented by the citizens of Allahabad to the Education Commission in 1882, the cause of Hindi had been much strengthened. Once the lead had been given by Bhartendu, there was no end to the unsavoury nature of the polemical debate. However, to the credit of Bhartendu it may be said that 'he did not totally exclude the courtly literature in Urdu or entirely subsume the rural Muslim, linguistically'. The memorialists, argues Dalmia exhibited no scruple in equating the national language conclusively with Hindu language, literature and tradition, which had maintained themselves, in spite of all hindrances. The Bengal and the Bombay Presidencies had their own national languages used for official purposes while in the North Western Provinces English was gradually becoming the medium of instruction at the senior secondary level. Urdu was the only language that could have easily replaced English when its status was challenged by the champions of Hindi. After all, Urdu had been the medium of instruction of several *madarsas* in India that taught rational sciences along with traditional disciplines. Mention may be made of the Madarsa Ghaziuddin, Madarsa-e Aaliya Rampur and the famous seminaries of Farangi Mahall and Khairabad.

The movement for Hindi not only harmed Urdu but also weakened the pace of liberal education in India. If Urdu had continued to be the regional language of the north-west like Marathi and Bengali in the Bombay and Calcutta Presidencies, people in this region may not have remained educationally backward. The battle cry of Hindi put the clock back for several decades.

This controversy has brought about some new myths into focus. For a long time we have been given to believe that Urdu is the language of the camp, of the Mughal conquerors which later became a kind of *lingua franca*. The *Oxford English Dictionary* and Hobson Jobson both give the meaning, scope and usage of Urdu in almost the same manner:

> . . . the language of the country but in fact the language that the Mohammedans of upper India, and eventually the Mohammedans of Deccan, developed out of the Hindi dialect of the Doab chiefly and the territory around Agra and Delhi with a mixture of Persian vocables and phrases, and a readiness to adopt foreign words. Also called Oordoo, i.e. the language of the Urdu, (horde), or Camp. This language was for a long time a kind of Mohammedan *lingua franca* all over India, and still possesses that character over a large part of the country, and among certain classes. Even in Madras, where it least prevails, it is still recognized in native regiments as the language of intercourse between officers and men. Old-fashioned Anglo-Indians used to call it the Moors.

Shamsur Rehman Faruqi in his book *Urdu Ka Ibtedai Zamanah* (Karachi: Aaj, 1999), refutes the definition as being arbitrary and baseless.

He posits several arguments that bring out the tendentious approach of the compilers. The definitions given in the two dictionaries, in fact, perpetuate the same viewpoint and mindset that had created the language controversy in the middle of the nineteenth century in order to advance the cause of Hindi and push back the claims of Urdu by linking it to the advent of Muslim conquerors in India and deliberately maligning it as the language of the hordes. Faruqi argues that the word 'Urdu' in the sense of language was first used around 1780 by the celebrated Urdu poet Mus'hafi; earlier it was referred to as Hindi, Hindavi or Rekhta. Urdu was, according to, Faruqi, also used as a synonym for Shahjehanabad and sometimes for Persian language. Urdu is now accepted by large number of linguists in India as a dialect of Hindi that found a different direction by rejecting native diction in preference to Persianized words. On the contrary, Faruqi argues, modern Hindi may be said to have found a different mooring by rejecting popular and current Persianized words in preference to Sanskritized Hindi and native diction. By the same logic modern Hindi can also be said to be a dialect of the then Hindustani, Hindi, Hindavi or Rekhta, that is the earlier incarnation of modern Urdu. Once the British decided to give to the Hindus of India a sense of destiny by alienating them from the Muslims, patronage to Hindi was a natural corollary. It was necessary to widen the gulf between Hindus and Muslims by redefining the genesis of the two languages. As soon as some of the leading Hindus realized the advantages that were in store for them, they deserted the Urdu camp and formed their own bandwagon in the last quarter of the nineteenth century. Raja Shiva Prasad, Jai Kishen Das and Bhartendu Harishchandra were the first to champion the cause of Hindi. Babu Shiva Prasad deposed before the Education Commission (1882) that 'the presence of Arabic Persian derivatives (in Urdu) is a reminder of the supremacy of Muslims over Hindus. On the contrary, the Nagari script has religious significance for us.' Much before the evidence Babu Shiva Prasad had deposed before the Commission, he had submitted a Memorandum to the Government in 1868 wherein he argued:

> Those who did not aspire or seek to gain the favour of the Muhammadans, by becoming, if not altogether half Muhammedanized, still valued Hindi works, left by Tulsidas, Surdas, Kabir, Behari, etc. Persian words of course found their way most extensively everywhere into all the dialects composing Hindi, and became household words as well in the Zenanas as in the Bazars. This new mixture of languages

has been called Urdu . . . I pray that Persian letters may be driven out of the Courts as the language has been, and that Hindi may be substituted for them.

It may be interesting to note that Raja Shiva Prasad was a descendant of Jagat Seth, 'the famous Marwari banker who sold out the Nawab of Bengal to Robert Clive'. 'Shiva Prasad', says David Lelyveld, 'was blatantly anti-Muslim both in his textbooks and in other public utterances: the British had come to rescue the Hindu population of India from Muslim persecution' (*Aligarh's First Generation*, Lahore, 1991). When the tirade against Urdu was at its peak, Sir Syed was away in England. In a letter to Mohsin-ul Mulk he wrote: 'I got another news that has disappointed me greatly. As a result of Babu Shiva Prasad's movement the Hindus are generally very irritated against Urdu script which they consider to be a symbol of Muslims and they want it to be dissipated . . . this is a stratagem that is not going to unite Hindus and Muslims. Muslims are not going to agree on Hindi and if Hindus are stubborn and insist on Hindi, they will not agree. It will alienate Muslims from Hindus. . . .' The gravity of the situation can be understood from the fact that Bhartendu Harishchandra demeaned himself to such an extent in his hatred for Urdu that he made fun of Urdu sounds and expressions. This unsavoury attitude of some of the educated men championing the cause of Hindi indeed hurt Sir Syed. The British had done their job by appropriating their right to define the origin and scope of Urdu and successfully aggravating the situation to an unprecedented divide. Interestingly, the new definition of Urdu (camp/horde) was being legitimized at a time when Maulana Muhammad Husain Azad was engaged in the process of rejecting thousands of Urdu words as unchaste and obsolete (*Ab-e-Hayat*, 1882). How can the language of the camp and the language of the court, with such emphasis on chastity and refinement be categorized as one? The blunder the Urdu–Hindi speakers committed in accepting the definition and scope of Hindi–Urdu as given by the British has not yet been rectified. Shamsur Rehman Faruqi has raised a seminal issue by addressing the Urdu–Hindi controversy in the context of the century-old debate.

One of the likely explanations for the British interest in fomenting the Urdu–Hindi controversy was the fact that the Delhi Muslims, according to Narayani Gupta, 'had by the 1880s shaken off the quietude that had gripped them after 1857, and they were again interested in things temporarily forgotten' (*Delhi: Between Two Empires*, Oxford, 1981). They revived their interest in literature, journalism, Unani medicine and humanitarian reform, the characteristic features of the cultured man in Delhi. The Hindi–Urdu controversy was the focus of attention and in the year 1884, three separate statements were issued in Delhi supporting Urdu as against Hindi. According to Narayani Gupta, 'one of these had a majority of Hindu signatories, another largely Muslims, while the third, the "Popular Language Advocates Committee", claimed to have ten thousand signatures, obviously including people from outside the city. The local newspapers all supported Urdu'.

Sir Syed's response to the Hindi campaign in 1868, according to David Lelyveld, 'was to argue that Hindi and Urdu were, in fact, the same language, and that good Urdu style avoided heavy use of Persian or Arabic vocabulary. Legal terminology, on the other hand, was inherently technical and might as well be of Persian or Arabic derivation, since those terms were already in use. All Sir Syed's early writings on the issue sought to diffuse it of its cultural symbolism, but the issue became increasingly charged as the years wore on. It may be interesting to point out here that Sir Syed's Urdu prose is a fine example of what he thought and advocated in defense of Urdu as the *lingua franca* of India. It is essentially simple, plain and idiomatic but never devoid of elegance and compactness. On the contrary, Abul Kalam Azad made significant departure from the prose of *Tahzeeb-ul Akhlaq* when he began the publication of *Al-Hilal*. Azad made his Urdu prose as ornate and exclusivist as it was accused of during the last decades of the nineteenth century by the Hindi chauvinists. The Urdu prose that developed from the times of Shah Ismaeel Shaheed and got the impetus from the inimitable style of Ghalib and an essays of Sir Syed appears to have suffered at the hands of Abul Kalam Azad. Though the earlier strain of Urdu prose was revived by men like Khwaja Hasan Nizami, Abdul Haq and Abdul Majid Daryabadi, the style of Abul Kalam Azad also had a loyal following.

The various histories of the separatist movements in India point to the Urdu–Hindi controversy and the negative role of Sir Syed Ahmad Khan in that regard. It is indeed ironical that a man like Sir Syed is accused of 'fierce intolerance' and 'perversity' and for making a prophecy 'about the imminent partition of the country' by Amrit Rai whereas Babu Shiva Prasad and Bhartendu Harishchandra are glorified. It is frequently alleged that the seeds of the two-nation theory were sown in the last two decades of the nineteenth century and that Sir Syed was at the centre of the controversy. Whereas the fact is that the first rumblings of the two-nation theory are heard in the Hindi camp. It may be pointed out here that the great Hindu political leader, Lala Lajpat Rai (1856–1928) suggested in one of his statements the separation of Muslim India from the rest of the country (*The Tribune*, 14 December 1925). It was the time when Europe had appropriated to itself the right and authority to define, analyse and categorize the Orient. The definitions of Urdu and Hindi as given by some of the British Orientalists may be seen as attempts in the same direction. In the absence of any definitive history of Urdu and Hindi, it was easy for the British to appropriate to themselves the authority to do so. But unfortunately the Urdu writers did not make any effort to join issue with the compilers of dictionaries and the orientalists of various hues and shades in regard to the genesis of Urdu even for a long time. Likewise, the entire burden of separatist tendencies in India is put on Muslims. The Urdu–Hindi controversy continued to haunt the politics of the subcontinent even after India's Independence and the formation of Pakistan. The issue before the Constituent Assembly of India with regard to the Official Language Act was more or less the same that dominated the last decades of the nineteenth century: that is, should it be Hindustani written in the Persian and Nagari scripts or just Hindi as advocated by Raja Shiva Prasad and Bhartendu Harishchandra. Hindi won and Hindustani lost. This time Urdu was completely obliterated, the designs of Hindi propagators having come full circle.

CHAPTER 7

Diwan-e-Ghalib

Books inform, provoke and help the reader to brainstorm. There is almost nothing that cannot be ascribed to books. This also includes books that brainwash and disinform. The kind of personality we acquire is also sometimes an index of the books we have read. There are books we read and want to forget and there are books we want to cherish in our memory. A student of humanities may be considered doubly priviledged as they get to read books which have been authored by some of the best minds of human history. The sacred texts, the revealed books, remains this day the most read and referred writings for guidance, inspiration and strength. The *Gita*, the Bible and the Koran are the most frequently published books without any copyright hassles.

Born and brought up in a small but ancient town of Awadh, Salon, on the Lucknow–Allahabad highway, I belong to a tradition and cultural ethos which may be described as the last phase of the Indo–Iranian civilization of the last millennium. In this society, quoting verses from a poet's *diwan* (collection of poems) was a common practice. Even those who did not learn the 3 R's sometimes remembered dozens of couplets to quote as and when occasion demanded. It was a part of a gentleman's conversation. To be able to quote from Saadi, Hafiz, Rumi, Kabir, Rahim, Mir, Ghalib, Anis, Iqbal and Chakbast was considered to be a mark of an accomplished personality. Personal libraries possessed a good number of collected works, collected poems, anthologies of Persian/Urdu poets.

The Indo–Iranian civilization of the Mughal period found its highest manifestation in nineteenth-century India. Here, it may not be out of place to refer to one of the most profound comments by an Urdu critic, A.A. Siddiqui, on the contribution of the Mughal civilization to India. He says 'Taj Mahal, Urdu and Ghalib are the three most cherishable landmarks of that culture.' The Indo–Iranian civilization produced writers of wide sympathies, catholicity of vision and with a commitment to the celebration of human love.

A noble in nineteenth-century Delhi/Lucknow was a thorough gentleman in the true sense of the word; a good swordsman, a courtier and well-versed in the rich traditions of Arabic/Persian/Sanskrit and other Indian languages. The literary convention of *ghazal* (Persian/Urdu), is one of the richest oldest traditions of poetry that spread over eight hundred years, from the twelfth to twentieth century, and is very much alive today. It has been anti-status/ quotist, rebellious and non-conformist, and to be precise, a secular tradition of poetry. Robinson's *The Ulema of Farangi Mahall* (OUP, 2000) and *Letters of Ghalib* translated by Khursheedul Islam and Ralph Russel (OUP, 1978) bring out with some precision and at times, in detail, the quality of life that characterized the life and manners of the nobles and people of north India. Bailey, the historian, in one of his articles said that the Mughal civilization in the twentieth century was with strong roots though was politically and militarily weak. The nobility was not overwhelmed by the British, it was simply destroyed by them. This brief introduction has been presented because Ghalib whose *Diwan* is going to be discuss, besides being a poet, was also a member of the Mughal nobility.

Besides celebrating human love as a controlling passion of life, the poets of the Indo–Persian tradition also dwelt on the themes of existential issues, freely commenting upon the interplay of orthodoxy, non-conformity and heresy. This trend had begun in the twelfth century with the rise of Sufism in West Asia, North Africa, Central Asia, and of course India and the South-East. The Sufis distanced themselves from the temporal and political authority and targeted the institutions that demanded complete subservience from people. They openly encouraged the questioning and examination of beliefs, rituals and received opinions in their quest for truth. We have examples of Rumi and Attar who, besides being great poets were practicing Sufis as well.

The liberty to accept, modify or reject dogma on the basis of their own spiritual experience was demanded and exercised by the Sufis and has a history of its own. We can regard it as a resultant of the attempts of the legalists to give comprehensiveness and precision to Muslim religious law, the intellectualist attack on certain theological concepts in the ninth century.

The defeat of the intellectualists by an alliance between the upholders of theology and the state, the oppressiveness of the despotic rule, the denial by the established theological and political systems of the individual's right to think and judge for himself and, what is perhaps most important, the urge of the spiritually sensitive to find their own way to the Absolute. The Sufis were at first suspected, and persecuted but they established themselves through their appeal to the masses, and from the twelfth century onwards the Sufi *tariqah* and the orthodox *shariah* became two recognized ways the Muslim could follow, with the option of crossing over from one to the other as and when he liked.

The mystic-poetic tradition also prescribed that the truly religious man must rise above distinctions of religion. In its philosophical form this prescription appears in the doctrine of the unity of existence—*Wahdat ul-Wujudi*—and there is a fairly clear trace of a continuous conflict between the believers in this unity and those who uphold the orthodox, transcendentalist point of view. Rejection of religion because of aesthetic inclination in completely absent. But it seems to have been regarded as essential for the poet's intellectual dignity to repudiate orthodoxy, its insistence on the external and its indifference to aesthetic values. In this way Urdu poetry, which represents the grafting of Persian tradition on are indigenous base, brought together all those whom historical circumstances, social laws, ritualistic restraints and traditional beliefs kept apart, stimulating them to realize unity at a high intellectual and aesthetic level. And Ghalib may well claim to be the culminating point of an intellectual, aesthetic and ideologically integrative development which is of great significance in the cultural history of India.

The metaphysics of Urdu poetry, and of Ghalib in particular, can be approached in terms of three questions: What is the nature of the Universe and man's place in it? What is God? What is love? For the Urdu poet, as for the passion, these questions are interdependent. There is no question of addressing man's place in the Universe without first contemplating the nature of existence or of love. Similarly, there can be no poetry of love unless love is understood, first, as a human reflection of a divine possibility and, second, as a definition of man's place in his moral universe. Ghalib does not offer a celebration of love, or longing, or ecstasy, as mystic poets do. Except in some places, his is not normally a poetry of mystic disciplines; rather, it is a poetry of contemplation, making subtle, and if possible, precise distinctions between one experience and another, and various shades of each. Thus love is defined not once or twice but over and over again, so that a whole collection of couplets may signify the complexity involved.

He also changed the paradigm of the *ghazal* whose beloved protagonist in the eighteenth and also nineteenth-century traditions had become 'an indifferent, cruel and hostile beloved' due to the turbulent political situation in the subcontinent. The protagonist of Ghalib's *ghazal* succeeds in releasing himself from the compulsions of immediate temporal reality and is able to make an upward progress in the framework of Ibn-Arabi's Sufism.

Diwan of Ghalib (1797–1869, first published 1842)

I.   1. Against whose coquettish art
         Is the picture a complainant
         Each image, robed in paper,
         Lays charge to its creator.

         Of whose cruel style of brush does the images complain?
         Every image, every picture is paper-dressed.

      2. Howsoever awareness spreads out
         Its net of hearing,
         Like the soaring Phoenix,
         The meaning of our speech escapes.

II.   The fragrance of the rose, the heart's lament,
      The smoke of the assembly's lamp;
      Whoever came out from thy assembly (company)
      Departed in confusion

III. Let there be an end to hopelessness
      After the catastrophe, let me be myself,

Lest the association of ideas of the beloved (now dead)
Are also lost.
(Where is soaring desire to set its other foot, O God?
The imprint of one foot has covered this desert of a world.)

IV.   Where do I step into my desired world
I find the existing Universe no more than an imprint of my foot.

V.   As the body has been burnt,
The heart too must have been burnt
Why engage in gathering the ashes
In a futile exercise?

VI.   Whenever we expected someone to appreciate our failures and
sufferings
He was found to be a worse sufferer thou what we could imagine.

VII. The battery and assault from quarters other than you was torturous
too,
How could your kind favours make any difference to me?

VIII. Its not a temple, nor the Ka'aba, neither the beloved's abode nor
any shrine,
I sit on a bylane, why should anyone ask me to leave.

IX.   Yes, he is not a believer, what if he is not a person of faith
If you so care about your faith and passion,
Why should you go there (to him).

X.   God is one, that is our faith,
All rituals we abjure;
This only when religions vanish
That belief is pure

XI.   Eager imagining of joys to be is burden of my song
I am a nightingale, my garden yet unborn.

XII. I long to live in utter loneliness.
With none to speak to, none to share my thoughts,
In a dwelling without walls and roofs,
Or neighbours guarding against fate and thieves,
With none to tend me if I'm sick and prostrate,
And none to mourn me if I pass away.

XIII. The God I worship is beyond the boundaries of sense:

The Ka'aba is for those endowed with vision
Only a sign-post telling pilgrims where to go.

Note

---

*This chapter was presented as a paper in a seminar on 'Books in my Life', organized by the Literary Criterion Centre, Mysore during 12–15 July 2003.

CHAPTER 8

Ali Sardar Jafri:
The Last Romantic

Ali Sardar Jafri, the legendary poet who revolutionized Indian poetry and changed the style of existing *adab* will always be remembered for his contribution to Urdu. He passed away in the year 2000 in Mumbai at the ripe age of 86, and had remained on the literary scene of Urdu in the subcontinent for about 65 years. As a poet he found a place with, the socially engaged and politically committed poets of the 1930s, namely, Faiz, Makhdoom, Majaz and Jazbi who formed a circle of their own and shared an ideology. He was greatly influenced by Anees and Iqbal and to a lesser degree by Josh, an influence he later appears to have eschewed. His prose work *Taraqqi Pasand Adab* proved to be seminal, as it generated serious debate on the value of literature and literariness of a work. Sardar Jafri edited selections from Kabir, Mir and Ghalib, appended with critical introductions. Later, the introductions to the three collections were published in one volume as *Paighambaran-i Sukhan*. The general introduction to *Paighambaran-i Sukhan* sets a new paradigm to evaluate and understand Kabir, Mir and Ghalib as the three humanist poets who celebrate man and humanity profoundly and variously. Jafri published as many as eight collections of poems in a span of thirty years, that is, from 1948 to 1978. The collections of poems he published include *Nai Duniya Ko Salaam, Khoon Ki Lakeer, Amn Ka Sitara, Asia Jaag Utha, Patthar Ki*

Deewar, Ek Khwab Aur, Pairahan-i Sharar, and *Lahu Pukarta Hai.* Jafri also penned his autobiography and the last anthology entitled *Sarhad,* which Prime Minister Atal Behari Vajpayee had taken with him on his bus journey to Lahore. Jafri combines in him the lyrical strain of the romantic movement in Urdu, the classical tradition of Persian/Urdu poetry, the passion of a revolutionary and the commitment of an ideologue. He impresses and often overwhelms us. We are not always won over by his argument and we often find his line of reasoning weak. There is poetry of statement and often highly romanticized notions about commonplace themes. But it is difficult to ignore him, to resist him.

One of the prime concerns of Jafri is colonial subjugation and the dangers of state terror. He wrote several poems on the theme of protest, some of which are expressed in powerful imagery:

Zehr aalud woh beete hue lamhat ke dank
Khoon mein doobi hui woh subah ki talwar ki dhaar
Shaam ki aankh mein barood ke kajal ki lakeer
Aur hafton ke sipahi wo mahinon ke sawar
Jo mere josh-i-baghawat ko kuchalne ke liye
Fauj dar fauj kiya karte hain yalghaar apni
Rifal karti hai faulad ke hoton se kalam

The poisonous stings of the moments past
The bloodstained edge of the morning's sword
The gunpowder kohl line in the eye of the evening
The soldiers on march for weeks and riders of months
Who to crush my passion of rebellion
Army after army continues to attack
Rifle communicating with the lips of steel.

Disarmament and the dangers of nuclear war also engaged the attention of Sardar Jafri throughout his poetic career. It is indeed paradoxical to see the concerns of progressive writers during the Cold War period, now being fully adopted by the Western powers. Sahir Ludhianvi's *Parchhaiyan* and Jafri's *Khwaab-i Pareeshan* may be cited, among others, as poems of specific themes on the subject.

Sardar Jafri is also distinguished in finding kindred souls outside Urdu and the Indian subcontinent. Some of his poems are titled *Irani Tulaba Ke Naam* (*To Irani Students*), *Afreeki Ladki* (*The African Maid*), *Habshi Mera Bhai* (*The Abyssinian—My Brother*), *Louis Aragon, Pablo Neruda, Julio Curie, Paul Robb's, Elia Ehrenberg, Ai Banke Afghan* (cf. *Ai Ghafil Afghan, Iqbal*) and a poem addressed to the Turkish poet Nazim Hikmet. In this respect Jafri's contribution maybe be seen on an international plane cutting across barriers of language, race and the nation.

Another important aspect of Jafri's personality is reflected in his concern for Urdu, a language without a home and state in India, consequent upon India's Partition. This was a cause that he championed throughout his poetic career with I.K. Gujral, Anand Narayan Mullah and others. Jafri contributed significantly in the preparation of the Gujral Committee Report. He also spoke against the menace of communal violence in India and gave poetic utterance to the agony and suffering of hundreds and thousands of victims. In one of his popular couplets:

Ai watan khake watan woh bhi tujhe de denge
Bach raha hai jo lahoo abke fasaddat ke baad

O my country, my beloved land
   we shall be most willing to sacrifice
Whatever blood is left in us
   after the bloodbath of riots.

Jafri began his poetic career as a poet of *nazm* and experimented with blank verse, some of which are quite innovative and refreshing. *Patthar Ki Deewar, Awadh Ki Khak-i-Haseen, Subhe Farda* and *Mera Safar* have earned recognition as popular anthology pieces. *Awadh Ki Khak-i-Haseen* is remarkable not only for its metre but also imagery:

Kumhar ka chak chal raha hai
Surahiyan raqs kar rahi hain
Safed aata siyah chakki se raag bankar nikal raha hai
Sunahare choolhon mein aag ke phool khil rahe hain
Pateeliyan gunguna rahi hain. . . .

The potter's wheel is moving
Goblets are dancing
White flour pouring a tune out of the black mill
Flowers of fire emerging from the golden hearths
Pots are humming.

Ghareeb Sita ke ghar pe kab tak rahegi Ravan ki hukmrani
Draupadi ka libas uske badan se kab tak chhina karega
Shakuntala kab tak andhi taqdeer ke bhanwar mein phansi rahegi
Yeh Lakhnau ki shiguftagi maqbaron mein kab tak dabi rahegi

How long will Ravan rule over the home of poor Sita
How long will Draupadi be deprived of her garment
How long will Shakuntala be enmeshed in the abyss of fate
How long will the freshness of Lucknow remain buried under the
imposing tombs?

Jafri's involvement with the classical *ghazal* tradition is manifest in
his *ghazals* also, some of which have earned the distinction of being oft-
cited quotations like those of Ghalib, Iqbal and Faiz:

Kaam ab koi na aayega bas ek dil ke siva
Raaste bund hain sub koocha-i-qatil ke siva
Baaise rashk hai tanha raviye rahrave shauq
Humsafar koi nahin dooriye manzil ke siva
Hum ne duniya ki har ek shae se utnaya dil ko
Lekin ek shokh ke hungama-e-mehfil ke siva
Tegh munsif ho jahan, daar-o-rasan hon shahid
Begunah kaun hai us sheher mein qatil ke siva

None is going to be of help except the comforting heart
All roads being closed except the assassin's lane
The passionate traveller's lonely journey is indeed enviable
With no fellow traveller except the ever farthening destination
Having renounced all worldly desires, the heart
Found itself caught in the charmed circle of that beauty.
Where the sword is the judge and the gallows witness
None is guiltless in that city except the assassin.

Kahin bijli gire woh apna gulshan ho ke auron ka
Mujhe apni hi shaakh-i-aashiyan maaloom hoti hai

Wherever there is lightning, in our garden or of others
I see it crashing upon my own nest's branch.

Pheink phir jazba-i-betaab ki aalam pe kamand
Let's again cast the intense passions' spell on the world.

Another aspect of Sardar Jafri's personality that deserves mention is
his intellect and stature as a charismatic personality. He had a presence,
which commanded respect and admiration. He was perhaps one of the
most learned men of our times. His intellect was not dry as dust but
refreshingly rewarding. Jafri enriched himself from the Oriental and the
Western literary traditions as well as systems of thought. He had in him

the liberal/secular thought of Persian poetry and the Vedantic strains of Indian philosophy. He was also influenced by Walt Whitman. Echoes of Whitman can easily be identified and seen in *Awadh Ki Khak-i-Haseen*. Unlike many of his comrades in arms, Jafri had an open mind and great catholicity. When in the late sixties, a literary movement in Urdu, called Jadeediat questioned several platitudes of progressive writers, Sardar Jafri was the first to call the new literary movement an extension of the progressive writers movement. Sardar Jafri will be remembered, besides being a major poet, critic and ideologue, as one of the most integrated personalities of our times. His learning, scholarship, journalistic career, stint in the film industry, compilation and editorial achievements, espousal of popular causes and a robust optimism inspired several generations.

Jafri was the last of the romantics on the Urdu literary scene. After Majaz, Makhdoom and Faiz, Jafri could have spoken in the words of W.B. Yeats:

> We were the last romantics-chose for theme
> Traditional sanctity and loveliness;
> Whatever's written in what poet's name?
> The book of the people; whatever most can bless
> The mind of man or elevate a rhyme:
> But all is changed, that high horse nearness
> Though mounted in that saddle Home rode.
> Where the swan drifts upon a darkening flood.
>
> —'Coole Park and Ballylee', 1931

Nightmare

1.   **CAVE OF FEAR**
She was my enemy's daughter,
the lanes leading to her house were filled with explosives
And not laid out with velvet,
Trees of fire with fireballs on its branches,
War-planes from my enemy's country and from that of my own
In hot chase,
Brought the doom down the sky.

She knew me to be her
    enemy's son
I knew her to be my enemy's daughter
One could see in her eyes
Child-like innocence, fear and helplessness

I too, perhaps, shared the same anxiety and horror;
Speeches of leaders,
Maddening orations of politicians,
Crazy statements of traders of arms,
Sound and thunder of rockets and war planes
Nothing was left
Except the sound of a heart-beat,
A touch of arms and body
And both of us panting—making a canopy
of our rhythmic discordant breath,
In the cave of fear
felt safe from the imminent doom.
She was beauty incarnate,
I was thrilled with the joy of loving,
Flowers blossomed quietly, and young buds smiling in joy.
Breezes from my enemy's land and those of my own
Embracing each other gladly,
as they required neither any visa nor any travel document.

2. DEVIL'S DANCE
    And then came the atomic explosion
    The heart of every particle bled
    (Sun's very own blood),
    Light turned into fire and broke the chains of all the genii and
    devils;
    And there rained brimstone and fire,
    and continued to rain
    all through the Space.
    Millions of hells
    created from out of the Sun.
    It was the devil's dance everywhere,
    But there was none to watch the devil's dance,
    Nothing but the devil's voice,
    A ghoulish laughter, with none to hear,
    Expect the God, the God,
    The one without a partner.

3. AFTER THE DEVIL'S DANCE
    The skyscrapers blown away,
    And the mountains like fiery carded wool,

Sucking the sky with their mighty blaze,
Fiery winds blowing in solar space danced arrogantly,
The planet Earth, now desolate and barren,
neither hears the lisping of a child
nor sees one held by a mother in her arms.
One neither sees moths,
nor the butterfly,
nor the nightingale nor a koel.

The planet Earth is a ball of fire,
with trees of fire,
and fiery winds,
and oceans of liquid fire,
There is neither left any bourgeois,
Nor proletariat,
Nor will there come any Revolution,
Pleasant and wild dreams
Nor their interpretations,
Neither evening nor glasses of wine,
Nor anyone putting his fingers
On the heart-strings of the beloved.

Everything has been turned into fire,
fires of hell,
The traders of arms reduced to ashes,
Those who loved arms and ammunition reduced to ashes,
And even those who hated war have been reduced to ashes;
Those who killed and also those who were killed—
All reduced to ashes.

Thousands of years after when a new world is born
None can say what kind of life will it be whether that would
    accommodate 'Man' or not. Hark!
There is a voice coming from the skies—
The Solar constellation is forlorn, (because) one of its stars,
The Sapphire-planet, the pride of the Universe, has been lost,
    dropped as a tear.

A deep wound in the heart of Space:
This region of excessive cold

(which is) billions of years old
where billions of light years seem to be insignificant
providing stage to the dancer of the skies.
The abode of the Earth's blue fairy
with huge constellations around;
More sacred than all other planets,
Earth, the land of prophets,
the preserver of heavenly verses,
defeated by the diabolic profiteering instinct
(of some),
Is hid in Space.

4.   NIGHTMARE
     This was nothing but a nightmare
     Man withheld the arm of tyranny and removed darkness,
     with radiance and joy emanating from
     the earth still, hearts lit with flowers of yearning,
     There dawns the Sun from the cave of fear and pain,
     There shines the Moon of the world of
     Love and beauty,
     There blossom in the garden roses, and lovers kissing.

5.   SONG OF PEACE
     This is the world of love
     That we have built,
     That we have adorned
     In the darkness of hatred;
     A lamp has been lit,
     A flame has been kindled,
     In this world of love.

     These flower-like faces
     Seated in our hearts
     Are raised from earth;
     with whiteness of sunshine
     their faces are washed
     and made beautiful as moons
     In this world of love.

                    —Translated from Urdu by Naqi Husain Jafri

Part II

CHAPTER 9

The Need for a Post-Colonialist Literary Theory

You'll never plumb the Oriental mind,
And if you did it isn't worth the toil,
Think of a sleek French priest in Canada;
Divide by twenty half breeds; multiply
By twice the sphinx's silence. There's your East.
>   —Kipling, 'One Viceroy Resigns'

The question whether there existed a colonial literary theory and as a reaction to which we could develop a post-colonial theory is indeed debatable. The answer is probably yes and probably no. In India, the colonial experience went a long way in shaping our tastes and literary tradition. The British were keenly interested in Indian literature, particularly the Urdu literature in the eighteenth and the first half of the nineteenth century. Their interest in India's literary heritage appeared in various forms—adaptations, translations, compilations and creative writings particularly in the *ghazal* form. The most important aspect of the colonial impact may be seen in the critical surveys of Indian literature and literary traditions which we may term here, for want of a better expression, the colonial literary theory.

The Indian colonial experience was neither unique nor different. India remained a great civilization and a 'phenomenon' in the imagination of the colonial masters. Even before the 'discovery' of India by Vasco da Gama by sea route in 1498, Indian civilization had influenced the European awakening, not directly but through the Arabs. Egypt had been conquered first by the French and later by the British. Iran was politically subdued by the British though never formally colonized. The three great civilizations, i.e. Egypt, Iran and India offered to their colonial masters challenges of different nature and variety than what they found elsewhere. These countries were conquered militarily, their people suppressed and humbled but these nations with their rich cultural heritage remained an enigma to their colonial masters and perhaps continue to be. It is, therefore, imperative to examine the discourse which appears to have engaged the issues of culture and politics. And this may be seen in my view as colonial literary theory. Once we understand this phenomenon, it becomes easier for us to explore the postulates of post-colonial theory.

Until the close of the eighteenth century, i.e. before the establishment of the European Empire, there was no problem in looking at each other's cultural heritage with interest and curiosity. We see two different and divergent attitudes: between ignorance and enlightenment, between the Islamic Orient and the non-Islamic Orient. The Islamic Orient, since the days of the Crusades, evokes images of awe and terror and this notwithstanding occasional admiration for some of their civilizational achievements. While, on the other hand, the other Orient, i.e. China, Far East and ancient India continue to fascinate European scholars for a variety of reasons, which is why we find adulation and admiration for the other Orient whereas the Islamic Orient continues to be treated with more or less the same Medieval perception. The beginning of the nineteenth century with the French occupation of Egypt and vital success of the East India Company in Bengal brought about changes of perception and attitude. The writers of the early Romantic Age are seen cultivating keen interest in the Orient, shedding their traditional prejudices and received perceptions and in this regard Byron's essays in prose and verse about the Turks and Turkey betray a freshness of approach that cannot be denied. While on the other hand, the respect and appreciation with which the oriental civilizations had hitherto been treated appears to be substantially reduced. In this regard I would like to reiterate the argument of Martin Bernal's *The Black Athena* which posits strong and convincing evidence in support of his theory that in fabricating the myth of Greece, the white

European nation, the contribution of the Egyptian civilization had been deliberately marginalized. This is at the conceptual plane that the intellectual leadership of the world was appropriated by Europe even in such areas where it was not due. Works of Pythagorus and Ptolemy who belonged to Egypt were appropriated as Greek achievements. Martin Bernal's thesis that the fabrication of Greece was a Eurocentric view aimed at glorifying the contribution of colonial masters and minimizing the civilizational strides made by the Egyptians, Phoenicians and Indians cannot be easily rejected. Likewise, the attempt on the part of the British and other European scholars to interpret Oriental texts on the parameters of their poetics also deserves consideration. Leigh Hunt in his essay, 'Persian Poetry' (*Poetry and Imagination*) says, 'Oriental life and society, especially in the Southern nations, stand in violent contrast with the multitudinous detail, the secular stability, and the vast average of comfort of Western logic, and the connection between the stanzas of their longer odes is much like that between the refrain of our old English ballads. . . . .' We clearly see in this observation that the Western nations took upon themselves the authority not only to interpret their culture to the world, but also our own culture to us. According to Edward Said, 'The Orient was not Europe's interlocutor but its silent other.' German orientalism was free of colonial hang-ups which is why it is fair and objective as opposed to the British and the French. Both in Max Muller and Goethe we see a refreshingly genuine and sincere devotion to Oriental studies. It is not to minimize the contribution of Germans to orientalism by suggesting that it was mainly because of their not being colonial masters. However, it could be taken as an important fact. In this connection it may be useful to quote from Tej Bahadur Sapru's *Foreword to Ram Babu Saxena's European and Indo-European Poets of Urdu and Persian* (1943):

> Europeans and the Anglo–Indians of the late eighteenth century and the first half of the nineteenth century had a more direct and more intimate knowledge of our language and literature than their successors of later generations . . . social and political condition have since changed very much and, at present moment there are two worlds in India—the Indian world and the Anglo–Indian world . . . the number of Indians, who in spite of political differences, can enjoy English poetry, English prose, must be indefinitely larger than the number of Europeans who can 'enjoy' our cultural product.

In the same book, Ram Babu Saxena has anthologized the verses written by European poets of Urdu, namely, Colonel John Bailey, John Shore, General Smith, Doctor Hui and David Hurst and among the Anglo–Indian writers, the essays of John Thomas, Alexander Heatherly, who was Ghalib's follower in Urdu verse and adopted the pen-name of Azad and General Joseph Benseley, deserve mention. These writers of British origin experimented with the forms of *ghazal, qasida* and *marsia* without any reservations or aversion to the traditional genres of Urdu poetry. On the other hand, people like Duncan Forbes indulge in universalizing and imposing the popular stereotyped notions on the Urdu poetics by finding it too elegant to be useful or obscene. He says about *Bagh-O Bahar* that 'the book contains a few passages of objectionable nature such as we meet within all oriental compositions'. It may be inferred from these instances that by the close of the nineteenth century, the attitude of the colonial masters changed from admiration to disdain and a kind of superciliousness towards the Other. They took upon themselves the privilege of the high priest who would decide the grammar of poetics and also dictate to us what to read and what not to read.

I take this opportunity to highlight an aspect of the *ghazal* tradition that has generally been ignored by the Western critics. Besides being a form of verse wherein the celebration of human love reached its pinnacle in a large number of Persian and Urdu poets, it is also a form of poetry which celebrates secular life in a way which is indeed unprecedented in literary canon. The *ghazal* tradition scoffs at whatever is status-quoist, superficial, vain and hierarchical. The very form of *ghazal* is such that it cannot accommodate any thought or expression which supports the authority, political, or religious. It is anti-convention, anti-establishment, unyielding and wary of whatever is pretentious or ritualistic. The beauty and love of the beloved in infinite variety is its soul and sustenance, nothing else is. Such an important form of poetry continued to be treated disdainfully by quite a few European scholars because it did not conform to the poetics of English poetry, and was generally compared to the ode form without any rhyme or reason. Love and religion shared, 'besides a common emblem in wine', in the words of Kiernan, 'another refinement of gross fact into ideal essence'.

The following passages/verses from the English translations of Hafiz, Mir, Ghalib and Faiz clearly bring out the essential concerns of the *ghazal* tradition. The celebration of human love and the rejection of temporal and religious censure is the common denominator in *ghazal* from the twelfth century to the present day. The form has undergone changes of various hues and shades, but its principal concerns remained unchanged as the basic instincts of human life. This may partly explain the variety and vigour of the tradition that has stood the test of time in the last eight centuries.

Hafiz

Where is the pious doer? and I
the estray'd one, where?
Behold how far the distance, from
his safe home to here!

My heart fled from the cloister,
and chant of monkish hymn,
What can avail me sainthood,
fasting and punctual prayer?
What is the truth shall light me
to heaven's strait thoroughfare?
Whither 'O heart, thou hastest?
Arrest thee and beware!
See what an adventure is thine
unending quest!
Fraught with what deadly danger!
Set with what unseen snare!

Say not, O friend, to Hafiz,
Quiet thee now and rest!
Calm and content, what are they
Patience and peace, O where?

I know this perilous love-lane
No whither the traveller leads,
Yet my fancy the sweet scant of
Thy tangled tresses feeds.
In the midnight of thy locks,
I renounce the day;
In the ring of thy rose-lips,
My heart forgets to pray.
Plunge in you angry waves;
Renouncing doubt and care;
The flowing of the seven broad seas
Shall never wet thy hair

—Translated by Elizabeth Bridges

Mir

Shaikh says his prayer?
Don't be deceived by that
Prayer is a load he lowers from his head.

I grant you, Sir, the preacher is an angel
To be a man, now that's more difficult.

It is God's mercy that we sinners speak of;
Fasting and prayer are never mentioned here.

To enter love's dominion is to throw your life away
For love makes no allowances, and beauty does not spare.
Now and then she passes smiling and for me the roses bloom
All the advent of the spring is in the grace of her approach.

—Translated by Ralph Russel

Ghalib

Once I gave up the tavern it matters not
If its monastery, academy or mosque.

When there was naught, existed God,
If all turned void; He'd still be there
Doomed am I, for I am,
Whatever could be if I were not

I would recall the vast number of blighted hopes
Lord, You'd better not ask to account for my deeds,
From slumbering Fate.
I could purchase
A dream or two,
But how would I pay their price?

Admire me, too, O Lord!
For the desire of vices missed
If there be the punishment of my committed sins.

—Translated by Qurratulain Hyder

Faiz

At times, in remembrance faintly old scenes reviving
Things once so near and so far from heart vision, eye vision striving
At times, in desire's parched sands, Caravans come halting.

With tokens laden to seal all bargains of lovers driving.
For eye or heart what repose, what slaking of joy an anguish
—Translated by Keirnan

Likewise, the celebration of human love in some of the earliest love poems in Provençal continues to baffle literary historians and critics. What is generally described as 'courtly love' is a *construct* of the late nineteenth century to explain the Troubadour tradition which probably had a link with the Hispano–Arabic poetry of the eighth and ninth century. The Hispano–Arabic, through the forms of *zajal* and *muwashah*, established a powerful tradition of love poetry the likes of which was never seen in the European literary experience. The explication of this tradition as attempted by C.S. Lewis in *Allegory of Love* (1936) and others is, in my view, a colonialist interpretation of a tradition which is patently oriental. The echoes of this form can still be heard in the Persian/Urdu/Hindi verses. The analogy of a 'vassal' to the poet and 'lord' to the lady love is based upon an inadequate understanding of the poetics of the Hispano–Arabic tradition. That the lady love in the Arabic poets was often addressed as 'Sayyedi' and that the said canon was as much a celebration of love as of poetry itself has generally been missed by Western critics. But instead of locating the said tradition in its context, the scholars continue to treat the entire phenomenon disdainfully.

However, some research in the recent past has made strides in this direction. Mention may be made of A.R. Nykl's *Hispano–Arabic Poetry* (1946) and Elizabeth Salter's writings on Medieval poetry. It may not be out of place to mention that the change of perception about Medieval love poetry came in the wake of Ezra Pound's seminal work on *Provence* and *Provençal poetry*.

Whereas the general disdain of *ghazal* relegated Urdu literary tradition considerable, Ghalib was raised in stature by applying the parameters of Western poetics in this century. Grierson's edition of *Metaphysical Lyrics and Poems of the Seventeenth Century* and T.S. Eliot's essay, 'The Metaphysical Poets' inspired Urdu critics to discover new aspects in Ghalib's poetry. Abdul Rahman Bijnori's essay, though very generalized and sweeping, 'The Merits of the Poetry of Ghalib' may also be studied in the light of the Western critical idiom. Bijnori's analysis of the verses of Ghalib in their context is indeed freshening. He compares Ghalib's achievement, though not convincingly, with the masters of Latin, German, Italian, French and English poetry. It is indeed interesting to see, that while we needed a Grierson and Eliot to appreciate Donne, we also needed a generation of scholars trained in the Western critical idiom to analyse and interpret Ghalib in a manner that was not done earlier. Urdu is said to be a poetical medium 'almost made up of poets for their own use' unlike English whose foremost poets have also been good prose writers. And this explains why poets like Mir, Sauda and Mir Hasan did not get critics to interpret them in the manner they deserved. That Ghalib's poetry besides being reflective also betrays tough intellectual content was evident upon us only after reading Eliot. It clearly shows the lack of application and dearth of critical approach. It may also be pointed out here that unlike the English literary tradition, Urdu has not undergone a 'dissociation of sensibility'. The principal concerns of the Urdu poet, particularly the *ghazal* writer, from the earlier times to the present day continue to be the same, that is, celebrations of earthly existence and unravelling of the mysteries of life, and this notwithstanding changes in technique and form. By citing the earlier example, the point is sought to be reiterated that the application of Western poetics to the Indian/Urdu literary tradition resulted in lack of appreciation of our heritage though geniuses like Ghalib withstood the alien parameters as well.

A word about another literary form: the *masnavi*. Because there is no equivalent or near equivalent of this important form in English, it was also ignored. The *masnavi* is a romance richly versified. There are tales within tales and there is no end of the tale. The English romance's varied narrative technique betrays a different structure and pattern. It may also be seen as the mystery of the Orient that its poets told tales without end. The *masnavi* with the multiplicity of plots and innumerable tales continues to baffle the Western scholar. The form was also ignored by Marxist critics as 'degenerate' and as 'a legacy of feudal society'.

I now turn to more recent instances of attempts by Western critics to interpret Indian literature to us. Edward Thomson, who is justly considered one of the most sympathetic, even indulgent critics of the Indian/Bengali literary tradition in his book on Tagore says,

> I would—if I may without offence—urge him to let *Radhas* rest from her age—long journeys through the pelting nights of Sravan and beg him to leave Sakuntala to water her flowers immortally in Kalidas's pages, and nowhere else. Also, let him describe a storm without hearing a thundering chariot drive along the heavenly ways, and without hearing a mighty conch blown or the trumpeting of Indira's elephant. Let him rid his forests . . . of cowherds and lost travellers and . . . lotuses. This sounds like someone pontificating to lesser

creatures. No language can afford to be oblivious of its essential milieu. Bangla can't adopt the English literary tradition in the manner Edward Thomson would like it to have. Many more instances can be cited to show how in almost every aspect of life the British imposed their cultural superiority and looked down upon the Indian heritage. They set a new poetics to evaluate and assess the Indian literature.

It is indeed interesting to see the declining graph of British attitude in India since the close of the eighteenth century to the beginning of the present century—from that of adulation and sympathy to disdain and contempt, from the time many of their talented officers learnt to compose verses in Urdu to the time they sat in judgement on the merits of the *ghazal* form and the oriental life in general. They invented types and patterns which over a time period, were transformed into stereotypes. The West's view of the Indian life and letters continues to be same and similar in spite of all the exposure and interaction with Indians/Asians all over the world.

It is in this context that we need to build a theory or theories of literature which would be indigenous and rooted in tradition. But in the process, the Western theories should not be entirely rejected. Many a literary tradition have acquired acceptability and space in our literatures and, with justifiable merit, which may be traced to the Western canon, like the *nazm* form in Urdu and fiction/short story in almost all the Indian languages and, perhaps more important than these the style of prose and criticism that owes much to the English discipline. But the hang-ups of the colonial past need to be shed in order to rediscover our lost identity.

CHAPTER 10

Hamlet's Soliloquies: A Note on their Nature and Functional Structure in the Light of *Natyashastra*

I would like to analyse the nature and function of soliloquies in *Hamlet* in the light of some of the dramatic devices from Bharata's *Natyashastra*.

A German scholar, Gottsched, who was a contemporary of Dr Johnson, while commenting upon the dramatic device of the soliloquy observed, 'Clever people do not speak aloud when they are alone.'[1] The *Encyclopaedia Britannica* also says that the dramatic device of soliloquy 'has always been liable to ridicule'. The convention of the monologue with its lack of psychological probability and its artificiality has been seen as a stumbling block. While on the other hand, Shakespeare's treatment and use of soliloquies in several of his plays, particularly *Hamlet,* continues to fascinate his readers and critics.

Soliloquy as a dramatic convention owes its genesis and use to classical Western tradition. Every great dramatist has developed his own manner of composing and using a soliloquy. It is, therefore, not always a device for 'self-expression'. Much more than that; at times it is self-expression as well. A soliloquy therefore, is a means of (i) informing the audience, (ii) identifying characters and explaining their role, (iii) bridging the gap between them, (iv) a device of exposition and narration; also (v) a prologue, commentary and chorus, and (vi) self-revelation of a character. The criticism of soliloquy as 'far removed from being true to life' or lacking in psychological probability was perhaps influenced by the dictates of naturalism in literary criticism. As we turn away from naturalism in the theatre, 'Our apologetic attitude about the convention of the soliloquy' betrays the fact that we are still in the grip of naturalism. It is, therefore, all the more necessary to see whether a soliloquy is used merely as a dramatic convention, or whether it is exploited by the playwright for other ends and effects as well. In this connection, it is indeed interesting to compare and contrast the fine distinction Bharata makes between the realistic and the conventional. The realistic has been called *lokdharmi* while the conventional *natyadharmi*. By the realistic practice, the *Natyashastra* (XIV, 62–3) refers to the reproduction of the natural behaviour of man and woman as well as other cases of natural presentation. 'Aside' or 'soliloquy' has been cited as an example of the conventional practice on the stage. The *Natyashastra* (XIV, 64–5) describes in general the convention as follows: 'If a play contains acts modifying traditional stories, supernatural powers and disregards the practice about the languages, and requires acting with playful use of *angaharas*, and possesses characteristics of dance, and requires conventional enunciations and is dependent on divine personalities, it is to be known as conventional *natyadharmi*.' The definitions of realism and convention as provided in *Natyashastra* spell out and resolve the conflict between the psychologically probable and the conventional far more convincingly.[2] Here the reader/spectator knows the intricacies of the plot/character and is able to locate an action or thoughtful deliberation in its perspective without questioning the veracity of the scene or its probability. In this regard, it is interesting to quote from Abhinavagupta: 'Not everything that is in this world deserves to be described by the poet in his plays. And what is not possible in the world deserves to be described by the poet in his plays.'[3]

Likewise, Shakespeare avails himself of both realism and conventionalism, but he also transcends both, creating a new and characteristic mode of presentation by which the poetic drama of the Elizabethans became Shakespearean drama.

The soliloquies in *Hamlet* form such an important aspect of the play that it is almost inconceivable to think of this play without its penetrating monologic diversions. Most of the lines from *Hamlet*, that have remained, over the ages, quotable quotes, are passages from its soliloquies. This is not to undermine the soliloquies in other plays like *Macbeth, Othello, King Lear, King John* or *Twelfth Night* which are all very powerful and typical of Shakespeare. The soliloquies differ from each other widely in style, method and function. These have little in common and serve different ends and dramatic effects. The Shakespearean soliloquies may broadly be classified as: (i) soliloquy of reflection, (ii) soliloquy of resolution, (iii) passionate outburst, (iv) soliloquy of comment, and (v) of self-explanation. But this classification is also superficial. As in several other respects, Shakespeare again defies any pattern. According to Una Ellis Fermor (in *Frontier of Drama*, 1945), 'But at its finest as at the height of the Elizabethan period, the soliloquy, by its rapid and profound revelation of thought and passion, serves the very end of drama. It reveals what we could not otherwise divine of the depths of the speaker's mind compressing into some twenty lines of vivid illumination what might have taken the better part of an act to convey.' This applies in particular, to the soliloquies in *Hamlet* which offer such variety and scale, both as a dramatic device and a means to advance the action of the play. Soliloquies peep into the thought processes and abysses of Hamlet's mind in a way that leaves the reader baffled.

It may also be pertinent to quote Wolfgang Clemen in *Shakespeare's Dramatic Art* wherein he says: 'In *Hamlet's* soliloquies Shakespeare has created a new kind of dramatic speech which by its rapid transitions, its dissolution of syntax, its extraordinary economy and its fusion of several emotions and ideas can follow the quickly changing reaction of a sensitive mind better than speech in dialogue ever could' (p. 160).

The first soliloquy of the play—'O that this too flesh would melt' sets the tone of a cosmic scale, of the complexity of issues, human predicament and self-reproach. It is, in the strict sense of the term, not only self-expression but a musing over human fate and the hasty and vicious marriage of his mother. By negatively eluding to Hercules, Hamlet gives an indication of his sense of inadequacy in the very beginning of the story. The second soliloquy comes in the wake of the visitation of the spirit of his father. This monologue presents the speaker heavily burdened and emotionally charged. Uncertainty about the ghost's provenance quietened during its presence, returns when it is gone. Hamlet does not ignore that to which he now pledges himself may embrace both good and evil.

The oft-quoted passage in Act II, Scene ii—'What piece of work is a man' is not a soliloquy and is framed in dialogic conversation. It is addressed to Rosencrantz and Guildenstern. But the speech is very close to soliloquy of reflection. Rosencrantz's response to Hamlet's speech that 'there was no such stuff in their thoughts' also conforms to the monologic nature of the speech. The speech also shows that Hamlet has been able to slightly abridge his self-reproach, so pronounced and strong in earlier scenes. The passage betrays an eloquent contemplation on the new Renaissance thinking, the immense possibilities of a man-centred universe, his exalted position as well as his helplessness and non-existent existence. It is a fine example of the fusion of several emotions and ideas which flow from the quickly changing reactions of a sensitive mind. The last soliloquy in the same scene, that is Act II, Scene ii—'O what a rogue and peasant slave am I'—takes Hamlet back to self-reproach. He deliberates over the problem logically and eloquently. He muses over the feigned grief of the player in comparison to his own which is far more genuine and strong. Hamlet reproaches himself for his cowardice but not without contemplating the other strategies of ascertaining the guilt of his mother and the king:

> I have heard
> That guilty creatures sitting at play
> Have, by the very cunning of the scene,
> Been struck so to the soul that presently
> They have proclaimed their malefactions.
> For murder, though it have no tongue, will speak
> With most miraculous organ.

The last lines of the scene tell unequivocally that Hamlet has not taken the speech of the ghost as divine prophecy:

> The spirit that I have seen
> May be a devil

And finally,

> The play is the thing
> wherein I'll catch the conscience of the king.

The soliloquy—'To be or not to be' is a superb example of the way in which Shakespeare turns into monologic speech an intricate chain of thought which is, as it were, connected subterraneously so that parts of it reach the surface of the spoken text leaving it to us to supplement the missing links. It is a soliloquy entirely given to reflection. 'Here a man only thinks and through the thought is transformed into unforgettable images;

it does not anywhere link up with the inner or outward action. This sheer detached meditation, although most characteristic of Hamlet's mind, is indeed rare in Shakespeare.'

I will now focus on the function and classifications of soliloquy in Bharata's *Natyashastra*. The *Natyashastra* mentions four types of soliloquies: *akashvachana* (speaking to the sky); *atmagata* (speaking to one's self); *apavartik* (concealed speech); and *janantika* (personal address). *Akashvachana*, according to Bharata, is:

> Addressing someone staying at a distance or not appearing in person or indirectly addressing someone who is not close-by. This mode of speaking will present (the substance of) a dialogue by means of replies related to various (imaginary) questions which arise out of the play.

> —*Natyashastra*, XXVI, 83–5

Likewise, *atmagata* or speaking aside is explained thus:

> When overwhelmed with excessive joy, intoxication, madness, fit of passion, repugnance, fear, astonishment anger and sorrow, one speaks out words which are in one's mind (lit. hear) it is called speaking aside.

> —*Natyashastra*, XXVI, 85–7

Akashvachana has also been called *akashbhashit* in a Hindi commentary on dramaturgy.[4] Herein, as in the classical theory, the character poses questions and gives answers. My approach is to see how Shakespeare discovers the possibilities inherent in the soliloquy which have been better explored in the Indian classical theory. *Akashvachana* and *atmagata* provide a more exacting pattern to some of the soliloquies in *Hamlet* analysed earlier. The issues that preoccupy Hamlet's mind, though initially arising out of filial disorder and corruption and unnatural act of murder, encompass a world of existential questions. In this connection it is significant to quote from Dr Johnson's note on the passage:

> Of this celebrated soliloquy, which bursting from a man distracted with contrariety of desires, and overwhelmed with the magnitude of his own purposes, is connected rather in the speaker's mind, than on his tongue, I shall endeavour to discover the train and *to shew how one sentiment produces another*. (Emphasis added)

Johnson's pronouncement on the passage is almost similar to Bharata's definition of *akashvachana*, that is, 'a dialogue by means of replies related to various imaginary questions (lit. causes) which arise out of the play'.

Hamlet questions and deliberates over them and often comes out with incomplete or not so satisfactory answers:

> To be, or not to be: that is the question:
> Whether 'tis nobler in the mind to suffer
> The slings and arrows of outrageous fortune,
> Or to take arms against a sea of troubles,
> And by opposing end them? To die: to sleep;
> No more; and, by a sleep to say we end
> The heart-ache and the thousand natural shocks
> The flesh is heir to, 'tis a consummation
> Devoutly to be wish'd. To die, to sleep;
> To sleep; perchance to dream: ay, there's rub;
> For in that sleep of death what dreams may come
> When we have shuffled off this mortal coil.
> Must give us pause. There's the respect
> That makes calamity of so long life,
> For who would bear the whips and scorns of time,
> The oppressor's wrong, the proud man's contumely,
> The pangs of dispis'd love, the law's delay,
> The insolence of office, and the spurns
> That patient merit of the unworthy takes,
> When he himself might his quietus make
> With a bare bodkin? Who would fardels bear,
> To grunt and sweat under a weary life,
> But that the dread of something after death.
> The undiscover'd country from whose bourn
> No traveller returns, puzzles the will,
> And makes us rather bear those ills we have
> Than fly to others that we know not of?
> Thus conscience does make cowards of us all;
> And thus the native hue of resolution
> Is sicklied o'er with the pale cast of thought
> And enterprises of great pith and moment
> With this regard their current turn awry
> And lose the name of action.

Hamlet's soliloquy doesn't serve the purpose traditionally associated with the device; i.e. informing the audience or identifying characters or merely self-revelation. It may be better analysed as a mode of *akashvachana*, that is, 'a dialogue by means of replies related to various (imaginary) questions which arise of the play', while some of its passages may be interpreted in terms of *atmagata*.

The opening lines of the soliloquy set the tone of questions. 'To be or not be: that is the question: / Whether 'tis nobler in the mind to suffer/ The slings and arrows of outrageous fortune/or to take arms against a sea of troubles. And by opposing end them?' The lines that follow offer a reply which leads to meditation: 'To die: to sleep; No more and, by a sleep to say we end/The heart-ache and the thousand natural shocks/That flesh to is heir to, 'tis a consummation Devoutly to be wish'd.' It leads to further introspection and reflection: 'For in that sleep of death what dreams may come/When we have shuffled off this mortal coil,/ Must give us pause?' Then follows another spell of serious questioning into the vital issues confronting the protagonist: 'For who would bear the whips and scorns of time,/ The oppressor's wrong, the proud man's contumely,/ The pangs of dispis'd love, the law's delay,/ The insolence of office, and the spurns/ That patient merit of the unworthy takes,/ When he himself might his quietus make/ With a bare bodkin? Who would fardels bear,/ To grunt and sweat under a weary life.' As Hamlet meditates upon ending his life out of sheer disgust and desperation, he speaks to himself in the form of a reply which again leads to crisis: 'But that the dead of something, after death. The undiscover'd country from whose bourn/No traveller returns, puzzles the will,/ And makes us rather bear those ills we have/Than fly to others that we know not of?' The last six lines of the soliloquy, before the entry of Ophelia on the stage, may be read as an illustration of *atmagata*:

> Thus conscience does make cowards of us all
> And thus the native hue of resolution
> Is sicklied o'er with the pale cast of thought,
> And enterprises of great pith and moment
> With this regard their currents turn awry,
> And lose the name of action.

To whom does Hamlet address these questions? Who is his imagined partner on the stage with whom he attempts to communicate? Is it his other self or alter ego or heaven? The classical definition of *akashvachana* or *akashbhashit* appears to offer a better description of the dramatic device than the omnibus term *soliloquy*.

Ophelia's soliloquy—'O, what a noble mind is here o'ethrown' (Act III, Scene i) may also be seen as an example of *atmagata*. It is a comment on Hamlet's long soliloquy in the direction of the same emotional current which, according to L.C. Knights, 'brings to head our recognition of the dependence of thought on deeper levels of consciousness, and to make plain beyond all doubt that the set of Hamlet's consciousness is towards a region where no resolution is possible at all' (*An Approach to Hamlet*, 1960). Claudius' soliloquy 'O my offence is rank' (Act III, Scene iii) may likewise be read as an illustration of *janantika*, that is, private personal address.

Shakespeare, according to W. Clemen, has been 'most ingenious in finding imagined partners for his soliloquizing characters. For the monologue lacking a real partner on the stage, calls for such fictitious partnerships.' In the Greek and Roman tragedy 'the apostrophe could be addressed either to the speaker himself, or to his heart, his thoughts . . . to an absent person, or to heaven, hell and the elements, or to some personification'. It is in this context that an address to heaven and *akashvachana* come very close and may be seen exemplified in Hamlet's soliloquies.

Notes

All references to Hamlet are from *Shakespeare's Complete Works*, ed. W.J. Craig (1894). All references to *Natyashastra* are from Manmohan Ghosh's English translation (the revised edition), 1967 (Calcutta).

1. Cited by Clemen in *Shakespeare's Dramatic Art*, p. 148.
2. Bharat Gupta in *Dramatic Concepts: Greek and Indian* (1994), Delhi, discusses at length the connotations of *Lokdharmi* and *Natyadharmi* with similar concepts in *The Poetics*. He quotes extensively from Abhinavagupta to show the intricacy and complexity of the two terms enunciated by Bharata. I have used these terms in a limited sense by referring them to the use of soliloquy as a dramatic convention.
3. Cited by Ingalls et al., *The Dhvanyaloka of Anandavardhana with Lochana of Abhinavagupta*, 1990, Harvard.
4. Vishwanath Prasad Mishra, *Vangmaya Vimarsha*, 1948, Benaras.

CHAPTER II

The Moone-Calfe:
An Interpretation

Drayton published *The Moone-Calfe* in 1627 along with *Nimphidia*, the *Shepherd's Sirena* and the *Elegies Upon Sundry Occasions*. *The Moone-Calfe* is a satirical poem which exposes the evils of luxurious living, corruption of court circles and the general degeneration of urban life. The objects of satire that Drayton chooses are the common themes found in the works of major satirists of the age like Hall, Marston and Guilpin, but unlike them he does not express himself in monologues or epistles. He writes a fantastic narrative. The poem describes the birth of monster twins to the 'lady world' followed by the tales told by the four women attending upon the mother in her labours. Thematically their tales reiterate and even mythologize the monster birth. *The Moone-Calfe*, in its technique and presentation, looks like a moral allegory, rather than a satirical poem.

Both the selection of the title of the poem and the theme of the monstrous birth are significant. The Elizabethan mind had not yet freed itself from the Medieval legacy of magic, witchcraft and sorcery, and was still preoccupied with the concepts of devilbegotten monsters and their effects on human life. References to monster birth are found in the chronicles of physicians, chapbooks and works of poets and dramatists. In contemporary idiom, the 'moon-calfe' was 'an abortive shapeless fleshy mass in the womb, produced by the influence of the moon'.[1] A detailed reference to a monster birth is also found in Spenser's story of Oliphant and Arganate, the monstrous lustful twins begotten on the earth by Typhoeus the Titan.[2] In Shakespeare's *The Tempest* (1610), Stephano addresses Caliban thus:

> The whole butt, man;
> My cellar is in a rock by the sea side where my
> Wine is hid
> How now, moon-calfe: How does thine ague   —II, ii,137–9

There is a mention of a moon-calfe in Ben Jonson's *News from the New World* (1620) also.[3] Thus, when Drayton wrote his narrative under this caption, he made use of a popular belief to satirize the common moral evils of society.

On internal evidence, *The Moone-Calfe* does not appear to have been occasioned by any particular event 'in the poet's life or in the contemporary society. It is also an exposition of the vices, natural and unnatural, that in the poet's view characterized the age of James I, commonly described as the 'iron-age'. The court of King James and Queen Anne of Denmark was symbolized by 'ugly and tasteless luxury'.[4] The fact that Drayton never found favour with the new king, and that his panegyric *To the Magestic of King James* (1603) was frowned at, may have contributed to the general mood of frustration of the poet. Added to this was the feeling, which Drayton expresses in several of his poems, that he did not get the recognition due to the writer of *Poly-Olbion* and other major poems. This resulted in a lamentation over the entire age imaged in the poem as the 'moone-calfe'.

The poem begins on a note of alarm and panic as the lady world is in her birth pangs:

> Help neighbours helpe, for Gods sake come with speede,
> For of your helpe there never was such neede:
> Midwives make hast, and dress yee as yee runne;
> Either come quickly, or W'are all undone   —11.1–4

The signs before the birth of the monster are of 'generall doom':

> Thunder and Earthquakes ranging, and the Rocks
> Tumbling donne from their syetes like maighty blocks,   —11.41–2

As the people gathered around the lady find themselves helpless, an invocation to the evil forces is made because the lady is to be helped and relieved of her pitiable condition:

Call Hecate, and damn'd Furies hether
And try if they will undertake together
To helpe the sick world   —11.68–70

At least it is with the help of these evil forces that the lady world gives birth to the monster twins:

The birth is double, and grows side to side
That humane hand it never can divide   —11.175–6

The 'androgines' born to the lady world present the 'male' who is partly 'female' and likewise the 'woman' is partly man. The creature is described as:

a more strange thing,
Then ever Nile, yet into light could bring[5]   —11.187–8

The coming of the 'moone-calfe' has been described in the following lines, which perhaps characterize the 'iron-age' in which Drayton lived:

That he shall thrive, when virtuous men shall perish
The drunkard, Glutton, or who doth apply,
Himselfe to beastly sensuality;
Shall get him many friends, for that there be,
Many in every place just such as he   —11.262–6

The poet then describes the future youth of the male counterpart of the monster twin who will 'attire' himself in 'Forraigne parts' and hold in scorn what England has to offer. There is a notable piece of alliteration in the following lines:

Rags, running Horses, Dogs, Drabs, Drinke and Dice,
The onely things that he doth hold in price   —11.313–14

This monster, Drayton says, terms virtue as 'madness', hates all 'high things' and profanes all that is 'holy'. So concerned is the poet about the abnormal birth that he invokes the wrath of the gods to destroy the society which is being vitiated by the advent of the monster:

Where is the thunder god, art thou asleep?
Or to what suffering hand giv'st thou to keepe
Thy wrath and vengeance; where is now the strength
Of thy Almighty arme, failes it at length?
Turne all the Starres to comets, to outstarre

The Sunne and Moon tide, that he shall not dare
To look but like a Gloworme, for that he
Can without melting these damnations see   —331–8

In the lines cited there runs a rhetorical vein, reminding us of a tragic hero's utterances at a catastrophe. It may be inferred here that whatever themes Drayton chose to write upon, which are no doubt varied and numerous, he worked them out and treated them with vigour and artistry. Obliquely, this upheaval and disturbance of the natural order leads to chaos and reversal of the social mores. Accordingly, the poet is disagreeably reminded of the blind imitation of foreign fashions and unnatural masculinity among women in general. The rather feeble attempt at investing an apparently trivial theme with epic magnitude accentuates the sordid nature of social perversions. No doubt, these were the popular objects of ridicule as one may see in the works of Marston, Middleton, Jonson and Donne, but what seems to have been treated by his contemporaries in light sarcastic style, Drayton took up with utmost passion and seriousness.

Another theme to which the poet turns is the tepid quality of the vast output of cheap verse in his age:

That the hideous braying of each barbarous Asse
In Printed letters freely now must passé
In accents so untuneable and vile,
With other Nations as might damne our lle,
If so our tongue they truly understood,
And make them thinke our brains were merely mud.   —11.391–6

The male-calf, prosperous-looking and sleek as he is, easily attracts the obsequious attention of a Bafoon who entertains him with 'some ridiculous jest', and thus spends his time and wealth in 'lewd fashion'. The description and details of the male-calf roundly satirize the luxurious life of the time and particularly the wealthy nobles and lords who represented a kind of cheapness in tastes and styles of life. Its counterpart, the female-calf, represents the ladies who were crazy for new fashions and perfumes imported from France and displayed a kind of masculinity in deportment and demeanor. The growing French influence on English taste and manners in the wake of Charles I's marriage with the French princess was a cause of resentment to many an Englishman. Drayton seems to echo the strong nationalistic sentiment aroused by this cultural invasion from across the Channel:

> With fumes and powdrings raising such a smoke,
> That a whole Region able were to choke:
> Whose stench might fright a Dragon from his den,
> The Sunne yet ne're exhal'd from any Fen;
> Such pestilencious vapours as arise,
> From their French Powdring, and their Mercuries   —11.477–82

He also ridicules the wearing of white hair by women, painting their faces and other vanities.[6] This inelegant artificiality was compounded by their debased aping of masculine manners, again of foreign importation:

> After again, and you shall her see
> Shorne like a man, and for that she will be
> Like him in all, her congies she will make,
> With the mans curtsie, and her Hat off take,
> Of the French fashion, and weare by her side
> Her sharpe stillato in a Rybond tide.   —11.517–22

The description of the she-calf, beginning with her vanities, fashion preferences and masculinity, ends in her lewdness and whoring. One may discover here the present-day moralists' disfavour of the sartorial and heterosexual attire of the modern emancipated woman. As a whole, the description of the androgynous monster begotten by the Devil on the world, says Kathleen Tillotson, has an almost Swiftian brutality; it is unlike Drayton, and is important as an extreme statement of the misanthropy which lurks in the background of all his poems after 1603.[7] Though the sourness of the mood is evident, it is difficult to agree with Tillotson's charge of misanthropy as one finds here an aggresively nationalistic note rather than any unsparing denunciation of the species as whole. Perhaps, one could also add that Drayton betrays a touch of conservatism as well. Furthermore, *The Moone-Calfe* is the only poem where we find Drayton very bitter and angry in his tone and presentation, which can be attributed to the common reaction to the threat from France to British cultural patterns. Moreover, there are quite a number of poems and lyrics written after 1603 which refute Tillotson's criticism, to name a few, Drayton's late sonnets, *Odes, Muses-Elizium, Nimphidia* and *Poly-Olbion*.

Tillotson's inference that, 'the poem is really two works, the first ending abruptly at line 574'[8] (the birth and description of the monster twin) appears to be hasty and not wholly indisputable. Later, she adds, 'this second section is united to the first only by its continued preoccupation with the beastliness of man'.[9] But in reality the entire poem appears to be well-knit and organized.

Feeling a little freer of their immediate concern after the birth of the monster, four matrons waiting upon the mother in labour each tell a tale to while away the time. These tales follow the pattern of riddles, and the related comments by the successive narrators reinforce the theme of bestiality and lewdness which forms the core of the principal account of the birth. These four women are Mother Red-cap, Mother Bumby, Mother Howlet and Gammar Gurton.[10] The first tale describes the loss of common sense and self-consciousness, the second covetousness, the third cannibalism and the fourth describes nature through seasons. The second phase, that is, covetousness and ambitiousness, is the direct consequence of the first stage, loss of wisdom and self-consciousness. Similarly, the third stage, cannibalism, is the extreme result of the second stage, covetousness. The first narrator,[11] Mother Red-cap, tells the story of a people who were deprived of their reason and common sense and do not pay any heed to a prophecy about the visitation of a catastrophic and violent shower. It was believed:

> That upon whom one drop should chance to light
> They should of reason be deprived quite   —11.611–12

Not only did the warning fall on deaf ears, people ridiculed the prophecy and laughed it off. The result was that when the actual shower came, with the exception of one honest man who believed the prophecy and took shelter in a cave, the entire locality was turned into a bedlam. Understandably, the honest man has been compared to the great prophet, Noah, who had taken every precaution to save his people from the forewarned 'deluge'. But 'the honest man' in the tale could not convert anyone to his belief. After the 'violent shower', he emerged from the cave to see the condition of his people:

> To showe myselfe yet a true Patriot,
> Ile amongst them, and if so, that they
> Be not accurst of God, Yet I may,
> By wholesome counsell (if they can but heare)
> Make them as perfect as at first they were   —11.698–702

Indirectly, these verses reflect Drayton's own patriotism and moralistic concern with the spiritual edification of his countrymen.

But what the 'honest man' sees is all horror and lewdness. The human beings are debased and appear to be shorn of all decorum and decency. People run amuck; women with 'buttocks bare' ride horses in public, and men in 'broad-brim'd hat' courts' 'loathsome mezzled sowes'. This perversion turns the tables, and whereas they had scoffed at the wise man before the watery curse, now it is his chance to laugh:

> At which this man in melancholy deepe
> Burst into laughter, like before to weepe   —11.172–5

It is a moral anti-climax on the part of the erstwhile warner, since his melancholy, suggestive of his charity, now turns into a baser rather revengeful expression. Drayton's description of people is also tinged with a bantering of the new fashions then popular in England:

> Had arm'd his heeles with cork, his head with feather;
> And in more strange and sundry colours clad,
> Then in the Rainbow ever can be had   —11.728–30

Mother Red-cap, then recounts abhorrent sports in which people indulged and the sights which compelled the pious man to advise them out of 'concern for his native earth, and common-weale'. The 'honest man' sometimes also described as a 'wise and sober man', feels concerned not only for the present generation but:

> That twenty Generations shall be woo'd;
> And this brave land for wit, that hath been fam'd,
> The Ile of Ideots after shall be nam'd   —11.9790–2

The honest man's admonition like the prophecy of 'violent-shower', fell on deaf ears and he was called a 'coxcomb', a mere 'dizard', an 'ass' and a 'dolt', He thereafter retired from the scene only to become

> A true Hermit afterwards to live.   —1.821

It may be noted here that the life of 'a true hermit' was the motto of the poet all along his poetic career, that is, a cottage in a rural setting, free from all the ills of urban city life.[12]

The interpretation of Mother Red-cap's tale is given by Mother Bumby, who explains the 'shower' as the 'plague sent by supernatural powers upon the wicked'. The rock that provides shelter to the 'honest man', according to her, is the contemplation of sad times and the moral of the fable reads as follows:

> Who counsailes fooles, shall never better speed.

One wonders if here the poet had also a personal observation in mind. The realization that he, like the 'honest man' had been counselling heedless compatriots and that it had been a futile exercise appears to be dawning upon Drayton in the later years of his life. As already noticed, the function of poetry, for Drayton, was primarily moral instruction. He regretted the lack of seriousness of interest in poetry and deplored corruption in the socio-cultural life of his age.

The tale of Mother Bumby follows her comments on Red-cap's tale. She tells the story of a witch from 'Groneland'[13] who could float the island and sell windes.[14] She had the power to stay the 'Moone'; raise 'mists and fogs', keep back 'the day' and eclipse the 'light' through her spell. Among the 'bastard creatures' who inhabited the 'lie' besides 'Satyres' and 'demy-urchins' there was one 'ill-favoured Babian', he was almost an 'Ape', whom the witch had trained in 'all tricks and crafts'. He was skilled in curing through 'extraction', could tell people's fortunes and play tricks upon other animals.[15] In the same region there 'dwelt a wise and learn'd astronomer', skilful in 'planetary howres':

> He could command the spirits up from belowe,
> And bind them strongly, till they let him knowe
> All the drad secrets that belong'd them to,
> And what those did, with whom they had to do.   —11.937–40

This wizard,[16] continues Mother Bumby, noticed one day that the world was nearing a state of chaos:

> For things set right, ranne quickly out of frame,
> That States were pusled, almost beyond thought   —11.945–8

Considering it to be the working of devils, the well-meaning wizard wanted to exorcise them in order to save the world from their depredations. So he sets out to banish evil from the land with the help of Babian and another spirit. The principal evil-doers were a 'foule witch' and her factor who had spoiled many a state and wished to divide the entire world among themselves to rule and spoil in perpetuity, The Wizard succeeds in his mission when Babian with the help of his fellow spirit drowns the wretched witch in the sea.

The notorious witch, the cause of Chaos in the world, is interpreted by Mother Owle (Howlat) as 'ambitious men (who) have to be rich'. The Ape, accomplice of the witch, is interpreted as:

> Those damned Villaines, made the instrument
> To their disignes   —11.1030–1

The 'wondrous man of skill' (the wizard) is interpreted as a dispenser of 'Divine Justice'.

Through the tale of Mother Bumby, Drayton explains the popular beliefs in magic, black and white, to use them as vehicles of his satire on the contemporary society, suffering from ambitiousness and covetousness. The place of the 'honest man' in the tale of Mother Red-cap is taken here by 'the wizard' with perhaps the same role and mission. In this context Mother Bumby's tale, castigating ambition and greed follows Mother Red-cap's tale, signifying loss of wisdom and 'self-consciousness'. The latter appears to be the direct consequence of the former, that is, ambitiousness and covetousness are the natural results of loss of common-sense. Thus, a rational basis is given to the customary moral presuppositions—a concession to reason in the age of newly dawned renaissance.

The third narrative in the sequence is told by Mother Owle, 'somewhat ill of sight' as she is believed to 'have hurt her eyes with watching late'. She tells the story of an evil man disguised as a 'warre-wolfe', who was master of 'all kinds of witch-craft and black sorcery' and used to 'theft, rapine and shedding blood'. This monster devil-wolf would stand in a forest everday after sunset to prey on the passersby:

> No silly woman, by that way could pass,
> But, by this woolfe she surely ravisht was,
> And if he found her flash were soft and good
> What serv'd for Lust, must also serve for food   —11.1069–72

The wolf was a cause of panic to everyone and there was no way to get rid of him as he could easily change his shape on being chased. An 'ass', who in fact was a 'perfect man', transformed into the beast by an 'envious witch', came to the place where the devil-wolf usually preyed. The wolf attacked him. The ass's braying and roaring could not get him any help. But the wolf decided not to kill the ass so long as he continued getting other animals for prey and thus took him to his den and cruelly tethered it to prevent its escape. Fed up with the wolf's ravages, the people of that area resolved to kill it. After being chased for long, the beast plunged into a pond and was re-transformed into its original human shape. For the people the chase was over, as they thought the wolf had disappeared. But the ass had seen the trick of the devil-wolf and he continued chasing the wolf turned 'man'. During the chase, the ass got into a spring which transformed him too, into a man—his original form. Now it was easy for the ass-turned-man to overpower the 'cannibal', and with the help of other people to punish him for his savagery and evil doings.

The fourth attending woman, Gammar Gurton interprets the 'warre-wolfe' as a man, 'given to blood and cruelty' who survives only on 'spoils'. The silly 'ass' is interpreted as 'some just soul', disdained by the world but:

> He by God is strangely made the meane,
> To bring his damned practises to light   —11.1228–9

A significant feature present in the first three tales told is the dispensation of 'divine justice' through different agencies when the evil reaches its highest point. The 'honest man' of Mother Red-cap's tale is replaced by the 'learn'd wizard' in the second tale and in the third tale the silly 'ass' is originally a 'perfect man'. Furthermore, as circumstances aggravate, it appears more difficult to set them right. The world of 'Mother Owle' is far more horrible and savage than that of Red-cap or Mother Bumby. It implies that if covetousness and ambitiousness are not checked in time, they might lead to more gruesome evils; in the present instance, cannibalism.

The fourth tale has been told by old Gammar Gurton, 'a right pleasant dame'. She relates the story of a 'mighty waste' become barren as the result of a curse by some saintly man. The land was so barren that:

> Upon the earth, the spring was seldome seene
> T'was winter there, when each place else was green   —11.1239–40

There were neither 'mirthful birds' nor any 'boughs'. The 'croking' of the night-crow was the only sound heard. Nor were there any cattle except asses and mules who were 'used to gnaw':

> The very earth to fill the hungry mawe   —1.1258

Asses may denote simplicity, but, significantly, the mules symbolize sterility. Then Gammar Gurton tells the story of a mule described as 'Jade', who, one day came to a pasture known for its 'rich sweet grass' and 'fat soyle'. The pasture was properly fenced and circled by a 'mighty mound' where:

> nothing could get in, nor nothing out   —1.1290

But the mule somehow makes his way into the pasture and through his 'nayes and brayes' calls others to share his fortune. They eat so much of grass that:

> Their Pampered bellies swolne above their backs.   —1.1326

> Thus along while, this mery life they led
> Till (even) like Lard their thickned sides were fed   —11.1333–4

The owner of the pasture ultimately runs to the town and with 'cords and halters' and with the help of others, fastens them and drives them to the common pound.

Mother Red-cap solves the riddle told by Gammar Gurton. The theme of the story she says is 'want and beggarie'. The beasts in the mighty waste are interpreted as 'the poor-bred in scarcitie'. The Mule is 'some craftly fellow who has found a way to thrive by' and the green pasture, she says is 'wealth'. The last commentator, Red-cap, is the first narrator and thus the cycle of tales comes to an end at a point where it began. The fourth tale exposes evil in the form of affluence in a world of want and beggary. The caner of the pasture administers justice by driving the erring beasts to the common pound. But the fourth tale is somewhat different from the rest. It is good humoured and full of sarcasm and satirizes the evil of greed and plenty through beast-fable. Drayton describes Gammar Gurton as 'a right pleasant dame', the best of them and, therefore, as a concession to her pleasant nature assigned her a 'not unpleasant tale'. The four ancilliary tales leave an enlivening effect on the readers and are not devoid of moral overtones. There is divine justice, though dispensed through different modes. The role of the instrument of divine justice changes from tale to tale. The 'wiseman' in the first tale may be compared to Noah, the great prophet, the 'learned wizard' in the second tale, lives in an 'Ile', away from the people, a 'complete hermit', and third character enacting divine justice, is made to roam as an 'ass', a silly beast. The tales appear to be progressing from 'word' to 'thought' and thence to action. The 'wiseman' tries to save his people from the 'great shower' through the word of mouth, whereas the 'learned wizard' adapts a speculative course and like Prospero, becomes a hermit. The task of rescuing the people from the cannibalism of the 'wolf' is given to the 'ass who accomplishes it through action'.

It may, therefore, be inferred that the situation created by the monster-birth with all its evil effects would also be saved through some agent of divine dispensation as may be affirmed from the tales of the four women.

Notes

All quototions are from the *Works of Michael Drayton*, 5 vols., ed. W.J. Hebel, H. Newdigate and Kathleen Tillotson (hereafter *Works*).

1. *Oxford English Dictionary,* entry no. 1.
2. *The Fairie Queene*, III, 7, 47–50.

3. Pr: Moone Calves: What monster is that? To Her: Monster? None at all: a very familiar thing, Like our fool here on earth.
4. Kathleen Tillotson, *Works*, vol. V, p. 210.
5. There is an interesting resemblance to the following lines of John Donne:
'Towards me did runne
A thing more strange, then on Niles slime, the sonne
E'r'bred'.   —*Satyre*, IV, 17–9.
6. Cf. 'I have heard of your paintings too, Well
God has given you one face, and you make yourselves another'.
                                                   —*Hamlet*, III, i, 148–9.
7. Tillotson, op. cit.
8. Ibid., p. 209.
9. Ibid., p. 210.
10. The tales told by the four attending women remind one of *Mother Hubberd's Tale* by Spenser, though thematically *The Owle* is closer to Spenser's poem.
11. The idea and dramatic setting bear an interesting resemblance to Samuel Rowland's, *'Tis Merry when Gossips meete* (1609), and *A whole craw of kind Gossips* (1609). J.M.'s *New Metamorphosis*, vol. II, bk 5, where a midwife and her friends gossip and tell tales reminds us of the setting of *The Moone-Calfe*. See Tillotson, op. cit., p. 212.
12. See Lady Geraldine's 'Epistle to Surrey', *Muses Elizium* and other Pastorals.
13. 'Witches were traditionally associated with the north, and especially with Lapland. Some stories specify Iceland or Norway but none name Greenland'. Tillotson, op. cit.
14. See also *Macbeth*, Act I, Scene iii.
15. Drayton's Babian echoes Shakespeare's Caliban both in sound and description.
16. The wizard resembles Shakespeare's Prospero in description and detail. The fact that the wizard though skilled in 'black and gloomy arts', becomes an agent of eradicating evil forces, brings him closer to a Shakespearean character.

CHAPTER 12

The Muses Elizium: An Allegorical Interpretation

Drayton published *The Muses Elizium* in 1630 along with the three divine poems, *Noah's Flood, Moses: His Birth and Miracles* and *David and Goliath* in the last volume of his poems. *The Muses Elizium* was dedicated to the Earl of Dorset and the remaining poems, to the Countess of Bedford, whose patronage he enjoyed in the later years of his life.

The Muses Elizium, perhaps the most imaginative poem of Drayton, is one of his most important works. The poem consists of ten 'nimphals' and has been prefaced by a 'Description of Elizium'. With the writing of *The Elizium,* the poet's vision appears to have been completed and his dream fulfilled. According to Kathleen Tillotson, this poem is 'the ideal culmination of his career'.[1] He began his poetic life with a pastoral,[2] *The Shepherd's Garland* and contrary to the popular practice climaxed it in the same tradition by writing *The Muses Elizium,* 'the poet's paradise'.

The 'Elizium' is an imaginary landscape described graphically:

The winter here a summer is,
No waste is made here by time,
Nor doth the autumne ever miss
The blossoms of the Prime   —11.37–40

It is the world of Flora, of Apollo, and of 'Nimphes' and the 'thrice three virgins'. Here the 'summer shade' is perpetual and 'decay' and 'age' are unknown. The 'other world' or the 'earthly paradise' of Drayton, abounding in description, presents something more pictureseque and refined than the Homeric 'heavenly-plains' or Spenser's *Bower of Bliss*.[3]

The first 'nimphall' describes the beauties of the human body through two 'most perfect creatures' in the course of a dialogue. Dorida and Rodope praise each other lavishly, 'who in shape both so excell':

> That to be paralleled elsewhere,
> No judging eye could tell   —11.18–20

The subject of the second 'nimphall' is a contest between two shepherds for the love of a nymph called Lirope. Lalus, a well-bred swain, vies with Cleon who excels in physical prowess to win the favour of the nymph. Lalus offers to his beloved a lamb, then a pair of sparrows, afterwards full-leaved lilies and in the end 'twelve swannes', against which Cleon comes out with the gifts of a kid, a pair of doves, pearls and a chariot. Lirope listens to the swains in turns but finally refuses both, yet without altogether killing their hopes. The nimphal is in the nature of a debate and in keeping with the pastoral convention. Lalus's gifts are simple and charming whereas those of Cleon are beyond the competence of a swain, particularly the pearls and the chariot. It has been suggested that Drayton, by highlighting Cleon's crude upmanship over Lalus, might be 'quietly satirizing Marlowe's Passionate Shepherd'.[4] But Lirope's suspended judgement does not seem to lend much support to this observation.

The third nimphal is the longest piece of the poem. It presents a series of tableaux wherein the poet displays great dramatic skill and feeling. There is a dialogue between Doron and Dorilus, the two 'noble swayns' who describe the picturesque beauties of Elizium with great amount of indulgence. The following lines of the third nimphal remind the readers of similar lines in Spenser's *Prothalamion*:[5]

> NAIJS   Behold the rosy dawne,
> Rises in tinsild lawne,
> And similing seems to fawne,
> Upon the mountaines.   —11.153–6

In the changing scene, Naijs and Cloe debate the varying merits of 'Rime'. The debate is not without a gentle satire on Donne and his school of poets who disregarded strict adherence to metre and form:[6]

CLOE	Why Naijs, that am I,
	Who dares thy pride defie?
	And that we soon shall try
	Though thou be witty.
NAIJS	Cloe I scorne my Rime
	Should observe feet or time,
	Now I fall, than I clime,
	Where isn't I dare not. —11.133–40

Then the nymphs divert their attention to the scenic charms of the land and refer to some fresh aspects of Elizium. The third tableau moves round the beautiful Florimel[7] who is being persuaded to sing by Cloris and Mertilla,[8] Claia, another nymph, also entreats Florimel to heed to their request for a song. But Florimel is unmoved. Later, when she is threatened with a shower of stink, she relents. Florimel's song has an ironical vein as it criticizes the female vanities:

> When our weake Fancies Working still,
> Yet changing every minute   —11.315–16

> For Whilst our browes ambitious be
> And youth at hand awayts us,
> It is a pretty thing to see
> How finely beautie cheats us:
> And whilst with tyme we tryfing stand
> To practise antique graces
> Age with a pale and withered hand
> Drawes Furowes in our faces.   —11.346–54

The last scene of the nimphal portrays the chorus singing of the nymphs and their praises in honour of each of the nine Muses.

The fourth nimphal describes the disillusionment of Cloris who has been to the land of Felicia where she saw nothing but decay and contamination. Mertilla consoles her and asks her not to give up hope:

> O that the sweets of all the flowers that grow,
> The labouring ayre would gather into one,
> In Gardens, Fields, nor Meadowes leaving none,
> And all their sweetnesse upon thee would throw.   —11.104–7

The fifth nimphal describes Clarinax, a hermit, who has an assignment:

To cure a mad man, which of late
Is from Felicia sent me.   —11.251–2

Lelipa and Claia are seen picking flowers to make a laurel, which, according to the hermit, was meant for the conqueror and for the poet only in the good old days.

An interesting situation parallel to the judgement of Paris in Homer's *Odyssey*, has been dramatized in the sixth nimpal wherein Silvicus, a woodman, Halicus, a fisherman and Melanthus, a shepherd, present themselves in the court of the nymphs for the prize of the 'worthiest'. All the three contestants stake their claims in a spirit of debate. But none 'absolutely wonne':

That equal honour they should share.   —1.249

In the seventh nimphal, the poet describes the arrival of Venus along with her son Cupid to the land of Elizium. It is narrated by Codrus, a ferry man who sailed the goddess and her blind son to the shores of Elizium. The nymphs pursue her and later banish her from their land:

To all the Elizian Nimphish Nation,
Thus we make our Proclamation,
Against Venus and her Sonne.   —11.256–8

The description is not without a humorous vein. If Cupid, the proclamation says, is seen in the land after a certain date, his 'bow will be broken', and arrows given to boys 'to shoot at sparrowes' and their wings cut. The eighth nimphal is a 'prothalamion'. It celebrates the marriage of Tita, a nymph, with a Fay. Drayton's sense of the diminutive is in play with his exquisite descriptions of the marriage festivities, jewellery, nuptial song, music and flowers.

The penultimate piece of the poem describes the nymphs and muses who make an altar for Apollo and place offerings. The muses' song in praise of the deity is remarkable for its imaginative power:

In thy swift course from East to West,
They minutes misse to finde thee,
That bear'st the morning on thy breast,
And leav'st the night behind thee.   —11.25–8

The last nimphal has a swift dramatic movement. Naijs, Claia and Corbilus, the nymphs of Elizium are panicky and frightened to see a 'Satyre' enter their land. After the nymphs are calmed, Satyre, the ugly shaped creature, tells them of his escape from the land of Felicia, where he could not bear any more the spectacle of continued deforestation. He says that he has been constrained to wander the 'wide-world' about as Felicia is being gradually robbed of her rich attire:

> Men wanting timber wherewith they should build,
> And not a forest in Felicia found,
> Shall be enforc'd upon the open field,
> To dig them caves for houses in the ground:
> The land thus rob'd, of all her rich attire
> Naked and bare herselfe to heaven doth show
> Begging from thence that Jove would dart his fire
> Upon those wretches that disrob'd her so: —11.101–8

It is interesting indeed to note that the most imaginative poem of Drayton should come to a close with a note of concern for, and worry about, the state of continued deforestation of England. Deforestation was perhaps the natural result of the expanding and shifting population of the cities in Elizabethan and Jacobean England. The poet's strong patriotic feelings come forth in the last nimphal. The last lines of the poem, wherein Satyre is welcomed, express the poet's profound sorrow, even bordering on cynicism, over the state of affairs in Felicia:

> And to Elizium be thou welcome then
> Untill those base Felicians thou shalt heare,
> By that Vile nation captived again,
> That many a glorious age their captives were.   —11.145–8

With its scenic displays, dramatic and sometimes semi-dramatic movements, choruses and songs, *The Muses Elizium* is closer to the tradition of pastoral-drama.

Though a good part of *The Muses Elizium* is given to the 'old bachelor's ruminations about suffering in love, which do indeed teach us nothing, charming though they may be',[9] still the poem is not without allusions to some serious themes. When Drayton wrote this poem he was fully aware of the difference between the rustic and the urban way of life.[10] The beauty and freshness of *The Muses Elizium*, according to Hardin, 'derive mainly from the sharpness of the author's aversion to life in the court and city'.[11] It is obvious that Felicia, which is a foil to 'Elizium', alludes to England.[12] The sometimes gentle and sometimes sharp satirical lines in the poem focus attention on the same subjects which he covered in

The Moone-Calfe. 'Elizium', according to Kathleen Tillotson, 'is the Muses' Elizium, the Poets' paradise, with Apollo as its tutelary deity', and that it also signifies, 'a hint of Elizabeth's reign, that long-ago golden age for poets'.[13] An old satyre, seeking shelter in Elizium, describes Felicia thus:

> Fair Felicia which was but of late
> Earth's paradise, that never had her peer,
> Stands now in that most lamentable state
> That not a Sylvan will inhabit there   —11.65–8

The nature of complaint of the 'old satyre' reveals his own identity also; that he is the poet himself, who now takes leave of this world and seeks shelter in Elizium, in another sense, the other world. Symbolically also, the number ten may suggest the Ten Commandments, and the ten tribes mentioned in the Bible.[14] The *OED* also notes the swearing by ten ends of flesh and blood.[15] Therefore, the ten nimphal's of *Muses Elizium* may suggest the symbolic end of a long poetic career. It may also be mentioned in this connection that Drayton died a few months after the publication of *Muses Elizium*. In seventeenth-century numerology 'ten' was considered a 'perfect number' as it is the sum of the first four odd and even numbers.[16]

The poem may also be interpreted as a partial allegory of the various forms and moods of poetry. Dorida's and Rodope's description and praises of beauty in the first nimphal suggest the celebration of physical beauty. The contest between Lalus and Cleon for the maiden's favour in the second nimphal seems to signify a conflict between traditional pastoral poetry and the new trend of poetry, popularized by Donne and his followers. The third nimphal makes direct reference to 'form'. Cloris's censure of the new fashion that she witnessed in 'Felicia' may denote Drayton's disapproval of the fashionable new conceits and imagery recently introduced in England (nimphal IV). Clarinax, the hermit, says in the fifth nimphal that only conquerors and poets deserve laurels. This is followed by a debate between the woodman, the fisherman and the swaine. But the shepherd, though 'ten times preferred' by nymphs does not get the coveted prize, he shares it with the fellow-woodman and fisherman, which may suggest that the poet's pre-eminence and primacy in society in ancient times is now lost in a decadent age. The seventh nimphal describing the banishment of Venus and Cupid from Elizium by Florimel appears to hint at the spiritual dimensions of love and poetry. The eighth song is a prothalamion, presenting a feast to the eye and ear and nuptial celebration was readily associated with mystical union. The Muses are seen building an altar for Apollo in the ninth nimphal and a satyr seeks shelter in 'Elizium' as he found the conditions in 'Felicia' unbearable and had fled from there.

Rather significantly, the satyr explains his self-imposed exile from 'Felicia' and justifies it on three counts; first, because the Felicians have contempt for the past, second, because they have neglected their poetic heritage and third, because of their crimes against Nature. One wonders if these views reflect Drayton's own reactions to the decadence of the age and its antipathy to genuine poetry and nature.

Notes

All quotations are from the *Works of Michael Drayton*, ed. W.J. Hebel., H. Newdigate and Kathleen Tillotson, 5 vols., 1931–41 (hereafter *Works*).

1. Kathleen Tillotson, *Works*, vol. V, p. 219.
2. *The Harmony of Church* (1591), though written and published earlier, was not received favourably and lacked literary merit.
3. Tillotson, op. cit., p. 220.
4. Bret Cyril, *Minor Poems of Michael Drayton*, 1907, p. xii.
5. 'Along the shoare of silver streaming Themmes; Whose rutty Bancke, he which his River hemmes was paynted all with variable fiowers'. 11.11–13, *Works*, ed. R. Morris, Globe edn. 1869.
6. See also Campion's 'Obervations in the Art of English Poesy', *Works*, pp. 35–56, ed. Percival Vivian, 1909.
7. Cf. Spenser's *Faerie Queen*, bk 3, cantos V, VII & VIII and bk 4, cantos II, IV & V.
8. Ibid., It recalls Spenser's Mercilla (bk 5, canto IX) not in characterization but only in assonance of sound.
9. Richard F. Hardin, *Michael Drayton and the Passing of Elizabethan England*, University Press of Cansas, Lawrence/Manhattan/Wichita, 1973, p. 128.
10. Frank Kermode says, 'The first condition of pastoral poetry is that there should be a sharp difference between two ways of life, the rustic and the urban'. 'Introduction', *English Pastoral Poetry*, London, Harrap, 1952, p. 14.
11. Hardin, op. cit., p. 127.
12. 'Felicia,' says Hardin, 'is a Latin equivalent for the Greek word that gave the title of *Poly-Oblion*', ibid., p. 129.
13. *Works*, op. cit., p. 220.
14. *Oxford English Dictionary*.
15. Ibid. See entry under 'e'.
16. See Alastair Fowler's *Triumphal Forms*, pp. 185–6n.

CHAPTER 13

'When People Can't Abide Things as They Are': An Interpretation of Albee's *Vision of Life*

In Act I of *Who's Afraid of Virginia Woolf,* George the protagonist, speaks to Honey: 'It's very simple. . . . *When people can't abide things as they are,* when they can't abide the present, they do one of the two things . . . either they . . . *either they turn to a contemplation of the past,* as I have done, *or they set about to alter the future* (emphasis added) and when you want to change something . . . you Bang; Bang; Bang' (Penguin, 1965, p. 106).

'People' may broadly be divided into two categories, i.e. those who abide things as they are, and those who can't abide the present. So long as people abide by things as they are, there is no problem. The problem arises when people can't abide the present. In that case, Albee says, there is a choice between the 'contemplation of the past' and 'setting about to alter the future'. Some of the plays of Albee, namely *The Zoo Story, The Sandbox, The American Dream* and *Who's Afraid . . .* may be studied on the three-pronged premise spelled out by George, a history professor, to Honey, the wife of the biology teacher in the play. *Who's Afraid* as the contemplation of the past or alteration of the future appears to be the only course left for such protagonists who can't abide the present. The two referent positions are not always antagonistic but sometimes appear as alternating rhythms in Albee. What the playwright makes George say to Honey in his usual manner of hindsight appears to be a profound comment on all creative writing.

There has, no doubt, been a shift in the focus; earlier it used to be more of the 'contemplation of the past' and only some hint or suggestion of events, nature of things anticipated. However, the post-War literature and especially the drama of the 1960s in the U.S. abounds in such writings as anticipating a future which is different as well as terrifying. The future is not merely anticipated, it is set about to be altered, causing a Bang, turning everything upside down. To make the point explicit, Peter in *The Zoo Story*, Mommy and Daddy in *The American Dream* and *The Sandbox* and Nick and Honey in *Who's Afraid* . . . may be placed in the category of people who can't abide the present. In further subdivision, George and Grandma are given to contemplation of the past and Jerry and Martha are set to alter the future.

Peter, in *The Zoo Story* represents precisely that category of men who abide to their heart's content things as they are. He is a nice married man with two daughters, has an executive position with a small publishing house with an annual income of US$ 18,000.

He owns two TV sets, has two parakeets, reads *Time* magazine, smokes pipe and has a house in a posh locality. He is bewildered by Jerry's questions about class. He is normally reticent. To some of the disturbing questions and posers of Jerry, he says that he is in the publishing business and is not a writer. He can't understand things unless they are pigeonholed and compartmentalized. He says that he can't believe that people such as they really are. In the most gripping conversation Jerry tries to engage him in he gets no response from Peter, except, 'I . . . I don't understand what . . . I don't think I . . . I don't want to hear any more', 'I'm . . . I'm sorry, I didn't mean to . . .' and in the closing scene, he says, 'Well, I must confess that this wasn't the kind of afternoon I'd anticipated.' Peter is offended only when he is being pushed out of the bench. He is seriously annoyed only when threatened to be dispossessed of his bench on which he has been sitting every Sunday for the last several years. It is the only occasion he makes an intelligent observation. When Jerry lays a claim to the bench he says, 'People can't have everything they want. You should know that; it is a rule; people can have some of the things they want, but they can't have everything.' The other occasion when Peter reacts rather profoundly comes when Jerry mentions the word 'honour' in the course of his rather longish conversation: 'Absurd. Look, I'm going to talk to you about honour or even try to explain to you. Besides, it isn't a question of honour but even if it were, you would not understand.' Until the close of the play, which is no doubt intense and tragic and must necessarily shock and enliven Peter, he remains a contented person, abiding the present and treating Jerry as an alien not only to his world but to the civilization of which he is a part.

The young man Jerry is one of the most powerful characters ever created in Albean drama. He has been variously interpreted and commented upon by the critics. Investing him with a Christ-like personality has been one of the constant refrains. Without delving into the issue, he may be placed in the category of those 'who can't abide things as they are', 'can't abide the present', and 'set about to alter the future'. So the conflict is essentially between the two ideological positions, willingly abiding the present and actively altering the future.

Despite possessing a few things like 'toilet articles', 'a few clothes', 'a hot plate' he says, 'he is not supposed to have', 'a can opener', 'a knife', 'two forks', 'two spoons', 'one small one large', 'three plates', 'a cup', 'a saucer', 'a drinking glass', 'two picture frames', 'both empty', 'eight or nine books', 'a pack of pornographic playing cards', 'regular deck', 'an old Western Union typewriter that prints nothing but capital letters', and 'a small strong box without a lock'. Jerry remains 'an accommodated man'. He combines in him the deprivations of Lear, Edgar and the Fool, though he is neither a victim of the vagaries of Nature, nor the ungratefulness of man as are Lear and Edgar. He is the 'odd man' out in a highly possessive, advanced, technological world of the West. He evokes neither sympathy nor concern from Peter, who remains indifferent to his plight or, at the most, is amused by his weird conversation. Jerry describes his visit to the zoo and says that he went there 'to find out more about the way people exist with animals, and the way animals exist with each other, and with people too'.

Regarding Jerry's account of the dog's antipathy towards him and of his attempt first to draw it into friendship by feeding it, then failing that to poison it, and finally to reach some kind of mutual understanding mirrors, Anne Paolucci says, 'In the length and intensity of the narrative, his mounting hysteria' (*From Tension to Tonic*). The story is a kind of parable, full of allusions, phrases, and cadences from the Bible. In Jerry's words: 'I wanted the dog to live so that I could see what our new relationship might come to.' Jerry's description of himself, his state of being is notable for its self-mocking, ironic note: 'I don't live in your block; I am not married to two parakeets, or whatever your set up is. I am not a permanent transient, my home is the sickening rooming houses on the West Side of New York City, which is the greatest city in the World. Amen.' Jerry accepts loneliness as the norm of existence. Albee's thesis, according to Bigsby, is that 'there is a need to make contact to emerge from these self-imposed cages of convention and false values so that one individual consciousness may impinge on another' (*Confrontation and Commitment*).

In *The American Dream*, Mommy and Daddy and Mrs Barker belong to the same category of people who abide the present, while Grandma can't abide things as they are and turns to 'a contemplation of the past', and adds meaning to the drama of the absurd. In this play 'Mommy', a crusty and domineering person, is more deeply entrenched in the new social ethos, divested of the basic values of life, than her husband who is the acquiescing type. Nevertheless, both conform to the norm of abiding things as they are, abiding the present. As the play begins, they are seen talking over and waiting for the man who will cart the Grandma off. There is not even an iota of regret and remorse over what they have decided.

There follows a long spell of waiting and an interesting diversion into trivialities, intimating hypocrisy, artificiality and meanness. Mommy describes Mrs Barker thus:

> She's a dreadful woman, you don't know her; she has dreadful taste, two dreadful children, a dreadful house, and an absolutely adorable husband who sits in a wheelchair all the time, you don't know him. You don't know anybody, do you! She's just a dreadful woman, but she is chairman of our women's club, so naturally I'm terribly fond of her.

Interestingly, Mrs Barker and Mommy resemble one another in more ways than one. Mrs Barker judges Mommy's house in almost the exact words Mommy used to describe her 'chairwoman friend'.

Grandma in *The American Dream* is, according to Anne Paolucci, 'The Prospero of the piece, who gives a semblance of meaning and purpose to others. It is she who reveals to Mrs. Barker why she has been called; and it is she also who instructs the young man as to his new role.' The young man in the play is the American Dream whose twin has been mutilated by Mommy and Daddy. The myth about the son in this play, according to Paolucci, is 'the first direct attempt at the manner and style of *Who's Afraid of Virginia Woolf*'. 'The American Dream', she says 'becomes the private dream of a couple much more interesting and provoking than Mommy and Daddy.'

The Sandbox, a one act tragedy, may also be seen as a fine example of the eternal conflict between those who abide things as they are, and those who can't. Grandma, in whose character Albee immortalized the death of his own grandmother, is the protagonist of the play, being pitilessly disposed of by her heartless daughter and acquiescing son-in-law. Mommy and Daddy as they call each other, have decided to dispose off their eighty-six-year-old mother. The Grandma initially resents being dumped in a sandbox, but later accepts her fate. As she can't put up with her daughter and son-in-law, she makes an effort to communicate with the audience and the young man on the beach whom we later know to be the angel of death, doing his callisthenics, Grandma turns to a contemplation of the past. She complains about bad treatment from her daughter, who had married for money. She tells the young man about her own past life. At an early age she had married a farmer, who had died when she was only thirty years old, leaving her alone to raise her unpleasant daughter now turned a 'big cow'. Grandma tells the Young Man of the life in which she struggled through an early widowhood only to be taken off the farm and moved to a big townhouse and like a domestic animal, given a blanket, a dish and a place under the stove. The speech confirms the loss of love and filial bonds.

On the other hand, Mommy and Daddy execute their plan with such precision and apathy that they don't even pretend to be apologetic. When Daddy is seen hesitating slightly, Mommy censures and cuts him short.

> 'I know she's my mother. What do you take me for [*A pause*]
> All right, now: let's get on with it'.

After Grandma has been dumped in the sandbox, she addresses the audience, as there is no use protesting against the daughter and the son-in-law: 'Honestly; what a way to treat an old women; Drag her out of the house, stick her in a car, bring her out here from the city . . . dump her in a pile of sand . . . and leave her to set. I'm eighty six years old.'

Fortunately for Grandma, who can't abide her present plight, the young man at the beach doing callisthenics with whom she has been able to create an intimate rapport turns out to be the Angel of Death. Now, from a contemplation of the past, she is delivered from evil, and released into a world of grace.

CHAPTER 14

American Poetry in the Contemporary Era

American poetry in the contemporary era offers such varied and diverse forms of expression and modes of experience that it has become increasingly difficult to classify or categorize it into specific trends or traditions. The variety and richness of American poetry as a whole may be seen as a measure of what American culture itself has accomplished. There is not one America but several Americas, not one tradition of literature, strong or weak, but several literary traditions, not one mainstream culture, but several cultures, each claiming to be authentically distinct and different. While the literary taste and aesthetics of the masters of the inter-war years like Pound, Eliot, Williams, is not completely gone, the Beat poets, Confessional poets and the post-Confessionals, Black poets, Native American poets, the practitioners of free verse and experiments with new forms and language provide such a vista of colour as has never been seen before. This literary and cultural proliferation did not come about suddenly; it has always been present in the American tradition. Earlier it was neither visible nor audible. The newly emerging trends in ethnicity, cultural identity, individuality and revolution in mass communication and print media have only brought these invisible and hitherto inconspicuous trends into focus, thereby changing the entire literary scene.

The emergence of the Beat poets during the Cold War period marks, in some ways, a departure from the tradition of American poetry between the two World Wars. These poets rejected the examples and precepts of T.S. Eliot, who was a reigning influence and the leading arbiter of poetic taste. This was a serious questioning of conventional American values. The Beat poets proclaimed and exploited the American dream of individual freedom. It was a full-throated protest against social conformity, political repression and materialism. The term 'Beat' while connoting disillusionment and defeat, also signified, 'beatitude', that is, a championing of aesthetic and spiritual values. It was in the mid-1950s, that groups of writers in New York city and San Francisco gained a national audience for their work. Allen Ginsberg, Jack Kerouac and Gregory Corso were members of the original Beat group in New York city, who found among Lawrence Ferlinghetti, Cary Synder and Michal McClure, leading the San Francisco poetry renaissance kindred souls and fellow travellers. Allen Ginsberg, regarded as the leader of the Beat poets, published his first collection of poems, *Howl* in 1956. The most anthologized piece of Ginsberg's poem 'Howl' still haunts the minds of readers:

> I saw the best minds of my generation destroyed by madness, starving,
> hysterical naked
> dragging themselves through the Negro streets at dawn looking for
> an angry fix.
> angelheaded hipsters burning for the ancient heavenly connection to
> the starry dynamo in the machinery of night.
>
> Who bared their brains to Heaven under the El and saw
> Mohammedan angels
> Who passed through universities with radiant
> Cool eyes hallucinating
> Arkansas and Blake-light tragedy among the scholars of War.

The impact and immensity of the Beat poets—Ginsberg, Ferlinghetti, Synder, Baraka/Jones can also be measured by their continuous inclusion in the anthologies of American literature and their large sales figures. Ferlinghetti's *Starting from San Francisco* (New Directions, 1961), Synder's *Axe Handles* (North Point Press, 1983), Ginsberg's *Howl and other Poems* (City Lights, 1956) have elicited enduring interest in poetry among a large number of readers. These poets not only brought about an aesthetic revolt but also a 'radical assault on mainstream American value system'. In the words of Rebecca Solnit:

A poetic rebellion was taking place. Ezra Pound and T.S. Eliot had established a modernist tradition of erudite, impersonal poetry. . . . There was no single reaction against that orthodoxy but there were some widespread tendencies—the assertion of the personal, a grounding in the details of everday life, and a desire to return to a genuine American speech. Walt Whitman's free-wheeling rhapsodies and William Carlos Willam's taut lucid verse become the foundation for a new tradition in which Allen Ginsberg could write about supermarkets and homosexual encounters; in which humour and imperfection, confusion and confession were possible.

The last named of the major Beat poets, LeRoi Jones moved to New York city and affiliated himself with this group. After the assassination of Malcolm X in 1965 he left his white wife and children and founded the Black Arts Repertory theatre in Harlem, and adopted the name Imam Amiri Baraka. Jones's growing interest in the Black revolution has made his poetry increasingly nonformal and non-traditional.

His poetry is free of orthodox diction, images and received ideas—a rejection of what he considers 'White poetic tradition':

Dull unwashed windows of eyes
and buildings of Industry. What
industry do I practice? A slick
colored boy. 12 miles from his
home. I practice no Industry.
I am no longer a credit
to my race. I read a little.
Scratch against silence slow spring
afternoons.

—'A poem some people will have to understand'

Beat poetry, to quote Diane Wood Middlebrook, 'proposed no changes in material social conditions'. It seems to have been 'Undertaken, eventually, by the artistic wings of two progressive political movements: black civil rights and women's liberation'. By the mid-1960s the poets of a New Black Aesthetic prominently, Gwendolyn Brooks, Maya Angelou, Etheridge Knight, Andrey Lorde, LeRoi Jones/Amiri Baraka were defying the precepts of new critical universalization by making African American difference the subject of the poem itself. A similar artistic impulse, Middlebrook says motivated the women—mainly white women who began writing women into poetry as makers and readers. Swenson Kizer,

Kumun, Sexton, Rich and Plath were among the first to evoke in their women-centred poems the definitive ways that gender difference shapes the social experience of persons, and inescapably situates readers in a gendered position *vis-a-vis* the poetic 'text'.

Though the genesis of the poetry of New Black Aesthetics may be traced to Alain Locke's *The New Negro: An Interpretation* (1925). It was Langston Hughes', 'The Negro Artist and the Racial Mountain' (*The Black Aesthetics*, 1971) that spelt out the agenda of the new movement. Hughes argues that a new poetry will come that will reflect 'the beauty of dark faces'. This new poetry will be 'racial in theme and treatment'. It will use as its metrical base jazz, 'the inherent expression of Negro life in America'. It will speak without shame or fear of the experience of the African–American on the streets of those communities that have not abandoned the sound of the tom-tom in such a way as to open the 'ears of coloured near-intellectuals' to be the blare and bellowing voice of the African–American reality.

According to William W. Cook, 'The Black Arts poets' (*The Columbia History of American Poetry*, ed. Parani Jay, Columbia University Press, 1993), the Black Arts movement is the culmination of a five-step historical process: Race Memory, The Middle Passage, Transmutation and Synthesis, Blues God/Tone as meaning and memory and Black Arts Movement/Black Aesthetics. Clarence Major's *The New Black Poetry* (1969), Ameer Baraha's *Black Fire* (1968) and Gwendolyn Brooks' *In the Mecca* (1968) are some of the important anthologies that treat the new black poetry 'each offering its special perspective on ideology and poetics'. Some of the passages from Gwendolyn Brooks' *In the Mecca* speak of the new black aesthetic unequivocally:

> Black people understand
> That they are the lovers
> and the sons
> of lovers and warriors and sons
> of warriors Are poems and poets
> all the loveliness
> here in the world.
>
> * * *
>
> a new nation
> under nothing;
> a physical light that waxes; he dees not want to

be exorcised, adjoining and revered;
he does not
like a local garniture
nor any implish onus in the vogue
. . . the auspices of fire
and rock and jungle-flail,
wants
new art and anthem; will
want a new music screaming in the sun.

Imam Amiri Baraka's poem 'Biography' is also very illustrative of the Black metaphor and poetic mode:

Hangs.
whipped
blood
stripped
meat pulled
clothes ripped
slobber
feet dangled
pointing
noised
noise
churns
face
black
sky

and moon
leather night
red
bleeds
drips
ground
sucks
blood
hangs
life wetting
sticky
mud

laughs
bonnets
wolfmoon
crazyteeth

hangs
hangs

granddaddy
granddaddy,
they tore
his
neck

The origin of the Confessional poets may in some ways be traced to the intensely private world of Emily Dickinson. However, the contemporary Confessional poetry, generally associated with some of the women writers of America—Sylvia Plath, Anne Sexton and Adrienne Rich owes its source to the writings of Robert Lowell, who had his goal 'to write poems as pliant as conversation, so clear a listener might get every word'. The poetics he developed for *Life Studies* (1959) permitted 'a prose-like flow of reminiscence with movement in and out of meter and rhyme'. The poetry of *Life Studies* is deeply personal. The poems probe 'past and present, self and civilization, family and friends'. It is argued that Lowell opens himself to the influence of William Carlos Williams in 'freezing his verse' and to that of his own student, W.D. Snodgrass, in 'divising confessional forms of his own'. Robert Lowell's impact on the contemporary literary scene was perhaps as immense and consequential as that of Ginsberg during the Cold War period. Interestingly, Lowell's career presents two major developments of modern poetry which on the face of it appear contradictory: the search for the impersonal (assumption of 'masks', the reliance on illusion, etc.) and the open expression of self-revelation, the exposure of 'I'.

The Confessional poetry of Lowell, Sylvia Plath, Snodgrass, Anne Sexton and Rich is a protest against 'Impersonality' as a poetic value, introducing an insistently autobiographical first person engaged in resistance to all kinds of pressures and conformist modes. The strong confessional impulse of much contemporary poetry may be seen in the works of Sylvia Plath. Her dependent love on her German father, who died when she was ten, was countered by her hatred of the Nazism she associated with him and by her identification with its Jewish victims. Her ambivalence and her drive toward self-destruction are revealed in 'Daddy':

I have always been scared of you,
with your Luftwaffe, your gobbledygoo.
And your neat moustache
And your Aryan eye, bright blue.
Panzer-man, panzer-man, O you.

I was ten when they buried you.
At twenty I tried to die
And get back, back, back to you,
I thought even the bones would do.

Anne Sexton began writing poetry in 1957, when she was 29, during recovery from a mental breakdown. While she was separated from her children her doctor prescribed writing as a form of psychotherapy. Sexton quickly discovered and then developed an impressive talent. 'The Double Image' is one of the most anthologized pieces of Sexton. This poem, in the words of Middlebrook, 'proposes a most un-Freudian resolution of the oedipal struggle by which the daughter gains from the mother the power of image-making'.

Adrienne Rich's poetry is a presentation of a changing view of man and woman. It exhibits a growing hostility to what she calls 'patriarchal politics and patriarchal civilization'. She speaks from a woman's viewpoint 'precisely and bluntly about human relationships and, particularly in her later poems, about the individual's search for sanctuary and release'. Rich's poems—'The Trees', 'The celebration in the Plaza', 'Sex, as they harshly call it', 'Planetarium' and 'Lucifer in the Train' demonstrate a remarkably authentic poetic sensibility, that is, to say the least, novel and refreshing.

The growth and development of Native American poetry is a phenomenon that cannot be overlooked in any account of contemporary American poetry. Though the cultural roots of the Native American poetry are believed to be the oldest indigenous tradition in North America, the Native American poetry itself is a twentieth-century phenomenon. Some of the major anthologies of Native American poetry are: Duane Niatum's *Carriers of the Dream Wheel* (1975), Kenneth Rosen's *Voices of The Rainbow* (1976); Joseph Bruchac's *Songs from this Earth on Turtle's Back* (1983) and Robert K. Dodge and Joseph B. McCullough's *New and Old Voices of Wah' Kon'–Tah* (1985). These titles contextualize the poetry for the reader, announcing its cultural *difference* and distinguishing these anthologies from other collections of American poetry.

The tone and tenor of the Native American sensibility as reflected in the poetry of some of these poets bears testimony to the new consciousness and anger:

> Our skin loosely lies
> across grass borders:
> . . . we struggle until our blood
> has spared off our bodies
> and frayed the sunset edges.
> It's our blood that gives you
> those southwestern skies.
>
> —Wendy Rose, 'The Day They Cleaned up the Border'

> for all the fallen dead to return
> not teach us a language so terrible
> it could resurrect us all.   —Harjo, 'Resurrection'

To quote Lucy Maddox, 'Rose's strongest and angriest poems are those in which she speaks in the voice of another, someone whose story has been in Rose's view, grotesquely misrepresented'. Rose says: 'I would tell this like a story/but where a story should begin/I am left standing in the beat/of my silences'.

The various traditions of poetry and modes of poetic utterance that emerged after the inter-war years in America are not restricted to the emerging trends in thought and feeling alone; innovations in form and experiments in language exploited and accomplished by some of the third generation poets, notably James Merrill and John Ashbery, is an equally fascinating aspect of contemporary American poetry. These poets have been influenced by Stevens, Auden and Elizabeth Bishop. Merrill admires Stevens 'great ease in combining abstract words with gaudy visual sound effects'. For both Merrill and Ashbery writing in the 1950s, Auden was undoubtedly a formidable influence. To Elizabeth Bishop they owe the art of concealing and illuminating personal experiences earlier considered not fit for poetry. The other notable trend in innovations of form and language has been that of Charles Olson's theory of 'projective verse'.

Merrill and Ashbery have also contributed long poems. Merrill's trilogy, *The Changing Light at Sandover* (1982) and three of Ashbery's contemporaneous long poems—from *Three Poems* 'Self Portrait in a Convex Mirror', 'Litany' and 'Flow Chart' deserve special mention. Merrill's *Sandover* a 560-page poem is immense. The poem is 'Universal in scale and scope, extending from atom to its outer space creator, from the creation to apocalyptic present, from this world of the living to the other world of the dead and the supernaturals. Whose speech appears in alien, telegraphic capitals'. Near the end of 'Mirabell', Merrill in *Sandover* introduces a new character with his own grand measure and diction—the sun god Michael:

> AND SO AS YOU FACE THIS SETTING SUN YOU FACE YOUR ANCESTOR,
> AND THE SUN LOOKS THROUGH YOUR EYES TO THE LIFE BEHIND YOU.
> EACH OF YOUR SUNCYCLES IS A STEP ON YOUR WAY TO YOUR ANCESTOR
> AND THAT IS ALL YOU NEED TO KNOW OF YOUR PHYSICAL INCARNATE
> HISTORY.

Similarly, Ashbery's 'Litany' with its parallel columns, rarely corresponding, offers a new experiment in form and language which leads the reader across the margin in either direction for help or support:

> Some in underwear stood around *Outnumbering the sheaves.*
> Puddles in the darkened, *Even the ants on the anthill,*
> Cement and sodium lights *Black line leading to*
> Beyond the earthworks. *The cake of disasters.*

CHAPTER 15

Image of the Orient in Shakespeare

By the image of the 'Orient', or more accurately, images of the Orient, I intend to examine Shakespeare's references to and treatment of what is generally understood by the term 'Orient'. The *Oxford English Dictionary* defines the Orient as 'usually those countries immediately east of the Mediterranean or of southern Europe'. This includes the images of the 'Turk', the Saracen, the Ottoman, the Moor, and countries like India, Arabia, Egypt, Persia and Cathay. It makes a category which is exclusively non-European, non-white, non-Christian, and last but not the least, the unfamiliar, and the 'other'. While most of the references constitute stock images, a few of Shakespeare's dramatic characters deserve to be examined in some detail. They include the Moor in *Othello*; Aaron, the Moor in *Titus Andronicus*; and Cleopatra in *Antony and Cleopatra*. The references to Arabia, India, Egypt, Persia and Turkey and the Ottomans are of a general nature which bring out the contemporary Elizabethan stock responses to these images. Among these, the references to the Turk abound most in Shakespeare.

This not only involves the examination and interpretation of imagery but also, to some extent, the treatment of history by the Elizabethans in general and Shakespeare in particular. I would like to recapitulate the relevance of historical plays as an important component of humanistic culture, for in the sixteenth century, according to the treatises of Puttenham (*The Art of English Poesy*, 1589) and William Webbe (*Discourse of English Poetry*, 1586), and more importantly, Sir Philip Sidney (*Apologie for Poetrie*, 1580), history was considered to be a part of poetry, and one of the important arguments in defence of poetry was related to the writing of historical plays focusing on moral truth which was seen as a justification for the works of poets. In this regard, mention may be made of the poetic license the writers enjoyed in the writing of history. Several examples of such writings can be cited where poets not only sharpened the outlines of a map but also introduced changes of vital consequences. Like many other seminal ideas, the concept of history and its relationship to poetry was a preoccupation with the Elizabethans. Not content with the early classical definitions of these new terms, they sought new interpretations and explored various possibilities of the use of history in the perspective of their national aspirations. According to Toynbee in *A Study of History*:

> The saga and the epic arise in response to a new mental need, a new awareness of strong individual personalities and of momentous public events. . . . The interest in the present predominates just so long as the storm and stress of the Heroic age continues; but the social paroxysm is transitory and, as the storm abates, the lovers of epic and saga come to feel that life in their time has grown relatively tame. Therewith they cease to prefer the new lays to the old, and the latter day minstrel, responding to his hearer's change of mood; repeats and *embellishes* the tales of older generation. (Emphasis added)

In the present context, three examples may be cited from Elizabethan literature:

1. Marlowe's treatment of *Edward II* and Michael Drayton's *Barons Warres*, delineating and improvising upon the chronicle accounts of King Edward II, Queen Isabella, Mortimer, and Gaveston.
2. The Medieval opinions of Brutus found him to be a 'short-sighted political blunderer', who foolishly or even wickedly struck down the foremost man of his time. But Shakespeare followed the Renaissance admiration for Brutus and detestation for Caesar. Shakespeare seems to have left, according to T.J.B. Spencer, 'the exact degrees of guilt and merit in Caesar and Brutus deliberately ambiguous in the play to give a sense of depth and to keep the audience guessing', which goes to show that 'the reassessment and reconsideration of famous historical figures

was a common literary activity in the Renaissance' (*Shakespeare Survey*, 10).

3. An example of Shakespeare's poetic license may also be cited from *Othello*. The Turks invaded Cyprus and captured Nicosia and later, Famagusta in November 1571. The island remained under Turkish rule till 1878 when the British took possession of it. To avoid referring to this defeat, Shakespeare imagined the Turkish fleet shattered by a storm although Richard Knolles' *The Generall Historie of the Turks* had been published earlier. English audiences would appreciate this divine intervention, for England had been thus saved from invasion several times in the past 15 years. The fate of the Spanish Armada in 1588 was a recent event in English history, the subsequent attempts by Spain in 1596, 1597 and 1598 had all failed.

The news of the Turkish invasion is broken by a Senator in the Duke's court, 'Narrator: Yet do they all confirm/A Turkish fleet, and bearing upto Cyprus', and a messenger brings the news that 'Ottomites, steering with due course, towards the isle of Rhodes/Have there enjoined with an after fleet'. By the time the scene shifts to Cyprus, a gentleman reports of 'a high wrought flood 'twixt heaven and the main' and then come the glad tidings:

> News, lads! our wars are done.
> The desperate tempest hath so bang'd the Turks
> That their designment halts; a noble ship of Venice
> Hath seen a grievous wrack and sufference
> On most part of their Fleet.   —II.i. 21–4

Mention may also be made of Tamburlaine's subdual of Bajazeth (Bayazid II), the Sultan of Turkey, in the play *Tamburlaine*, wherein several interpolations have been made by Marlowe. Moreover, Tamburlaine has been portrayed as a pagan and not as a Muslim that he was. Tamburlaine belongs to one of the Turkish tribes, who rose to become one of the greatest warriors in history. He was one of the most fascinating personalities to the Elizabethan audience, probably because he had subdued the mighty Sultan of Turkey, Bayazid II.

The image of the 'Turk' in Shakespeare stands for ferocity, savagery, intemperate and uncivil conduct. It is in consonance with a kind of national consensus and general Elizabethan understanding, for during Shakespeare's age the Ottoman Empire, with 52 kingdoms (*I Henry VI*, IV, vii, 73), was not only the largest but the mightiest empire of the world whose writ ran on the three continents: Asia, Africa and Eastern Europe. The Ottomans were not only dreaded but detested. The fear of the Turk was compounded by the ever-increasing ambition of the Ottomans to expand their boundaries. There were intermittent wars between the Ottomans and the European states. England being farthest on the western side of Turkey was relatively safe and enjoyed a kind of peace and prosperity under the reign of Queen Elizabeth I. However, the hatred of the Ottomans was shared by all the Europeans. In the plays of Shakespeare or Ben Jonson there are no Turkish characters. Turks are generally referred to as stock images. Turks, Tartars, Phrygians and Ottomans are more or less synonymous in Shakespeare.

Turks are also described as black pagans, Saracens, infidels. There are innumerable references to the 'Turk' in Shakespeare. Mention may be made of *Othello, King Lear, Hamlet, Macbeth, The Merchant of Venice, As You Like It, Richard II, I Henry IV, 2 Henry IV, Henry V, Richard III, Merry Wives,* and *Much Ado About Nothing.* On an examination of the image of the Turk in Shakespeare it can safely be said that it embodies lack of courtesy and defiance: 'Turks and Tartars, never trained to the offices of tender courtesy' (*The Merchant of Venice*) or 'She denies me, like Turk to Christian' (*As You Like It*). 'Peace shall go sleep with Turks and infidels' (*Richard III*). In *Macbeth,* 'Liver of blaspheming Jew, nose of Turk and Tartars lips' constitute the cauldron of the Witches, and in *Hamlet,* Shakespeare speaks of 'Fortunes turning Turk'. In all such phrases, references and comparisons are always in a pejorative and derogatory sense.

Edgar in *King Lear*, while recounting his various assets, says that in woman he has 'out-paramoured the Turk'. The various images of the Turk employed by Shakespeare bring to the readers' mind the picture of a powerful adversary, a villain, a detested creature, and a mistrusting man. In modern terms, the Turk is demonized and transformed into the Other.

Shakespeare did not introduce the fashion of Turk baiting. He was only endorsing and subscribing to the Euro–Christian notions of anti-Turk sentiment which had been accentuated in the early sixteenth century in European writings, particularly after the fall of Constantinople in 1453.[1] The British and the other European states had known the Arabs and the Turks since the Crusades (1096–1244). The period of the Crusades has been generally described by the Western writers as an epic effort to reconquer the Holy Land which Amin Maalouf describes in his book, *The Crusades Through Arab Eyes* (1984), as 'a brutal, destructive, unprovoked invasion by barbarian hordes'. Amin Maalouf, quoting contemporary Arab sources, says that when Jerusalem was captured by the Crusaders in 1099 after a 40-day siege, Muslims and Jews were slaughtered indiscriminately, women and children were not spared, houses were plundered and mosques sacked. However, the Crusades did expose the West to the Orient in an unprecedented manner. Their mercantile activity was stepped up, they had a sense of political and religious unity which gave them a sense of destiny. They saw for the first time civilized nations east of the Mediterranean and south of Europe which were truly cosmopolitan in terms of learning, applied technology, manners and social institutions. But the images of the Orient were distorted and invented to suit their whims and fancies that were to last six centuries. During Shakespeare's age these images had been more or less solidified. It is indeed interesting to note that contrary to what the Crusaders had done during their numerous campaigns to regain the Holy Land, the conduct of the Arabs in the battlefield and outside was generally governed by a code of civility that was unknown to the West. The example of Saladin, the Sultan of Egypt and Syria who reconquered Jerusalem in 1187, is well known in the annals of European history. He was accepted by his fiercest enemies as a paragon of chivalry. The chivalric attitude of Saladin in the battlefield has been fictionalized by Sir Walter Scott in *The Talisman*. But during the later Medieval ages, Arabs and Turks had been made the target of European writers and treated as villains in order to celebrate their national heroes like Charlemagne and his paladins. Mention may be made of Tasso's *Jerusalem Liberata* and Ariosto's *Orlando Furioso*. In this context it is relevant to mention that by the close of the sixteenth century, the Saracen, the Turk and the Tartar had been more or less synonymized. In a general sense, it may be inferred that it was the Muslim, the believer in Islam, who became the target of detestation and scorn in European literature irrespective of race, region or country. However, it can be said to the credit of the Bard of Stratford-upon-Avon, that his detestation of the Turk is mostly political and not religious and moral, a phenomenon we see in the treatment of the Sarazin/Saracen in Spenser's *The Faerie Queene*, or in the Italian Romantic epics of the early sixteenth century.

It may not be out of place to mention here that the term 'Saracen' has no reference to Turks. The term 'Saracen' was applied to Arabs. While its etymology is uncertain, it was loosely applied to the peoples of the East or the Orient. In Medieval times the name 'Saracen' was often associated with Sarah, the wife of Abraham. St. Jerome identifies the Saracens with

'Hagarens', the descendants of Hajra 'who are now called Saracens, taking to themselves the name of Sarah'. Sir John Smyth, in *Discourse Weapons* (1590), says, 'The brave Saladin, Sultan of Egypt, with his notable militia of Mamloks (by many called Saracen) reclaimed Jerusalam'. Syed Amir Ali in his *A Short History of Saracens* has erred in explaining the etymology of Saracen as *Sahranasheen*, i.e. the desert dweller. Saracens, according to Greeks, were the nomadic peoples of the Syro–Arabian desert. The point which deserves attention is that during the thirteenth century, particularly after the fall of Baghdad in 1258, Arabs had ceased to be a political force and had no role in the conquest of Constantinople, but the European writers treated them with the same hatred and disdain as was done for the redoubtable Ottoman, that is, by inventing an omnibus term for 'Muslims'.

My next reference to Shakespeare's oriental images is to that of the Moor. Before coming to Othello the Moor of Venice, it would be interesting to refer to Aaron, the Black Moor in *Titus Andronicus*. The play, ascribed to Shakespeare, is of doubtful authorship. Shakespeare scholars consider this to be one of his earliest. The scope of the play as spelt out on the title page runs:

> The History of Titus Andronicus, the renowned Roman General who, after he had saved Rome by his valour from being destroyed by barbarous Goths, and lost 22 of his valiant sons in ten years' war, was upon the Emperor's marrying the Queen of Goths, put to disgrace, and banished; but being recalled, the Emperor's son by a first wife was murdered by the Emperor's sons and a bloody Moor, and How charging it upon Andronicus's sons, though he cut off his hand to redeem their lives, they were murdered in Prison. How his fair daughter Lavinia being ravished by the Emperor and the Empress; with the miserable death he put the wicked Moor to; then at her request slew his daughter and himself to avoid torment. Newly translated from the Italian copy printed at Rome.

As the advertisement says, the play is a gory tale of revenge compounded by villainy. However, the character of Aaron, the Black Moor, the master schemer and executor of the multiple deaths and the paramour of Tamora, the Queen of Goths, and later the Queen of Rome, deserves our attention. He is regularly described as a Moor. The phrases he uses to describe himself and his child are: 'My fleece of Wooly hair', 'Aaron will have his soul black like his face', 'Coal black is better than another hue',

'Look how the black slave smiles upon the father', 'You thicklipped slave'. He stands out among the Goths and Roman savages as a figure of filial love and humanity, when the new-born child of the Queen, admittedly fathered by him, is protected and saved at great risk.

Aaron's strange blend of villainy and engaging paternal affection is quite illuminating. Shakespeare has indeed made him a brilliant dramatic creation and his villainy 'invites a less complicated response than does the obsessive behaviour of Tamora and Titus'. When the sons of Tamora, the Queen of Rome, try to prevail over Aaron to kill the young babe in order to save their mother of public shame, Aaron tells them very firmly that the child shall not die. He says:

> Stay, murderous villains! Will you kill your brother
> Now, by the burning tapers of the sky,
> That shone so brightly when this boy was got,
> He dies upon my scimiter's sharp point
> That touches this my first-born son and heir.   —IV.ii. 89–94

Commenting upon the black colour of the child's skin, Aaron says:

> For all the water in the Ocean
> Can never turn the Swan's black legs to white
> Although she lave them hourly in the flood
> Tell the empress, from me, I am of age
> To keep mine own, excuse it how she can.   —IV.ii. 102–6

Aaron, with the child in his arms, decides to fly to the Goths. Speaking to the child, he says:

> I'll make you feed on berries and on roots
> And feed on curds and whey, and suck the goat
> And cabin in a cave, and bring you up
> To be a warrior, and command a camp.   —IV.ii. 179–82

In an atmosphere vitiated by 'murders, rapes and massacres, acts of black-night, abominable deeds, complots of mischief, treason and villainies', Aaron's resolve to save the child is indeed illuminating. Lucious, the banished son of Titus Andronicus and the future emperor of Rome, pledges to save the child on condition that Aaron reveals all. In the end, the 'irreligious' and the 'misbelieving' Moor is also sentenced to death but the Black issue begotten by him is saved. What needs to be examined in the context of this play is the fact that Shakespeare the artist, while endorsing the general opinion of Elizabethans with regard to Turks, Saracens and Tartars succeeds in presenting an individual character coming from the same stock, differently.

The plot of *Othello* is too well known to merit a recap of the events leading to the tragic end of Othello. It is one of the four great tragedies of Shakespeare and has elicited great admiration and critical response down the ages. According to Geoffrey Bullough, the intention of the playwright was,

> to give the story of the noble Moor an international setting and modern associations, was in line with what Shakespeare has done in *Hamlet* and was soon to do in *Macbeth*. In this way additional interest and importance were added to the theme; and one of his chief preoccupations in using Cinthio's materials was to dignify it, to transform it from a seedy drama of sordid crime into a poetic tragedy of human nature at its highest and lowest. So, social setting and the ranks of many characters were changed.

The two Moors in Shakespeare are different in several respects, yet the connotations/associations of the word 'Moor' in the two plays bring out an unusual correspondence. The Moor in *Titus Andronicus* has been described as 'My lovely Moor, this barbarous Moor, this cavernous tiger an irreligious Moor, chief architect and plotter of these woes, misbelieving and damned Moor', 'The Moor is of a free and open nature, that thinks men honest', 'war-like Moor and Othello of a noble nature'. It would not be out of place to infer that the image of the earlier Moor in *Titus* had not been forgotten by Shakespeare when he worked on Cinthio's plot. He raises the stature of Othello, invests it with 'honour' and unblemished 'reputation'. Through the words/speech of Iago, Brabantio and Roderigo, Shakespeare focuses on Othello being alien to Venetian society. That gives a chance to the dramatist to bring out Othello's characteristic traits of personality. This again is a manifestation of Shakespeare's wide sympathies that brings out the finest qualities of the noble Moor. Othello's references to Aleppo and Arabian trees clearly allude to his Arab connection and by portraying him as a Christian, the playwright has made him acceptable to the European audience.

There are other aspects of Othello's personality that merit attention. Some of these may be seen in the context of his Moorish background. M.R. Ridley in his introduction to *Othello* (The Arden Shakespeare, 1958) says: 'If I were challenged to produce a "theme" for *Othello* I should suggest

"Reason versus Instinct"' (p. iv). The suggestion made here refers to Othello's dependence on instinct whereas Iago may be seen to represent reason. It is indeed interesting to see that while Iago has been invested with reason in many a thing he contends, Othello speaks in a manner, plain and simple, which often goes against the paradigms of deductive reasoning. He is put to a defensive position to explain the context of his marriage to Desdemona. The contention Iago puts against this marriage appears to be well-argued though not convincing. While Othello is described as a 'noble Moor', 'a full soldier', and his marriage with the Venetian beauty justifiable, he is undeservedly pitted against Iago's self-serving arguments.

It is tempting to infer that Othello being of Moorish origin, though accomplished in military service and the art of governance, is seen by Shakespeare as a representative of the traits which are contrary to the image of the protagonist as a soldier, a scholar and a courtier, the Elizabethan ideal of a hero. On the other hand, Iago who is considered to be one of the most pernicious villains, is seen as an epitome of reason and logic. While Othello has all the characteristics of a tragic hero, why was it necessary to divest him of reason and put him in a position where his dependence on instinct and native intelligence is considered to be his greatest asset? Does it have anything to do with the common perception of the Elizabethans about the people of non-European origin? Othello fails against the logical postulates cleverly framed by Iago with regard to Desdemona's alleged acts of infidelity. Ridley argues, 'Whenever Othello trusts his instinct he is almost invariably right . . .; whenever he thinks, or fancies himself to be thinking, he is almost invariably and ruinously wrong' (p. iv). Edmund in *King Lear* also appears to be fluent in his reasoning power while contending against the rhetoric of Gloucester. While associating 'instinct' or native intelligence with characters of non-European origin, i.e. Othello and Cleopatra, Shakespeare seems to be unsympathetic to characters who appear to be strong in deductive reasoning or logical postulates, i.e. Iago and Edmund.[2] At a time when primacy of reason was beginning to be realized, it is indeed interesting to note that Shakespeare does not seem to be convinced of its soundness, which is why some of his heroes seek shelter in rhetoric and poetry when pitted against the onslaught of cold reason. It may not be out of place to mention here that Milton also cast Satan in *Paradise Lost* in the same rational mode as that of Iago and Edmund.

Shakespeare's romantic imagination finds full expression in *Antony and Cleopatra* in the description of the Queen of Egypt. It served for Shakespeare a dual objective. Shakespeare turned to Roman history after he had been preoccupied with English history for some years; nevertheless, it was this history which usually had the primacy for the study of political morality. It should also be borne in mind that, Roman history was written and interpreted tendentiously in Europe in the sixteenth century. In writing his Roman plays Shakespeare was touching upon the greatest and most exciting as well as the most pedantic of Renaissance studies of European scholarship. *Antony and Cleopatra* provided to Shakespeare the subject matter for the delineation of two of his greatest Roman characters, Octavius Caesar and Antony, besides giving him an opportunity to treat the 'Oriental matter' of Egypt. The play very finely juxtaposes the two value systems and political cultures; while Rome signifies shrewd statesmanship and manoeuvring, Alexandria represents a fuller participation of life. It is the 'gorgeous east' or the 'fabulous Orient' that finds full play here:

> The barge she sat in, like a burnished throne
> Burn'd on the water, the poop was beaten gold
> Purple the sails, and so perfumed that
> The winds were love-sick with them, the oars were silver
> Which to the time of flutes kept stroke, and made
> The water which they beat to follow faster
> As amorous of their strokes;   —II.ii. 199–205

One of the aspects of the plot with which Rome is concerned is the de-Romanization of Antony which is a consequence of Antony's dotage for Cleopatra. The famous lines spoken about the Queen of Egypt, 'Age cannot wither her nor custom stale her infinite variety', may also be interpreted as denoting the mystery of the 'East'.

Images of India are also frequently referred to in Shakespeare's plays. There are frequent phrases such as 'metal of India' (*Twelfth Night*), 'mines of India' (*Henry IV*), 'her bed in India; there she lies a pearl' (*Troilus and Cressida*), and 'I had gone barefoot to India' (*Troilus and Cressida*), 'a lovely boy stolen' from an Indian King', 'In spiced Indian air, by night/full often hath she gossiped by my side' (*A Midsummer Night's Dream*), 'The beauteous scarf veiling an Indian beauty' (*The Merchant of Venice*), 'not decked with diamonds and Indian stones' (3 *Henry VI*). Elizabethan England held highly romanticized notions about 'India'. They may also be seen as the images of the fabulous East, the distant, the remote, the rich, and the beautiful.

Rather curiously, the references to Arabia in Shakespeare are generally complimentary: the perfumes of Arabia, the mythical bird, phoenix with its throne on the Arabian tree, which also symbolizes 'rarity'; and Antony, in *Antony and Cleopatra*, described by Cleopatra as an 'Arabian bird'. These images denote, as in the case of Egypt, pictures of the fabulous orient. It is indeed interesting to see Shakespeare mocking the people of the land while celebrating their countries' fabulous wealth and rarities.

'Sophy', the term generally applied to the Emperor of Persia, and 'Sultan' to the Emperor of the Ottoman Empire, also evoke images of oriental extravaganza. They are found in the writings of Ben Jonson, Spenser, and a host of Elizabethan and Jacobean writers down to later ages. Addison speaks of 'A Turkish tale, which I do not like the worse for that little *oriental extravaganza* which is mixed with it'. In Shakespeare, the reference to 'Sophy' in the following line from *Twelfth Night*: 'A pension of thousands to be paid from the Sophy', obviously refers to the fabulous wealth of Persia. What do these oriental images signify in Shakespeare's imagination? How do they contribute to the atmosphere he creates? To what are the said images seen to replace direct statements about the peoples and lands? How do these images form a link in the complicated chain of his plays? Caroline Spurgeon, in her pioneering work, *Shakespeare's Imagery*, refers to Shakespeare's 'sensitiveness, balance, courage, humour and wholesomeness'. He had also been described by the scholar as 'gentle, kindly, honest, brave and true, with deep understanding and quick sympathy for all living things'. How far Shakespeare measures up to the description of Caroline Spurgeon in the context of oriental images needs to be closely studied.

The image of the orient continued to attract the attention of the European minds in a different manner as the British became successors to substantial part of Roman and Ottoman empires by the close of the nineteenth century. The famous, or the infamous, comments of Macaulay on the value of Sanskrit and Arabic literatures, that is, the oriental legacy, reflect a point of view different from that of the Elizabethan England. The Orient had now been subdued, exploited, and humbled by the present masters in a new manner. In this context, the following extract from Kipling's poem, 'One Viceroy Resigns' (1888), is indeed intriguing:

> You'll never plumb the oriental mind
> And if you did it isn't worth the toil;
> Think of a sleek French priest in Canada
> Divide by Twenty half-breeds. Multiply
> By twice the Sphinx's silence. There's your East
> And you're as wise as ever.

Shakespeare's treatment of the oriental images is based on the received opinions and the popular Elizabethan responses. He was careful not to examine or question them as he was discreet in respect of the sensitivities of the Tudor dynasty and the newly established Church of England, particularly during the days of James I. His catholicity, however, restricts the treatment of the popular Orient within the secular realm. He does not seem to bother about the religious beliefs of the Turks or Saracens and is generally concerned with their political conduct and ambition, a phenomenon that is not to be found in the works of his illustrious contemporary, Spenser. An interesting example can be cited from *Henry IV* wherein Falstaff describes his imaginary feats in the battlefield as those of 'Turk Gregory'. Through this invective Shakespeare attacks both the Ottomans and the then Pope Gregory, the formidable enemies of England, that is, the head of the Catholic Church and the mighty and the terrible Turk. However, it is to the credit of Shakespeare that the immortal characters of the noble Moor in *Othello* and the black Moor in *Titus Andronicus*, although created out of the same stock images from the Orient, have continued to engage the attention of scholars and critics down the ages as these two characters have been treated in a manner which makes them truly humane and universal.

Notes

All quotations from Shakespeare's plays are from the *Oxford Shakespeare Complete Works*, ed. W.J. Craig, Oxford University Press, 1966.

1. The French dictionary, *Petit Le Robert Dictionnaire De la Langue Francaise* defines the etymology of turk as follows: *turc*—noun, masculine (1966), metaphor, because it attacks the pear trees of the good Christian; old usage—a larva which attacks certain fruits, larva of a white worm. Le Robert, Paris, 1992, p. 2040.

   The Oxford Advanced Learner's Dictionary describes the turkey as 'a large bird reared to be eaten especially at Christmas'. The fact that the American gallinaceous bird was given the name turkey in the sixteenth/seventeenth century may also take us back to the period of Turk baiting.

2. Edmund, after listening to the speech of his father, Gloucester, about the nature of events following the division of the kingdom, says:

   > This is the excellent foppery of the world, that, when we are sick in fortune, often the surfeit of our own behaviour, we make guilty of our own disasters the sun, the moon, and stars: as if we were villains on necessity, fools' by heavenly compulsion, knaves, thieves, and treachers by spherical predominance, drunkards, liers, and

adulterers by an eriforc'd obedience of planetary influence; and all that we are evil
in, by a divine thrusting on.   —*King Lear*, Act I, Sc. ii, 132–41

This may also be compared to the speech of Iago craftily duping Roderigo into believing
that he still has a chance to pursue Desdemona even after her marriage to Othello:

Virtue? a fig! 'tis in ourselves, that we are thus, or thus: our bodies are gardens, to
the which our wills are gardeners, so that if we will plant nettles, or sow lettuce,
set hyssop, and weed up thyme; supply it with one gender of herbs, or distract it
with many; either to have it sterile with idleness, or manur'd with industry, why
the power, and corrigible authority of this, lies in our wills. If the balance of our
lives had not one scale of reason, to poise another of sensuality, the blood and
baseness of our natures would conduct us to most preposterous conclusions.
                                        —*Othello*, Act I, Sc. iii, 323–35

Part III

CHAPTER 16

The Human Predicament and its Sublimation

Zikr-i-Mir: The Autobiography of the Eighteenth Century Mughal Poet
Translated, Annotated and with an Introduction by C.M. Naim

Mir Taqi Mir (1723–1810) by general consensus is the most celebrated poet of Urdu whose mastery of the verse form has been acknowledged by several of his notable contemporaries and later poets including Ghalib, Mir's illustrious rival to fame. Among the many distinctions that Mir has, his understanding of the human predicament and its sublimation through a poetic medium in a felicitous manner are the easily recognizable features of his poetry. Mir makes no effort to initiate us into tough intellectual postulates for the explication of the human situation, but baffles us with his renderings of couplets, which are subtle and attractive. Besides inheriting common themes of the Indo–Persian tradition of poetry, Mir witnessed the two devastations of Delhi, which brought about untold miseries to the people of India, i.e. the sack of the city and its neighbourhood consequent upon the Third Battle of Panipat (1761) and the earlier calamity due to the invasion of Nadir Shah Durrani (1739). Furthermore, the latter half of eighteenth-century Mughal India was characterized by declining imperial authority and an empowered nobility. It unfolded innumerable situations of betrayal and treachery, ambition and greed and flickering fortunes particularly at a time when the British had begun to assert their authority after their initial successes in Bengal. Mir's poetry betrays the tension and the pathos of the age through the glorification of human love. The celebration of life remain the dominant passion of his *ghazals*.

Zikr-i-Mir is the account of the poet's life and antecedents in Persian. It is a pioneering work as it is the first-ever autobiography of an Urdu poet. Besides his autobiography, *Zikr-i-Mir*, he also wrote *Nikat-al-Shu'ara*, a chronicle account of Urdu poets and *Faiz-i Mir*, a collection of Sufistic anecdotes, both in Persian, which may be seen as supplementary texts to *Zikr-i-Mir*.

The book under review is the English translation of *Zikr-i-Mir* by C.M. Naim, professor of Urdu studies at the University of Chicago. The translator/editor has annotated the text with useful information prefaced by a scholarly introduction. Naim has collated the texts from the existing six manuscripts of *Zikr-i-Mir* available at Aligarh, Kolkata, Gwalior, Lahore, Lucknow and Rampur. On the basis of the difference in the concluding passage of the autobiography, Naim has appended them, as Narrative A and Narrative B. Besides, there are appendices on historical personages, a glossary of Persian words, Mir's patrons, Mir's literary milieu, Mir's 'lunacy' and love and sex. Naim has done his job so painstakingly that the book deserves to be rated at par with an Arden edition of Shakespeare.

The book, as it now exists 'contains a brief notice of Mir's ancestors, an extended section about Muhammad Ali, Mir's father, and his dear friend Amanullah, followed by a comparatively detailed narrative of the political events of the time only some of which were actually witnessed by Mir. The account of Mir's own life is scattered and quite summary in nature. He does not give us the kind of personal details we expect in an autobiography' (p. 11). Naim considers *Zikr-i-Mir* to be 'a deliberate enterprise' and avers that Mir had specific purposes in mind when he wrote *Zikr-i-Mir*. One of the purposes attributed to Mir is 'to claim a Sayyid lineage for himself while the other objective, according to Naim, was 'to establish his father as a major Sufi . . . whose fame had spread far and wide'. Naim also sheds light on the efforts of Mir to denigrate Sirajuddin Ali Khan Arzu, his stepbrother's uncle and his self-acknowledged mentor.

Naim convincingly argues as to why Mir put so much effort into projecting his father as a prominent Sufi. One of the possible motivations,

Naim surmises, 'may have been the envy of his Peer Khwaja Mir Dard, who belonged to a prominent Naqshbandi Sufi family and who was also a Sayyid on both sides of the lineage'. Naim further argues: 'even if we disallow any envy on Mir's part, it remains safe to believe that Dard's glorification of his own father could have suggested to Mir the way to establish a distinguished figure other than Arzu for his own identification' (p. 13). The so-called objectives of the autobiography, i.e. 'to claim a Sayyid lineage' and 'to establish his father as a major Sufi', who otherwise was a 'non-entity' in his age testify to the fact why there did not exist a tradition of autobiography in India in earlier times. The people were not interested in reading the authentic accounts of personal lives but expected their writer/heroes to conform to certain socially acceptable norms of the elite, the distinguished and the illustrious, whose flaws of lineage or character were either suppressed or negated. Naim posits that Mir managed to enter a forged entry in a copy of Arzu's *tazkira*, *Majma'-al-Nafa'* is about himself and his *ghazal* writing though Mir held a grouse against him for unknown reasons.

Mir was singularly fortunate in living through the reigns of five Mughal emperors from Muhammad Shah to Shah Alam II. He also saw the age of some of the most powerful nobles of eighteenth-century Mughal India like Najib-ud Daulah, Safdar Jang, Mahadji Sindhia, Suraj Mal, Jugal Kishore and Imad-ul Mulk, besides such illustrious poets and scholars as Khwaja Mir Dard, Mirza Muhammad Rafi Sauda and Shah Valiullah and mystics like Mirza Mazhar Jani-i Janan and Shah Fakhruddin. It was the best of the times and in a sense one of the most treacherous and depressing times. *Zikr-i-Mir* sheds light on almost all the aspects of life that Mir experienced. In the absence of any model of a biographical format, whatever we get in Mir's autobiography is illuminating.

Zikr-i-Mir recounts some of the events of that age which had a bearing on the political and social life of the people, particularly in and around Delhi and Lucknow. We get a glimpse into the intrigues of the imperial Mughal court, the Maratha–Rohilla rivalry culminating in the Third Battle of Panipat and the conduct of Warren Hastings, the first Governor-General of India later impeached by the British parliament. The book also sheds light on the social fads and literary taste of the nobility and, in general, offers a comment on the life and world view of the people. Eighteenth-century Mughal India has received the critical attention of historians and social scientists in the recent past focusing upon the possible causes of the crisis of empire that ultimately led to the fall of the Mughal dynasty.

The translation has been rendered into English with such care as is expected of a text dating back to the eighteenth century. The ambience of the archaic modes and manners of expression have been preserved. The narrative is punctuated with anecdotes, incidents, admonitions, tales, subtle points, rare words, excellent remarks, *dervish*-like advice, morals and in the end witty tales. Some specimens of Naim's translation, deserve to be cited in order to bring out the experience of the narrative:

> Endless praise be to that Eloquent one alone. . . . The Master of Eloquence who makes known a thousand different hues of speech; the Noble Teacher who provides a tongue to those who cannot speak. The Creator who blessed the world with creation; the Crafter who turned dust into the human. —p. 25
>
> Houses had collapsed. Walls had fallen down. The hospices were bereft of Sufis. The taverns were empty of revelers. It was a wasteland, from one end to the other. —p. 93
>
> Circumambulate human hearts, for that is truly the *tavaf*. Be a votary of yourself, for there is no finer goal. Nothing exists besides Him; nothing is manifest without Him. —Verse
>
> I asked the House, 'Who is the Intimate of the House'?
> It softly asked back, 'But who is a stranger?' —p. 62

The archaic expression, culture-specific terms and Persian idioms have been copiously glossed in the footnotes by frequently referring to Arzu's *Chiragh-i-Hidayat*, the lexicon Mir had richly exploited. With regard to the literary merit of the book, Naim's opinion deserves to be cited: 'Contrary to the claim made for Sir William Jones, Arzu was the first person to note and extensively comment on linguistic similarities between Persian and Indic languages' —p. 149

In Appendix I the absence of Shah Wali Allah Dihalwi in the entry on 'Other Important Persons' is conspicuous. The reference to '*Sabihe ke sabahat-i-o*' and '*Malihe ke malahat-i-o*' (p. 26) may also allude to a saying of the Prophet, which may be rendered as 'I am *Maleeh* and my brother Yusuf was *Sabeeh*'. The footnote on Mu'aviya, the founder of the Umayyad dynasty, that he had been an 'honoured companion' of the Prophet is factually incorrect. He was undoubtedly one of the companions but by no stretch of imagination an 'honoured companion' (p. 28).

CHAPTER 17

Paying Court

Umrao Jan Ada (1899), the fictionalized story of a courtesan of Lucknow, presents an interesting and authentic portrayal of Awadh in the middle of the nineteenth century. In technique and treatment, the novel is a landmark in Urdu fiction. It centres round the adventures of a young girl, Umrao Jan, after she is abducted from her hometown, Faizabad, and sold to the *khanum* (madam) of Lucknow. Her experiences of love are ennobling as well as demeaning. She survives the aftermath of the First War of Independence of 1857, and after a brief stint at Kanpur, returns to Lucknow. An invitation to perform a *mujra* at Faizabad takes Umrao, for a while, to her parental home and down memory lane.

Umrao's lovers are diverse—the philanderer Gauhar Mirza, the suave Nawab Sultan, the uncouth nouveau riche Rashid Ali, the foolhardy Khan, the priggish lawyer's attorney Akbar Ali, and a few others. Another courtesan, Bismillah Jan, is the object of Maulvi Saheb's lifelong devotion. The character of the *khanum* with her fine manners and an eye for the rich and generous comes through exquisitely. The novel analyses interesting aspects of the lives of both aristocrats and commoners.

The novel celebrates life in the Lucknow that was. Some knowledge of music and the ability to compose verses, besides other accomplishments, were considered essential for a gentleman in the erstwhile Lucknow. The finesse of etiquette, courtly manners and the nuances of the Urdu language contributed to the richness of Lucknow's culture. A typical courtesan, 'combined in her the personalities of a concubine, a performing artist, a songstress and dancer as well as a companion of the nobleman'.

Umrao Jan Ada is so culture-specific that it can be appreciated only with a proper understanding of literary tastes and urbane manners that the novel seeks to recreate.

David Matthews' English translation of the novel merits attention in so far as it meets many requirements of translation. He is conscious of the demands of readership of the target language as it is doubly distanced in terms of time, language and culture. Matthews takes care to explain the specificities of Lucknow Urdu culture by appending notes to the text.

The translator's language is lucid. But in rendering some of the specificities of Lucknow culture, Matthews has taken liberties that only reduce the charm of the book.

The translation of *mehtabi* (raised terrace) as balcony, *kanwal* (paper-silk ornamented candle lamp) as chandelier, *sheer-falooda* (flummery) as buttermilk fails to recreate the cultural ambience. Likewise, the use of 'sum of life' for *ikhlas pyar* (sincere affection), 'firmness in features' for *rob* (awe inspiring), 'thief' for *chor* (culprit) in the context of Gauhar Mirza's deflowering of Umrao, 'embroider the story' for *hashia* (embellish) strain the reader. On page 76, the expression 'Chabban has insulted her . . .' has been thoroughly misconstrued. The usage of *gali padna* is specific to Awadh and signifies the sanctity of a marriage proposal which, if withdrawn, amounts to a grave insult. This connotation is not borne out by saying 'has insulted her'. 'The chowk was thronged with people all dressed in white' doesn't convey the sense of *safed posh* which connotes the gentry. '*La hawla wala quwwata*', though translated correctly, fails to convey the connotation of proclaiming disapproval. 'Aiming a kick at Hatim's grave' doesn't convey the sense implied—the attempt to score over the legendary generosity of Hatim.

The sentence on page 187, 'I read until the morning, I made my ablutions, went to the lavatory, said my prayers and then fell asleep' is not translated correctly as it is semantically ill-structured. One performs ablutions after going to the lavatory and not before. Other examples of inaccurate translation are: 'balance' for *aetidal* (moderation), and 'proceeds' for *dallalah* (hand-maiden). 'It is obvious that the infidel is the one who has no belief', should in fact be: Only an infidel would not believe it.

There are a few typographical errors like *Ahmadnama* for the Persian primer *Amadnama*, *Haidar* for *Haidari* and 'perserve' for preserve. The translator's preference for Latin over Arabic philosophical terms helps retain the effect of the original.

The rendering of the cultural and linguistic nuances of *Umrao Jan Ada* justifies its claim as a masterpiece of Urdu literature. But Matthews' translation is perhaps not as successful as the earlier one by Khushwant Singh and M.A. Husaini (Disha, 1993). However, it is felicitous and he seems to be striving for the contemporary idiom in English.

CHAPTER 18

Inner Dimensions of Islamic Worship

Inner Dimensions of Islamic Worship: Al-Ghazali
Translated by Muhtar Holland

Al-Ghazali (1058–1111), lectured and contributed to Islamic learning at a time when, in the midst of powerful currents and cross-currents of Greco–Syrian and Persian intellectual legacy, the real spirit of Islam appeared to have been lost. Such was the confusion and dilemma of Muslims that it had become impossible for people to hold to any belief or conviction without support or anchor from 'philosophy'; and that too was often so flimsy and weak that it could be rejected or vindicated by a seemingly more convincing argument any time. People either withdrew to a life of resignation or succumbed to the pressures of Aristotelian logic in matters of religious belief. Anything that did not stand to the taste of Reason was rejected and rational justifications were sought for the affirmation of articles of faith. Never in the history of Muslims, neither before nor perhaps after(?), were the challenges to the Islamic faith so big and alarming as in the tenth and eleventh centuries. Not only at the intellectual plane, but also on social, ethical and political levels, Muslim society was torn asunder by schisms and movements of far-reaching consequences. The *mu'tazalites*, the *jabarites*, the *mulahidas* (heretics) and their further divisions into *batinis* (esoterics) and *talimites* (doctrinaires) with deep political overtones, all contributed to create a situation of utter confusion and chaos for the common believers and thinkers alike. But significantly it was in this age of crisis of faith and intellect that some of the greatest Muslim minds were born: Farabi (d. AD 950), Ibn Sina (d. AD 1036), Nizamulmulk (d. AD 1092), Ibn Miskawyh (d. AD 1030), Ali Hujwiri (d. AD 1062) and Al-Ghazali (d. AD 1111).

It was against this background that the future don of Nizamiyya took upon himself the stupendous task of examining and investigating the sources of Islamic faith and the sciences developed by later Muslims afresh and putting them in their proper perspectives. Al-Ghazali questioned the ascendency of philosophy as an all-comprehensive discipline to examine into and pass judgements upon all matters concerning life and the 'hereafter'. He did not do it as an outsider but as an insider only after drinking deep from the streams of philosophy.

The *Ihya'-ul-'Ulum al-Din*, which has rightly been called Al-Ghazali's *magnum opus*, is one of the rare Arabic classics that has stood the test of time and the severest standards of critique down the ages. Comprising four volumes, and divided into four quarters, the *ihya'* deals with *'ibadat* (worship), *'adat* (customs), *muhlikat* (vices) and *munjiyat* (virtues, or qualities leading to salvation). Al-Ghazali's treatment of such a wide range of matters is based upon his conviction that religious knowledge was essentially for the attainment of salvation in the life-hereafter rather than a means of worldly advancement as had come to be taken by the *ulama* of his time. The *ihya'* has proved to be 'a complete guide for the devout Muslim to every aspect of religious life-worship and devotional practices, conduct in daily life, the purification of heart, and advance along the mystic way.'

Muhtar Holland's translation from the *ihya'*, *Inner Dimensions of Islamic Worship*, is concerned mainly with its first section, the *'ibadat*. The book is divided into seven chapters—Prayer (*salat*), Almsgiving (*zakat*), Fasting (*sawm*), Pilgrimage (*hajj'*), Night vigil (*qiyam al-layl*), Invoking blessings upon God's Messenger (*darud*) and the merit of seeking forgiveness (*istighfar*). The earlier cited selections from the *ihya'* have been faithfully translated from the original into English with the added fascination and sense of wonder of a convert to Islam that indeed the translator is. In his Foreword, Muhtar Holland writes, 'To speak of myself, I know in my heart at least fifteen years before I embraced Islam that I must one day visit the Ka'aba in Makka as a Pilgrim. Throughout that time I performed the Islamic ablutions every morning and often at other times as well. Like others with whom I joined in exercises of a spiritual nature, 'receiving' from beyond the influence of heart and mind, I would sometimes feel the movements of Islamic prayer arising spontaneously in my body.'

Lest the reader is confused with regard to the use of the word 'inner' with esoteric as against exoteric forms of worship, Khurram Murad in his 'Foreword' clears the misunderstanding: 'His (Al-Ghazali's) 'inner' dimensions include things like praying at the proper time, congregational prayers, balance and proportion in the outward movements in prayer, finding the right type of person to give alms to, journeying for pilgrimage with legitimately earned money and caring for animals on the way, etc.'

Some of the terms that the translator has used in his book need to be examined. The use of the word 'servant' is commendable as its earlier accepted equivalent 'slave' sounds weak in the English lexicon. One wonders if Muhtar Holland is the first to use 'servant' for *'abd'*, Furthermore, the word 'servant' goes well with 'service' which is the Christian equivalent of *'ibadah* also. But the use of the word 'almsgiving' for *zakat* calls for an explanation. 'Alms', as *Webster's New Collegiate Dictionary* defines, is 'charity or something (as money or food) given freely to relieve the poor'. But the connotations of *zakat* in Islam are different, Pickthall uses the word, 'poor-due' while Abdullah Yousuf Ali prefers 'regular charity'. In my opinion it would be better to use the word *zakat* and make no attempt to translate it as it is hard to find a one-word equivalent for it. However, if one must have an equivalent, 'regular charity' comes nearest to the meaning.

On the whole, *The Inner Dimensions of Islamic Worship* is a valuable addition to the existing literature on Islam in translation.

CHAPTER 19

Qurratulain Hyder's *My Temples, Too (Mere Bhi Sanamkhane)*

Qurratulain Hyder, a Jnanpith Award winner and author of various novels and travelogues needs no introduction. Her first Urdu novel, *Mere Bhi Sanamkhane*, has now been rendered in English as *My Temples, Too*. Like many of her other novels, *My Temples, Too* is also set in Lucknow during post-Second World War, offering a vivid landscape of composite living together. In Urdu fiction, Lucknow is usually portrayed as a feudal urban society with a decaying culture. *My Temples, Too* is perhaps the first novel that brings out the anxieties of the educated elite of a feudal background who hold their culture close to their heart. This work may also be read as the story of the pre-Partition Lucknow where a generation was embittered by the political divide between the Muslim League and the Congress. Partition divided hearts; it was a loosing game for all. The novel also talks about loss, the loss of its characters and more importantly about the loss of Lucknow both as signifier and signified.

The story begins at the end of the war when 'everybody was waiting to go back home—England, USA, India'. In the subcontinent the separate state of Pakistan was an imminent possibility and freedom was round the corner. The novel is set in the estates of Karwaha and Amberpur but members of both the feudal families reside in Lucknow. Ghufran Manzil, the Lucknow house of the Karwaha Raj family, is the hub of political and cultural activities. Those who made Ghufran Manzil as their centre comprised:

> liberals, fire-eating revolutionaries, mild scholarly left-wingers, vegetarians and pacifists. Their chief occupation was day-dreaming. They talked of new life and new values and new society. . . . They wore rough handloom cotton and sang Tagore's songs and wrote about realism in literature. . . . They were anti-British and passionately believed in Hindu–Muslim unity and discussed how the capitalists and the bourgeoisie of both the Hindu and Muslim communities had conspired among themselves to keep the masses down.

The protagonist of the novel is Rajkumari Rakhshanda of Karwaha Raj. Her 'gang' of kindred souls includes Ginnie, Christabel, Diamond, Kiran, Vimal and her brother Peechu. They also edit a magazine called *New Era*. Ghufran Manzil is also the site of various love affairs. In the very beginning we are told that Peechu has been invited to Amberpur House 'in order to be viewed officially by his prospective in-laws'. Later we find out that he is in love with Christabel who is already married. The marriage of Rakhshanda is also an important issue for the Karwaha Raj family who are toying with a proposal from the family of Jehangir Qadar, an officer in the Royal Indian Navy.

On the other hand, Kunwar Irfan Ali, the Rajah of Karwaha is a highly cultured noble who is a member of Lucknow University Court and 'whose father had given donations for the construction of the magnificent red-stone building of Canning College. He reads Avicenna and plays chess with the old English members of the Indian Civil Service but he hated the new middle-class.' Sitting in his 'cozy drawing room he recited Urdu poetry with his Hindu *taluqdar* friends, and funded himself as a solid rock of the old order' for whom, government service was a disgrace. Nevertheless, his son Peechu quietly decides to join the Indian Air Force but ends up as a member of the Indian Police Service. Another family is of Chaudhary Asghar Ali from the town of Sandila who are related to the Karwaha Raj but are not as liberal as Kunwar Irfan Ali. Rakhshanda, the protagonist, who has gathered around her young men and women, full of new ideas and revolutionary zeal who through their magazine *New Era* want to reform society. The protagonist and her 'gang' are despised both by the leftists and conservatives. For those on the left, Rajkumari Rakhshanda 'is a study in dying culture', while for conservatives, she is a blemish on society. In the beginning they are all 'actors' but towards the end they are 'acted upon'. The greatest catastrophe that renders them helpless and bewildered is the country's Partition.

Towards the end of the novel, dramatic events unfold in quick succession, Kunwar Irfan Ali of Karwaha Raj dies in peace at his estate. Rakhshanda, Christabel and Kiran move to Bombay, which becomes the new cultural capital of India. Ginnie Kaul gets married and Diamond Hussein migrates to Pakistan. Dr Salim, who comes in Rakhshanda's life like a gentle breeze soon disappears. Personal tragedies come to their extreme when we get to know that Peechu is killed by Hindu refugees at Shahdara Railway Station while Kiran Bahadur Katju, the P.R.O. of the Indian Army, who loved Ginnie Kaul, is killed by Pathan attackers during the war in Kashmir. After spending some time in Mumbai when Rakhshanda finally reaches Lucknow and steps into her house at Outram Road, she is curtly told by the sentry that she may approach the women's resettlement office at Aminabad as her own house has now become the office of rehabilitation for men. There can't be a greater trauma and a more tragic ending to the story.

As is true of her other novels, we get fascinating and vivid scenes of the *mela* at Dewa Sharif, Hanuman temple at Aliganj and *Muharram*, the description of which reminds us of cinematic technique. We also get an insight into the rhetoric of Muslim League ideologues explaining and justifying the two-nation theory particularly through characters like Syed Iftikhar and Chaudhary Shameem. Hyder also makes us aware of the highly repressive value system, marginalizing the existence of woman. The novel is replete with cameos of Indian life interwoven into the narrative. As a consequence, the city and pulsating life of Lucknow in the ambience of its culture, experiences and its people come to life.

History and fiction overlap in the novel. They coalesce in a manner that presents a unified experience of the time. The novel depicts how experience of human motivation is tied to facts in a manner that has far-reaching consequences for the individual and the nation. The novel is not essentially history, as it does not scrupulously narrate the precise way things actually happened. Rather, we find a fictionalized account with authentic details of the city at a particular moment in time. The life and its characters are caught in the mesh of historical and cultural forces in a manner still relevant to our troubled times. The novel lights up for us the lost landscape of a composite culture.

Remembering *Abbu*

I did not visit to say Fatiha, for I knew, you could not have died
Whoever has given the true news of your death, is a liar
It could not have been you
It was perhaps the autumnal leaf which fell
My eyes are still captive of your scenes
Whatever I see or think is the same
As that which was the world of your good and evil doings
Nothing has changed
Your hands, still breathe in my fingers
Whenever I hold a pen or a piece of paper
I find you sitting in my chair
All the blood that I have in my body
Still flows in me with your failures and successes
Concealed in my voice is your mind
In my ailments and bouts of frustration, you're always with me
Whoever has raised an epitaph on your grave is a liar
It is me who lies buried in that grave
While you live in me
Whenever you have time, come to say Fatiha. . . .

—'Your Grave', Nida Fazli
(on the death of his father). Translated by Abbu

There is no right age to lose a parent. No child is ready enough.
There are people who go after prolonged illnesses, meet with accidents,

fight wars. And there are those that go in the blink of an eye. That day, 9 December 2007 began as a regular Sunday. Abbu had invited his friends over for lunch. The table was laid. He stepped out to get some last minute accompaniments and never returned to us. Right outside our house he stumbled and fell. Neighbours rushed to him, cars rushed to the hospital but we lost our father to the clumsiness of mortality. It's not easy to write about him, as there are aspects of his personality that keep unfolding. No word is right enough and there is nothing that we want to miss out. The time that we spent together is now only stories, anecdotes, moments and regrets. We can share a few and keep the rest to move on. . . .

What is really unfortunate is that we've got to know him better after he left us. Be it his students, teachers, colleagues, friends and neighbours or the gardener and the milkman; they all have a different aspect of his personality to share.

To the three of us he was a very loving and indulgent father who was seldom demonstrative about his love. His expression of love was keeping his hand on our head with a blessing. Though he usually came across as preoccupied he was also approachable. As daughters there wasn't much that we could not share with him and he too was not afraid to share his fears and insecurities. His letters to us were not about 'how are yous' and 'take cares', but instead his opinions contained on Palestine, Afghanistan and Kashmir. There were quotations from Ghalib and Mir's poetry. There were verses from the Holy Koran with the translations for our benefit. His knowledge of *hadith* and *sunnah* was immense and he often quoted from these sources in his daily life.

He once got delayed for a lecture he had to deliver at the *dargah* of Hazrat Nizamuddin Awliya. The reason for the delay being Abdullah (his grandson), who insisted on playing with *Nana Abbu* a little longer. When he reached the venue, he shared with the audience how that delay was an observance of *sunnah*; and cited that even Prophet used to prolong his *Sajjada* as his grandsons would be on his back.

He was a man who could speak as brilliantly on subjects of his interests as he could speak on yours. His was a very balanced mix of humour and literary brilliance. And that's what he took to his class everyday. Hasan had the opportunity to be his student for a year in the Department of English and Modern European Studies. While teaching Shakespeare, he would start the lecture with European Renaissance. Not quite getting the connection, he once asked Abbu why he did that. He smiled and said, 'I am a person who believes that if I tell you ten important things in class and you learn just five you're missing a lot. But if I tell you twenty and you learn ten then you're learning more'. Since Hasan was also his student, he saw that Abbu was quite a favourite amongst the students. They admired his sense of style, the way he acknowledged greetings, his speeches, enactment of plays in class and sweet humour.

Abbu was fiercely proud of his background. Even though he left Salon (our hometown and Abbu's birthplace) for educational and professional pursuits, Salon never went out of him. He was rooted in the culture and *tehzeeb* of Awadh. He often said that gentlemen were bred in the small towns of India and credited his ancestry and upbringing for his sophistication, chivalry and a taste for the fine things in life.

As children, we always took pride in Abbu's open-minded nature. From a very early and impressionable age we were taught to respect all differences; be it of religion or class. Abbu was equally comfortable talking to intellectuals about literature—Urdu and English as he was to the farmer about the seed. The Shia–Sunni sectarian difference was never an issue in our house. As children when we watched *Ramayana* and *Mahabharata*. Abbu insisted that we always addressed the deities as 'Ramji' and 'Krishnaji' as they were prophets of a different religion. Tayyaba's wedding gift from her father was a collection of books that not just included the Holy Koran but also a Bible and *Bhagawad Gita*.

Whenever he felt proud of us, for reasons big or small, he was extremely generous with the praise. He took pride in Hasan's published advertisements, Mariam's lectures in her sessions, Tayyaba's letters and also the fact that Abdullah is as talkative in school as his mother was.

It's difficult for us to confine him in words. With a teaching experience that lasted three decades, his quest for knowledge never ceased. He was a devout Muslim with a liberal perspective. Abbu was diabetic but we don't remember him ever missing a fast. He loved poetry and we now know that he also wrote poetry in Urdu. Abbu loved to talk and laugh heartily. Abbu loved to sleep till late on cold winter mornings. In fact, he often narrated the story of those three men, who he thought were very lucky, who are sleeping in a cave till the Day of Judgement. And that's the irony of fate; he went into that eternal sleep on a cold winter morning.

We don't deny that there were no tough times, especially after Ammi passed away. We've had our share of childhood and teenage whims and rebellions. Abbu had sometimes gracefully conceded and other times sternly refused. We all end up doing things that our parents taught us in our most rebellious days. We realize that they were our best friends, only well wishers and perhaps the most authentic and accessible source of information. We may not be exactly like our father but we love him for everything he has given us and everything he's left in this world.

Elders say that parents' blessings are always there with their children. We believe it. We know that Ammi and Abbu watch over us and pray that we dream of them often.

And to Allah we pray: Take care of them like they took care of us.

Qurratulain Tayyaba
Syed Hasan Muzammil
Khadija Mariam

Remembering a Friend

My friendship and association with Syed Naqi Husain Jafri began in 1971–2 when I became a part-time lecturer in Anwarul Uloom College, where Jafri had joind as Lecturer in the Department of English. Those were the days when great scholars like Haroon Khan Sharwani, Ali Akbar, Sayyid Abdul Mannan were on the Managing Committee of the College. Anwarul College was one among the few minority colleges, which used to have on its faculty a number of committed teachers like Dr Wacha, Dr Manvi, Dr Wasif Ali Khan, Mr M. Fasihuddin Ahmad, Dr Munir Ahmed, Dr Ahmed Jalees and many others who were close friends of Professor Jafri.

The staff room of the college buzzed with academic debates on literature, history, poetry, religion and politics. It was a regular, feature and Jafri, though young, always participated in the debates and discussions raising issues of current importance. These debates continued even after college hours—always over a cup of tea. Inconclusive debates continued while walking back home and if there was any matter still inconclusive, we would find the nearest home of a friend—which always used to be of Ahmed Jalees or M. Fasihuddin Ahmed, to continue our discussion. These debates were always very lively and despite the difference of opnion there was no occasion which resulted in any ill-will.

Jafri was a very committed teacher and would not venture into the class room without preparing for the lecture. Yet another quality of the teacher in Jafri was the manner he would use to relate the topic of his lecture with the times, society and its people, a quality which has disappeared in the present- day teachers. This aspect reflects his vast reading and insight into subjects other than English literature. Jafri remained in Hyderabad for over a decade and in time Hyderabad became his second home. He cherished the history of the city, its architectural beauty, its culture and its cusines, especially the *kababs, briyani* and the variety of *achars.* After joining Jamia Millia Islamia, New Delhi he was always looking forward to be in Hyderabad. He often visited the city to undertake research at the American Centre or to participate in a seminar or symposia. During his visits, he always stayed either at the guesthouse of the American Centre or Osmania University, despite the fact that his younger brother, a scientist used to stay in the campus of the National Geophysical Research Institute, a CSRI Complex nearby. In each visit he would stand before the Arts College of Osmania University and admire its architectural beauty and grandeur. A walk in its corridor was a must. Whenever he visited Hyderabad he always talked about Salarjung Library, *Dairatul Maarif* and *Idara i-Adbiyat i-Urdu* and appreciated the efforts of His Excellency the seventh Nizam of Hyderabad, Mir Osman Ali Khan Bahadur, the stateman in his kingdom and scholars who were instrumental in establishing these institutions. Whenever I visited him in Delhi he shared with great enthusiasm his new publications and details about, his participation in seminars and conferences. Most of out time was spent discussing academic issues.

On his appointment at a lecturer at Jamia Millia Islamia, he left Hyderabad in 1982. We missed his company and the debating circle lost a great scholar, but the friendship continued. At least twice or thrice in a year whenever I visited Delhi, Jafri did not allow me to stay at the Jamia guesthouse. The reason was to share the company, which would enable us to discuss and debate different issues till late at night. We shared with each other our concerns and often consoled each other. I was one among the very few, may be the only friend, with whom he shared his personal problems.

Being a direct descendent seventeenth-century Sufi Shaikh Pir Mohammad Saloni, of the Chishti–Nizami order of the great spiritual lineage of Shaikh Nizamuddin Auliya, Sufism was his favourite subject. As I have a Ph.D. on the Bahmani Sufis, he was always keen to find out if I had come accross any reference on his *jede-amjad* (ancestor) in sources which I had consulted. Luckily, I was able to give him the titles of a few works and made copies of those passages which contained references to Shaikh Pir Mohammad Saloni. I would see, in Jafri, mystical elements like, a softness in speech, non-indulgence in the affairs of others, a concern for the poor, the weak and the ill, added to which I never found him raising his voice, even when provoked. These were his hallmarks which he inherited from the family. He kept to himself, rarely got provoked and always remained concerned for others. In my association of 35 years with Jafri, I never heard any adverse remarks about any one, including his foes.

During one of my visits to Delhi, Jafri had just returned to Delhi after completing his four-month visit to Sana University at Yemen. He narrated the details of his experience and the values being maintained even in a county like Yemen. He was always keen to raise the standards of teaching, assignments and research. As a scholar, his personalilty reflected in him a great teacher and a researcher of not only English language and literaure but also of Islamic Studies, History, Arabic literature and socio-cultural issues confronting our society. He produced six Ph.Ds and five M.Phils. He published three books and 56 articles, participated in several semiars, workshop, symposia and regularly visited the American Studies Research Centre, Hyderabad to undertake research.

Though Jafri was not keenly inclined towards administrative responsibilities, he became the Head of the Department of English and Modern European Languages in 1997 and did an excellent job for three years. He was a member of the University Court and Vice-Chairman of the Delhi Education Society. He was a member of the Board of Studies for the Departments of History and Culture, Urdu, Arabic and Islamic Studies of Jamia Millia Islamia. The list of his publications reveal divergent interests. As a guest editor of Urdu monthly magazine *Kitabnuma* and a member of different committees, Jafri left his mark.

Jafri had little interest games and sports, which I cherished but he never hesitated in sharing with me his half-baked knowledge of cricket to keep me in good humour. In Jafri I have lost a great friend, a concerned teacher, a great academician and researcher.

Professor Muhammed Suleman Siddiqi
(Former Vice-Chancellor, Osmania University, Hyderabad)

Select Publications of Professor S.N.H. Jafri

Books

1. *Critical Theory: Perspectives from Asia* (edited), Jamia Millia Islamia in collaboration with Creative Books, Delhi, 2004. A collection of critical essays on the poetics of Arabic, Persian, Sanskrit, Tamil and Urdu by eminent scholars including Asloob Ahmad Ansari, Shamsur Rahman Faruqi, S. Ramaswamy, M.S. Kushwaha, Selvamony, Shikoh Mirza and Tabish Khair.

2. *Kuch Mashriq Se Kuch Maghrib Se* (*Of the Orient and the Occident*) ——*Collection of Essays in Urdu*, Maktaba Jamia Ltd., 1993. The essays included are: (i) The Growth and Development of the Cult of Chivalry in Western Europe, (ii) *Tawq al Hamama*, (iii) The Verse Translation of Saadi's *Gulistan*, (iv) Textual Criticism of the *Ghazals* of Sauda, Nasir Kazmi and Meer, (v) Dream as a *Leimotif* in the Poetry of Shahryar, (vi) Firaq and the English Lyrical Tradition.

3. *Aspects of Drayton's Poetry* — Doaba House, Delhi, 1988. The Ph.D. thesis submitted to Aligarh Muslim University was originally titled: *Michael Drayton's Non-Narrative Secular Poetry*. It examined the poet's contribution to various genres of English poetry and discusses the causes

of his neglect in later ages. The same was published as *Aspects of Drayton's Poetry* in 1988. The book finds a favourable mention in the *Year's Work in English Studies*, vol. 69, 1988, London, a word of commendation by Professor Kenneth Muir and has been reviewed in the *Aligarh Journal of English Studies*, Aligarh, and the *Osmania Journal of English Studies*, Hyderabad.

Articles Published in Journals

'*Sufi* Themes and Images in Persian and *Hindavi* Poetry: A Re-ordering of Universe and Re-adjustment of Impulses', *Islamic Path: Sufism, Politics and Society in India*, ed. S.Z.H. Jafri and Helmut Reifeld, New Delhi: Konard Adenauer Foundation, 2006, pp. 47–74.

'A Modernist View of *Madrasa* Education in Late Mughal India', *Islamic Education, Diversity and National Identity: Dini Madaris in India Post 9/11*, ed. Jan-Peter-Hartunjg and Helmut Reifeld, New Delhi: Sage Publishers, 2006, pp. 34–55.

'The Persian/Urdu Ghazal: A Mode of Non-Conformist Utterance', *The Literary Criterion*, Mysore, vol. XXXVIII (iii and iv), 2003.

English translations of three Urdu poems by Munibur Rahman, *Annals of Urdu Studies*, Department of Asian Languages and Cultures, University of Wisconsin, Madison, 18 (I and III), 2003.

'The Signs and Signifiers of Urdu-Hindi Controversy', *Sir Syed Ahmad Khan: A Centennary Tribute*, ed. A.A. Ansari, Delhi: Adam Publishers, 2001.

'Hamlet's Soliloquies: A Note on Their Nature and Functional Structure in the Light of *Natyasastra*', *Dramatic Theory and Practice: Indian and Western*, ed. M.S. Kushwaha, New Delhi: Creative Books, 2000, also published in *Critical Practice*, 1999.

'The Need for the Post-Colonialist Literary Theory', *Islam and the Modern Age*, vol. XXX, no. 3, 1999.

'Image of the Orient is Shakespeare', *Encounter*, New Delhi, vol. 2, no. 4, 1999, also published in *Aligarh Critical Miscellany*, Aligarh and *Saudi Gazette*, literary supplement.

'Poetics and Politics of Troubadours: The Hispano–Arabic Connection', *The Aligarh Critical Miscellany*, Aligarh, vol. 10, no. 2, 1997.

'When People can't Abide Things as They are: An Interpretation of Albee's *Vision of Life*', *The Aligarh Critical Miscellany*, Aligarh, vol. 9, no. 2, 1996.

'American Poetry in the Contemporary Era', *The Aligarh Critical Miscellany*, Aligarh, vol. 7, no. 2.

Contributed three entries (*Marasi-e-Anis, Gul-e-Naghma, Kulliat-e-Meeraji*) to the *Masterpieces of Indian Literature*, ed. K.M. George, a National Book Trust Project, New Delhi, 1994.

'In Quest of New Idioms', *The Book Review*, New Delhi, July 1993, pp. 18–19.

'Some Perspectives on the Medieval Tradition of Poetry', *Islam and the Modern Age*, Zakir Husain Institute of Islamic Studies, Jamia Millia Islamia, New Delhi, vol. XVI, no. 3, 1986, pp. 167–83.

'*The Muses Elizium*—An Allegorical Interpretation', *Rajasthan University Studies in English*, Jaipur, vol. XIX, 1987, pp. 1–7.

'*The Moone-Calfe*—An Interpretation', *Osmania Journal of English Studies*, Osmania University, Hyderabad, vol. XX, 1984, pp. 12–29.

Articles Published in Urdu Journals/Books

'Macbeth', *Urdu Adab*, Delhi: Anjuman Taraqqi Urdu, Book no. 324, April–June 2004.

'Khwaja Hasan Nizami ki Nasr Aur Hindavi-Revayat', *Munadi*, Delhi, vol. 78, no. 2, February 2004.

Urdu translation of Annemarie Schimmel's 'Muhammad's Unique Position', *Islam Aur Asr-e-Jadid* (special issue), June 2003.

Urdu translation of Edward Said's 'Crisis in Orientalism', *Urdu Adab*, Delhi: Anjuman Taraqqi Urdu, Book no. 322, October–December 2003.

'Ghalib Ka Roya-e-Ziest', *Naqd-o-Nazar*, vol. 22, no. 2, 2003.

'King Lear', *Urdu Adab*, Delhi: Anjuman Taraqqi Urdu, Book no. 321, July–September 2003.

'Hamlet', *Urdu Adab*, Delhi: Anjuman Taraqqi Urdu, Book no. 320, April–June 2003.

'Aan Soo-e-Aflak'–Mir Ali Hamdani in Iqbal's *Javednamah*, *Naqdo-Nazar*, Aligarh, vol. 22, no. 1, 2001.

'Ghalib Ka Aaeen-i-ghazal-khawani', *Naqd-o-Nazar*, Aligarh, vol. 21, no. 1, 2000.

'Khawaja Hasan Nizami Ki Roznamchanigari', *Manadi*, vol. 74, no. 6, New Delhi, 2000.

'Sir Richard Burton Ka Safarnama-e-Harmain', 153, *Aajtak*, Delhi, vol. 57, no. 9, April 1999.

'Sher-o-Adab Mein Namrud Ki Talmeeh', *Maarif*, Darul Musaniffeen, Azamgarh, vol. 163, no. 1, January 1999.

'Paighambaran-e-Sukhan', review article, *Kitabnuma*, New Delhi: Maktaba Jamia, August 1998.

'Taseer al-Sher-ul-Arabi al-Asbani ala-Sher al Hub Enjelezi', *Thaqafatul Hind*, Indian Council of Cultural Relations, New Delhi, vol. XLIX, no. 4, 1998.

Urdu translation of three English Poems from South Africa published in the *Jamia*, New Delhi, July 1994. Subsequently also included in *Siyahfam Adab*, ed. Shamim Hanafi, New Delhi: Maktaba Jamia, 1995.

'Hindustan Ke Ah'de Wasta Ki Miras Aur Ilimi Rewayat Ki Talash' (The 'Medieval Indian Legacy and the Intellectual Tradition', *Kitab Numa*, New Delhi: Maktaba Jamia, January 1994.

'Textual Explication of the *Ghazals* of Sauda, Nasir Kazmi, Meer and Shaz Tamkanat', in *Naqdo-Nazar*, Aligarh, vol. X, 1987; vol. XIII, no. 2, 1991; vol. XV (i and ii) 1993.

'*Gulistaane* Saadi Ke Urdu Tarajim' (The Verse Translation of Saadi's Gulistan), in *Islam Aur Asre Jadeed* (Special issue on Saadi), vol. 21 (ii and iii), 1989.

'Khwab Se Khwab Tak' (Dream as a *Leitmotif* in the Poetry of Shahryar), Review article on Shahryar's *Khwab Ka Dar Band Hai*, *Shair*, Bombay, vol. 58, no. 4, 1987, pp. 21–7.

Review article on Mohammad Mujeeb's *Duniya Ki Kahani*, Jamia, vol. 83 (ix-x), 1986.

'Maghrebi Europe mein Futuwwah ki Rewayat Aur Uske Maakhaz' (The Growth and Development of the Cult of Chivalry in Western Europe), *Islam Aur Asre Jadeed*, vol. 17, no. 4, 1985, pp. 13–30.

'Firaq Aur Angrezi Rewayat' (Firaq and the English Lyrical Tradition) *Firaq-Shakhs Aur Shair*, ed. Shamim Hanfi, Delhi: Maktaba Jamia, 1993.

Book Reviews

Book review, *Ghazal Tanqeed*, ed. Asloob Ahmad Ansari, *Naqd-o-Nazar*, Aligarh, vol. 22, no. 2.

Book review, *The Myth of Holy Cow* by D.N. Jha, *Urdu Adab*, Delhi: Anjuman Taraqqi Urdu, Book no. 320, April–June 2003.

Review of *Zikr-i-Mir* (English tr. C.M. Naim, OUP, 1998), *The Book Review*, New Delhi, vol. XXVI, no. 5, 2001.

'Paying Court', Review of David Matthews English tr. of *Umrao Jan Ada, Indian Review of Books*, January 1997.

Review of *The Silken Knot*, English tr. of *Ghazals* by Prem Kumar Nazar, *Shabkhoon*, vol. 202, January 1997.

Shadow of a Bird in Flight, English tr. of Persian verses by Shamsur Rahman Faruqi, *Shabkhoon*, vol. 19, Allahabad, 1996.

Muslim Minorities and the World Today: M. Ali Kettani, *Islam and the Modern Age*, New Delhi, vol. XIX, no. 4, 1988.

Educating a Backward Minority: M.K.A. Siddiqui, *Islam and the Modern Age*, New Delhi, vol. XVI, no. 3, 1985.

Hijra—Story and Significance: Zakaria Bashier, *Islam and the Modern Age*, New Delhi, vol. XVI, no. 1, 1985.

Inner Dimensions of Islamic Worship: Al-Ghazali, tr. Muhtar Holland, *Islam and the Modern Age*, New Delhi, vol. XVI, no. 1, 1985.

Articles Published in National Dailies/Periodicals

'Ali Sardar Jafri—The Last Romantic', *Milli Gazzette*, New Delhi.

Several articles to *Siasat*, Hyderabad and *Qaumi Awaz* (literary supplement), New Delhi.

'Mohammad—the Apostle of Peace', *The Hindu*, 21 August 1994.

'Salman Rushdie Thrives on Controversies', *The Times of India*, 6 March 1989.

Translations

English tr. of sixteen Urdu poems by Majrooh Sultanpuri, Irfan Siddiqi, Shahryar and Hameed Almas, published in the *Indian Literature.*

English tr. of eight Urdu poems by Akhtarul Iman, Mohammad Alvi, Qazi Saleem and Shamsur Rahman Faruqi et al., published in *Uttara*, a literary digest of the Sahitya Akademy, 1995.

English tr. of Urdu poems by Makhboom Mohiuddin, Sahir Ludhianvi, Khaleelur Rahman Azmi, Shahryar and Nida Fazli, published in the *Indian Literature*, vol. 170, November/December 1995.

English tr. of seven poems of Mohammad Alvi, published in the *Indian Literature*, vol. 160, March–April 1994.

English tr. of Rasheed Amjad's Urdu short story '*Dashte Seyah Mein Akhiri Shaam*', published in *The New Quest*, Poona, vol. 107, September–October 1994.

English tr. of Zakir Husain's essay '*Achcha Ustad*', published by Regional Resource Centre, Jamia Millia Islamia, 1989.

English tr. of Ali Sardar Jafri's long poem *Khawaabe Parishan*, published in the *Soviet Land*, no. 16, August 1987.

Index